Deploying

Microsoft®

Office 2000

Notes from the Field

**Best Practices
from Microsoft
Consulting
Services**

PUBLISHED BY
Microsoft Press
A Division of Microsoft Corporation
One Microsoft Way
Redmond, Washington 98052-6399

Library of Congress Cataloging-in-Publication Data
Deploying Microsoft Office 2000 / Microsoft Corporation.
    p. cm.
  Includes index.
  ISBN 0-7356-0727-3
  1. Microsoft Office. 2. Business--Computer programs. I. Microsoft Corporation.
HF5548.4.M525 D46 1999
005.369--dc21

                                                                    99-046114

Printed and bound in the United States of America.

1 2 3 4 5 6 7 8 9 QMQM 4 3 2 1 0 9

Distributed in Canada by Penguin Books Canada Limited.

A CIP catalogue record for this book is available from the British Library.

Microsoft Press books are available through booksellers and distributors worldwide. For further information about international editions, contact your local Microsoft Corporation office or contact Microsoft Press International directly at fax (425) 936-7329. Visit our Web site at mspress.microsoft.com.

Acquisitions Editor: Anne Hamilton
Project Editor: Thom Votteler

Contributors

Project Management Team
Darren Yetzer, Microsoft; Abram Spiegelman, EntireNet LLC; Bryna Hebert, Hebert Communications

Lead Editor
Bob Haynie

Technical contributors (listed alphabetically)
Scott Alexander; Shelly Bird; David Chu (Ikon TS); Paul Emery; Bryna Hebert (Hebert Communications); Mark Jennings; James H. Kennedy, II; Geoff Kenny (Ikon TS); Chris Kunicki (MMA); Martin LaFrance (Ikon TS); Greg Martin; Taylor Maxwell; Rich McBrine; Wes McNab; David Ouart; Jim Pillar (Margolin, Winer & Evens LLP); Gerardo Rojas Quiroz; Michael Reagan; Jose Renato Roda; Bruno Schmidt; Abram Spiegelman (EntireNet LLC); Ned Studt (EntireNet LLC); Alan Von Weltin; Joel Ware (Boeing); John Wiffen (ICL); Paul Winter; Azin Wright

Technical reviewers (listed alphabetically)
Gigel Avram, Ed Barnes, Karel Blaha, Eric Broberg, Michael Cherry, Rich Choi, Gordon Church, Jane Clayton, Arthur De Haan, Holly Eggleston, Gary Ericson, D.J. Franchini, Chris Gibbons, Gordon Hardy, Darrin Hatakeda, Bryna Hebert, Jennifer Hendrix, Kari Hensien, Rob Howe, Tim Johnson, Peter Kelly, Roxanne Kenison, Chris Kimmell, Sunil Koduri, Jeff Larsson, Matthias Leibmann, Dorothy Liu, Clifford Mark, Bob O'Brien, Micheal Ohata, Jenn Parry, Chris Pratley, Rolf Robe, Samantha Robertson, Abram Spiegelman, Rick Stenson, Michael Tholfsen, Russell Williams, Tom Williams, Darren Yetzer

Indexer
Richard S. Shrout

Compositor
Paula Gorelick

Project Editor
Thom Votteler

Special Thanks
Special thanks to the hundreds of people who work every day to make Office a great product, and to the thousands of customers who believe in this product and show their support by using it every day.

Welcome

In building Microsoft Office 2000, the development team focused design efforts on making Office easier to deploy and administer in a wide range of networking and operating system environments. Whether you are deploying Office 2000 to a few hundred or to ten thousand PCs, enhanced flexibility and new deployment options will allow you to efficiently and cost effectively execute the deployment. You, our customers, have been quite clear that we must recognize the multitude of requirements that arise when successfully deploying Office. While product enhancements address many of the issues, you have told us that deployment guides and tools, coupled with accumulated knowledge and lessons learned from hands-on experience, are tremendously valuable in the deployment process.

This volume of Notes from the Field, *Deploying Microsoft Office 2000,* provides information, upgrade strategies, and techniques for successfully deploying and maintaining Office 2000 in your organization while also reducing total cost of ownership. We have gathered information from early adopters, partners, and the Microsoft Consulting Services professionals who have already encountered and addressed many of the challenges you may face. Not only will you find general strategies and best practices in this book; you will also find descriptions of specific solutions that have been successfully used to facilitate Office 2000 migrations and deployments worldwide. The information in *Deploying Microsoft Office 2000* and the accompanying CD cover many practical scenarios providing not only strategies, but supporting tools, project planning templates, and white papers that will help you plan for and deploy Microsoft Office 2000. While no single volume can cover every facet of every possible deployment scenario, this book is a snapshot capturing recent experiences that can be extrapolated and applied to your own situation. We believe that this can be a great starting point for your own deployment.

We hope that by making use of the strategies contained in this resource along with the current information on our Web site, www.microsoft.com/office/enterprise, you will be able to efficiently create and manage different Office configurations, support users (including worldwide users) across your organization, and integrate Office 2000 and intranets or the Internet with maximum flexibility and effectiveness. The knowledge of our authors can work for you throughout your Office 2000 lifecycle. We hope that you deploy, use, and enjoy Office 2000. Please continue to let us know how we can make it a better product. In addition, please email feedback and suggestions for how we can strengthen and enhance the content of this book to better meet your deployment needs to nffo2k@microsoft.com.

Steven Sinofsky
Vice President, Office
Microsoft Corporation

Contents

Introduction

Welcome to *Deploying Microsoft Office 2000,* sixth in the Notes from the Field series, featuring best practices from Microsoft Consulting Services. Designed for information technology (IT) and information systems (IS) professionals, this book organizes and condenses the broad expertise of field consultants and support engineers, offering you the benefit of their real-world experience. Some of the chapters use fictitious customer names, but all of the case studies derive from actual customer scenarios or an amalgam of several technical implementations where consultants tested and proved their approaches and techniques.

What's in This Book

No single book can cover every deployment topic for Office 2000, so this book doesn't try. It is a guide that will help you to plan and execute the best migration scenario for your company. Your first step will be to develop a plan for your migration after weighing the criteria driving your deployment and the benefits and challenges of various deployment methods. In addition to the material in this guide, the worksheets and tools on the accompanying CD-ROM will help you make the best decisions for your workplace. Step-by-step processes and case studies of distribution and deployment methods will help you to develop and fine-tune your deployment plans. This guide covers the issues and challenges faced by administrators as they migrate employees to Office 2000—including coexistence issues that arise from the concurrent use of multiple versions of Office, customizing Office to provide the most benefits for your company, and issues such as network bandwidth considerations.

Planning Your Migration: Chapters 1–5

Chapter 1 begins your deployment process by helping you plan your migration. This chapter introduces you to the tools available on the accompanying CD and defines deployment criteria, the steps involved, and the risk factors in deploying Office 2000. In Chapter 2 you will find detailed methods for migrating your organization's files, templates, and custom solutions that will preserve your documents and development work. A common issue during new Office 2000 deployments is the coexistence of different versions of Office. Whether your deployment will include a long-term or short-term period of coexistence, Chapter 3 will prepare you to support all of your organization's employees throughout the deployment. Office 2000 can be customized to best meet the needs of your company. Chapter 4 will show you the variety of customizations available to you as you create the best possible Office configurations for your specific needs. Migrating user settings is covered in Chapter 5, which explains the migration process in detail, including the migration of custom user settings and how the Office Profile Wizard can be used to migrate all of your company's settings.

Distributing and Deploying Office 2000: Chapters 6–9

In these chapters you will learn how the actual distribution and deployment can best be handled in your organization. Chapter 6 begins by explaining how to prepare your staff, organization, and hardware for the distribution. In Chapter 7 you will review step-by-step methods of distribution, the benefits of using Systems Management Server (SMS) for distribution, and, if SMS is not available, how to distribute Office 2000 without SMS. A flowchart that maps the decision-making process for distribution will lead you to the best path for your situation. Outlook 2000 can be deployed before, after, or during your Office 2000 deployment. Which is best for you? The information in Chapter 8 will show you how to choose the best deployment option for your organization, and how to avoid common issues that may arise. Multinational deployments are common in today's global marketplace. In Chapter 9 you will learn how to use the multinational features in Office 2000, along with customizations and deployment strategies, to ensure that your multinational deployment is as painless as possible.

Special Considerations for Office 2000 Deployment: Chapters 10–14

The last five chapters will help you ensure that your deployment plan is complete and takes full advantage of all that Office 2000 has to offer. Chapter 10 discusses network bandwidth issues that you should consider in light of the many network-based deployment solutions that are possible with Office 2000. Chapter 11 shows how you can customize alerts and Help files to meet the specific needs of your organization, allowing you to create custom content and put it at your users' fingertips. A successful deployment on Windows Terminal Server is the focus of Chapter 12, which discusses special Office 2000 considerations, and provides real-life scenarios to help you troubleshoot your Terminal Server deployment. The power of collaboration is greatly enhanced by Office 2000's new Server Extensions technology, and Chapter 13 will provide insight into how you can best use this new functionality. Finally, Chapter 14 offers a look forward at the unique benefits and considerations of deploying Office 2000 in a Windows 2000 environment.

About the CD

The companion CD contains a number of tools to aid in the planning and deployment of Office 2000, including the Enterprise Planning Workbook mentioned in chapter one. The CD also contains white papers gathered from the Microsoft Web site that discuss in further detail many of the issues raised in the book. To use the CD, simply load it; the default HTML page should launch, providing you with an easy-to-use interface to all of the tools and papers available. For detailed usage instructions, see the README.TXT file on the CD itself.

Icons That Highlight Text

These icons provide you with convenient signposts to important information:

Icon	Description
	Caution or **Warning.** Advises you to take or avoid taking specific action to avert potential damage.
	Note or **Tip.** Emphasizes, supplements, or qualifies points in the text.
	Best Practices or **Guidelines.** Highlights proven practices, techniques, or procedures from MCS real-world experiences. This icon also accompanies the shaded **From the Trenches** sidebars, which offer actual stories of lessons learned in the field.
	Tools. Indicates sample code or descriptions of utilities or tools provided in the text.

CHAPTER 1

Planning Your Migration

This chapter examines concepts, decisions, and procedures by walking you through the whole process of planning, deploying, and migrating to Microsoft Office 2000. This chapter presents the basic information you need to understand migration planning in context; the rest of the chapters in the book deal with specific aspects of major stages in the overall process.

This chapter follows the Microsoft Solutions Framework method, which allows you to work though all the major planning decisions, to take into account issues specific to your environment, and to ask questions that help you create more specific estimates for timing, budget, and effort.

An online version of this chapter (the *Enterprise Planning Workbook*) is on the CD in the back of this book. It is provided in that format so that you can copy it out to a soft copy, then replace the questions in the text with your answers—thus creating a plan simply by working through the sample. The CD version also includes Appendices A through F (mentioned in the text), which you can use to tabulate system information required for a complete migration plan.

What You'll Find in This Chapter

- What to include in your executive summary and when you should plan to write it

- How to determine the scope of your project—including the criteria you must determine and a budget worksheet for you to use

- How to define your current environment and how to plan your environment after deployment—including a table of hardware requirements for Office 2000 to reference while planning

- How to put together your migration plan and your development deployment plan—including tables that help you determine your needs, design useful plans, and track your progress

- How to use Proof of Concept and Pilot groups to resolve issues before beginning your actual deployment

- How to assess the risks of deploying Office 2000 for your company using the risk assessment checklist included in this chapter

- How to perform the implementation—including issues to be aware of and precautions to take, and information on how to conduct a useful review of the process

The procedures and tools described here can help you understand decisions, plan for contingencies, and estimate effort. The focus is on organizations deploying to more than 1,000 desktops. Read this chapter to build an understanding of migration planning; to build a well-documented plan that can simplify *and* optimize an Office 2000 deployment, and to complete the workbook version of this chapter on the CD-ROM. In addition, there is a Microsoft Project Deployment Planning Template on the CD-ROM (shown in Figure 1.1). Use it to help you estimate the time needed for each step of the deployment process and to set up a schedule for your deployment.

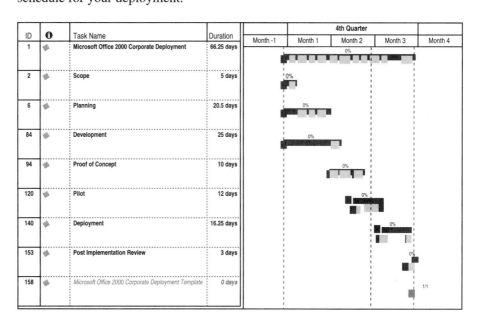

Figure 1.1   Microsoft Office 2000 Deployment Planning Template.

For detailed technical information on Office 2000 deployment and migration, see the *Microsoft Office 2000 Resource Kit.*

Note   All documents referenced in this chapter are at http://www.microsoft.com /office/enterprise.

Basic Information

The scope of your deployment may require adding or skipping sections, but you should at least consider all the sections listed below. Each is discussed in more detail in subsequent sections of this chapter, each represents a deployment preparation milestone, and each should be documented adequately:

- **Executive Summary.** An overview of the business case for migrating to Office 2000, the goals of the plan, and how the plan will be executed. Although this is presented first, it is best to write it after you have completed most of the plan and can summarize it meaningfully.

- **Scope.** The overall scope, which clearly defines what the migration to Office 2000 will include. Begin with the business case for making the change, even though the decision has already been reached to deploy. This is because the business case for deployment affects the scope. Scope out the timing, budget, methods for engendering user cooperation, projected service level, and acceptable results.

- **Current versus Planned Environment.** An analysis and inventory of the current environment as well as the planned environment, including hardware, software, and network infrastructure.

- **Migration Plan.** A detailed plan for migrating from the current environment to the planned environment. Include files, templates, macros, training, and support. If various versions of Office or its applications will have to exist on the system for some period of time, address the coexistence plan here.

- **Office 2000 Deployment Development Plan.** A detailed plan for configuring and distributing Office 2000, including testing.

- **Proof of Concept.** A test plan for all physical aspects of the migration and deployment—integration, coexistence, and deployment in an environment that closely replicates the planned environment.

- **Pilot.** A detailed outline for deployment to a representative pilot group of users.

- **Risk Assessment.** A discussion of the implementation's risks and how can they be mitigated. Base this on the results of the Proof of Concept, the Pilot, and other planning factors such as the budget.

- **Implementation Plan.** A detailed rollout schedule and logistics plan for actual deployment.

- **Post Implementation Review.** A complete review, including any necessary changes discovered during implementation, lessons learned (for the next deployment), and considerations for application development and Office 2000 use.

Each section begins with a graphic that shows your progress in the plan.

Figure 1.2   An example of the graphic that charts your progress.

Executive Summary

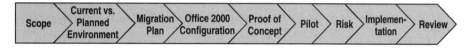

The executive summary quickly informs readers and decision-makers of the plan's pertinent points. Include the business case for deploying Office 2000 as well as highlights of the technical plan for implementation. Although this will be the first section in the plan, write it last—after you have specified and organized the plan's structure and particulars. Summarize these sections:

- Scope
- Current vs. Planned Environment
- Migration Plan
- Office 2000 Configuration
- Proof of Concept
- Pilot
- Risk Assessment
- Implementation
- Post Implementation Review

Scope

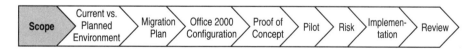

What the project will include is defined by need and limited by time, money, personnel, and so on. It is sometimes equally important to have a clear idea of what the project will *not* include. This can help focus and clarify everything from timelines to test procedures.

If the deployment will be handled by a project team made up entirely of people from your organization, you may be able to skip sections such as the business model, because everyone on the project team knows that information. If you will use external resources such as contractors or consultants, the information will help them understand your project and environment.

Here is an example of a *scope* statement with a practical level of specificity:

"Deploy Office 2000 Premium Edition, with all applications and features, to the local computers of all users. Implement custom settings to support coexistence and year 2000 policies and deploy custom Help explaining these policies. Distribute software with Microsoft Systems Management Server, which is already in place. The support and training organizations will increase staff to train all users immediately before deployment and support them fully afterwards. A process will be put in place to identify files, macros, templates, and custom solutions that need migrating, and another process will be put in place to migrate or reengineer them."

Vision

Throughout planning and deployment you make decisions based on your organization's vision for the migration, and this is based on factors relating to how your organization works and manages change. For instance, does it let users handle their own desktop computing needs or does it make decisions, control software distribution, and support user desktops? This drives the division of labor and defines who will be responsible for various tasks.

A clear vision for the deployment makes it easier to decide issues and to include everyone in your plan. Get all project stakeholders to agree to this vision and approve it before you move forward. Stakeholders are not just management: they are also users, designers, support, and so on.

Here is an example of a *vision* statement:

"Deploy Office 2000 to all local users by December 1999 and all international users by February 2000. Deployment will not interrupt user activity. Information technology (IT) staff will manage all upgrades either overnight or on weekends, rolling out the software to one business unit at a time. Users will receive training just before receiving software. Software deployment will minimize support calls, but the helpdesk personnel will be trained on major issues in advance and will be staffed to meet increased call volumes. The upgrade will benefit users by increasing file-sharing compatibility with others and new Web-based Office 2000 solutions for line-of-business needs. It will benefit IT through software that costs less to implement and to support."

Business Model

Clear documentation of your business model helps third-party personnel understand the decision-making dynamic. Describe the organization's

- Core competencies
- Strengths and weaknesses
- Primary competition
- Primary use of IT in daily business
- Business drivers for deployment

Business drivers are the pathways and mechanisms through which things are accomplished. For example, is the deployment driven centrally or on demand by departments or sites? For each business driver, identify who is concerned primarily with that driver (for example, IT or a specific department). Among other things, this information makes it easier to calculate budget requests and easier to get buy-in from managers and department heads who understand the deployment's business value.

IT Business Model

All resources that work on this project need to understand the underlying business model. Describe:

- Centralized versus decentralized, and pertinent relationships
- IT's relationship to business units
- Funding
- Level of support provided to business units
- Use of third-party resources to provide services

If you use only internal staff resources you can skip this section.

IT Organizational Profile

Describe all IT groups that will be involved with or affected by the deployment. People need to know who to go to for help with issues and decisions at any stage of the planning, testing, and implementation.

Budget

Following is an Excel spreadsheet to use as a starting point for your budget. (In the version of this chapter on the CD, you can double-click on the spreadsheet to launch Excel inside of the Word document, then add or delete items, create formulas to finish the budget, and update it any time your numbers change.)

Budget Item	Projected Budget	Actual Amount Spent
Hardware		
New client computers		
Client hardware upgrades		
New server computers		
Server hardware upgrades		
Software		
Office 2000 licenses		
Distribution software licenses		
Virus scan software upgrade		
Support		
Training		
Overstaffing for rollout		
Migrating files, macros, templates		
Needs assessment		
Testing		
Remediation		
Test lab		
Hardware		
Software		
Personnel		
Training		
Helpdesk training		
Helpdesk materials (CBT, etc.)		
User training		
User materials (CBT, etc.)		
Implementation		
Personnel		
Materials		
TOTAL		

Timing

What is the desired timing for this project, including major milestones for kick-off, planning, pilot, and the start and finish dates for implementation? The plan you create with Microsoft Project includes detailed milestone and timing information, so in this document you need only a high-level summary. Documenting project timing also helps you identify constraints, which can affect other variables such as budget and training.

Support Commitment

What level of support can business units and users expect during and after implementation? Answer this question with a vision statement, such as "We will commit the resources necessary so that users will not experience any downtime." You need to define the vision so that you can create a plan that achieves it.

Current vs. Planned Environment

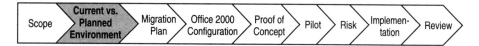

You need to document and understand the *current* and *planned* environments so that you can create a migration plan based on them. This section helps you define some of this information, but you should use the tables in Appendix A (on the CD) to document configuration information for each rollout unit (business unit, department, workgroup). If you have an existing hardware or software inventory system such as Systems Management Server, use the tables in this section as a guideline for the type of information you will need from that system. You can provide the information developed in this section as an addendum to the finished document.

Questions in this section with the ◇ bullet are pertinent to documenting the current environment. If you are changing other desktop aspects not covered in this section (operating system, messaging, software distribution, and so on), make sure you document them.

Desktop Architecture

Hardware

◈ Does the current hardware support the Office 2000 system requirements (shown below)?

If not, list hardware that will be upgraded (and describe *how*) and which users (if any) will have to wait for hardware before migration.

Item	Office 2000 Requirement	
Chip	Pentium 75 (166 for PhotoDraw business graphics software).	
RAM	For the Windows 95/98 operating systems: 16 MB for the operating system, 4 MB for each open Office application (8 MB for the Outlook messaging and collaboration client, Access, or the FrontPage Web site creation and management program; 16 MB for PhotoDraw).	
	For Windows NT Workstation operating system: 32 MB for the operating system, 4 MB for each Office application (8 MB for Outlook, Access, or FrontPage; 16 MB for PhotoDraw).	
Hard Disk	Office Standard:	189 MB (W,E,P,O)
	Office Professional:	217 MB Disk 1 (W,E,P,O,A)
		174 MB Disk 2 (Pub, SB)
	Office Premium:	252 MB Disk 1 (W,E,P,O,A,F)
		174 MB Disk 2 (Pub, SB)
		100 MB Disk 3 (PhotoDraw)
	Office Developer:	Add 130 MB To Premium
	Figures are based on installing a typical configuration to the local computer. Running the software from the source saves substantial space on the local computer.	
	W=Word, E=Excel, P=PowerPoint, O=Outlook, A=Access, Pub=Publisher, SB=Small Business Tools, F=FrontPage	
CD-ROM	Yes, for non-network installations.	
Network Card	Yes, for network installations.	

Software

◇ Does the current operating system support Office 2000, including the service pack version for Windows NT Workstation? If not, describe how the operating system will be upgraded, as well as anything else an operating system upgrade will affect, especially hardware and other software on the computer.

Note   Office 2000 runs on Windows 95/98, Windows 2000, and Windows NT Workstation 4.0 with SP3 or later. Some Office 2000 server components, such as the Office Server Extensions, require SP4 or later.

◇ Does the existing software work with Office 2000, particularly third-party Office-integrated software? If not, how critical is that software? If it must be used, how will this affect the plan? Are there compatible substitutes for non-compatible third-party software?

◇ What is the current default Internet browser? Office 2000 includes Internet Explorer 5; if you want to make it the default system browser you can deploy it with Office.

Operating System

◇ Do any users run 16-bit Windows or Windows NT Workstation 3.5? They will need an operating system update or Windows Terminal Server to run Office 2000.

◇ Have Windows NT 4.0–based workstations been updated to include at least Service Pack 3? If not, you will have to update them.

Profiles

◇ Does the current environment use system policies? If yes, see Chapter 5, "User Settings," or the *Microsoft Office 2000 Resource Kit* for information on the updated System Policy Editor and the system policy templates available for Office 2000.

◇ Do you need to implement and enforce user settings such as the default file format for saving documents? If yes, consider using system policies.

◇ Have you implemented profiles so that roaming users can call their system settings up on any computer? If yes, you can plan to install Office 2000 to support this.

Networking Configuration

Document the network elements pertinent to running or deploying Office 2000 and Office-based solutions. Describe concerns such as overloaded servers or links that may be too slow to support deployment adequately, but don't document the entire network topology in detail.

◇ Will the existing network configuration support deploying Office 2000 through the network? If not, decide on adding servers or bandwidth, deploying during off-peak hours, or using CDs for mobile users or those connected over slow links.

◇ Will the existing network configuration support running Office 2000 from the network? If not, you can create an installation that does not give users the choice of running Office 2000 from the network.

◇ What impact could the *Installed on First Use* setting have on your network? This feature allows you to provide user-desktop shortcuts to applications and features, but delays downloading the software until the shortcut is selected. This saves deployment time and bandwidth, but can present other issues. See Chapter 10, "Network Considerations for Deployment," for more information.

◇ Can current network servers store content that is not deployed to the desktop, such as PhotoDraw samples and graphics? If not, how will users access that content?

◇ Are users connecting to databases or network locations that need to be restored after deployment? If they are, make sure that all connections work after the upgrade. This is important for deployments that involve new hardware or operating system settings.

For more information, see Chapter 10, "Network Bandwidth Considerations."

Migration Plan

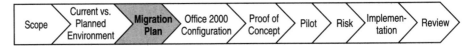

This is the roadmap from current to planned environment. It describes what you will do to get there and how you will do it. Update the plan throughout the migration so everyone is confident that it is accurate.

Resources

Project Team/Roles

Each project area requires key administrators who are responsible for activities related to each stage. The list below is based on the roles in large organizations. Your list may be significantly shorter use whatever works for your environment.

Role	Responsibility	Names and Company Titles
Business Manager	Owns the project from the line-of-business perspective. Is responsible for budget, communication between project management and users, and decision making.	
Product Manager	Drives the project and sets the priorities. Ensures that users' needs are met, establishes departmental profiles, and so on. Responsible for marketing and customer relations.	
Lead Program Manager	Manages the project, sets milestones, monitors overall project status and issues. Owns the overall plan and the project plan. Monitors the financial aspects (if applicable). Responsible for operations development.	

These program managers report to the Lead Program Manager:

Role	Responsibility	Names and Company Titles
Database Server Administrator	Responsible for administering database servers such as SQL Server, Sybase, Oracle, DB2, and so on. Owns the database connectivity sections of the plan.	
Distribution Administrator	Responsible for application deployment and licensing, particularly those responsible for push-installation modes such as Systems Management Server or IBM Tivoli. Owns all distribution methodology sections of the plan.	
Desktop Administrator	Responsible for workstation operating systems, software, and hardware. Owns the desktop components, including the current and planned environment, and the migration and configuration plans.	
Developers / Consultants	Involved in developing company-specific desktop applications (custom applications).	
End User Technical Support Team	Helpdesk personnel. Provide technical support for Office 2000 users. Maintain, operate, and repair Office 2000 configurations. Own all plan support aspects.	

(continued)

Role	Responsibility	Names and Company Titles
Intranet/ Internet Administrator	Responsible for the structural design and maintenance of intranet/Internet servers and services, as well as Web document standards. Owns the plan's browser and Office Server Extensions (OSE) sections.	
Messaging Administrator	Responsible for server-side messaging administration. Owns the plan's messaging sections.	
Network Administrator	Responsible for configuring and maintaining the network, ranging from network servers, protocols, and hardware (including printers) to domain administration of workstations and users. Owns all the plan's network-related components, including current and future configuration information and plans.	
Office Administrator	Determines technical configuration of all Office 2000 components (if applicable).	
Technical Consulting	Provides consulting services and problem resolution.	
Testing / Quality Assurance Team	Ensures Office 2000 conformance to functional requirements and corporate standards. Tests all betas, custom applications, and migration/coexistence issues. Owns the test plan.	
User Education	Develops training materials and documentation for users and technical support personnel, including helpdesk and user education. Owns the plan's training sections.	
Logistics Management	Deals with worldwide logistics. Owns the logistics plan and rollout strategy.	

Additional Personnel

List any other personnel needed to deploy Office 2000. For example:

Name and Title	Responsibility	Employee/Consultant/ Contractor	Duration
Installer	Installs the new configuration on all end-user computers.	Contractor	June–August

Equipment

In this section, detail additional equipment (and quantities) needed to migrate. Include:

- Test lab equipment
- Equipment for project personnel
- New computers for end users
- New network-related equipment
- Upgrade components for existing equipment

Needs Assessment

What is the plan for determining what each department needs to get from the current configuration to the desired environment? Of special interest are:

- Timing
- Hardware
- Operating system
- Third-party software integration
- File conversion
- Template and macro conversion
- Custom-solution conversion
- Specific feature requirements
- User settings/roaming users
- Browser considerations
- Messaging platform considerations
- Distribution infrastructure
- File sharing coexistence issues
- Development platform considerations

To assess needs, choose a method that is practical as well as accurate. Make sure any hardware/software inventory system databases are up-to-date before you run reports. Work with one contact from each business unit who supplies information in a one-on-one interview or in weekly meetings. Interviews also allow you to explain terminology and business needs to respondents, and to get the business units to accept responsibility for information gathering and quality. You can send out surveys through the mail or post them on an intranet site, but these methods incur costs and often fail to get accurate or complete information.

File Conversion

Detail plans to migrate or convert data files. Include the methods, logistics, and escalation paths.

File conversion methods depend on current software. If you are migrating from a previous version of Office, you shouldn't have to convert data files (except for Access databases) until they are used, particularly if you are moving from Office 95/97. Users can simply open documents, spreadsheets, and presentations in Office 2000 as needed, then can save these files in new-version formats or continue using the original format—which may be necessary to coexist with users who do not have Office 2000 or Office 97.

Access is an exception. Users who open previous-version Access databases in Access 2000 can manipulate data and use the application, but they cannot make any changes to tables, queries, reports, forms, macros, or modules. To make those types of changes, the database must be converted to Access 2000 format. This leaves a copy of the database in the old format. Make sure all databases are thoroughly tested before discontinuing use of the old format. For more information on Access format issues, see Chapter 3, "Coexisting with Previous Versions of Office."

Migrating from non-Microsoft desktop software requires more planning. Some issues are simplified by usage patterns. Most word processing files, for example, are created, used once, and never used again; users tend to have a few spreadsheets that they use frequently for a while, then stop using. So your file conversion plan should try to isolate and convert only necessary files.

The plan should also take into account file complexity and how many people use it. For instance, you can continue using complex files with specific printing requirements in their original-format versions, but reengineering them (if necessary for conversions) may provide better results for less work in the long term. The plan must balance costs with user inconvenience. File conversion may seem to be a relatively unimportant deployment issue, but it has high visibility and can complicate or halt deployment if not handled properly.

For more information, see Chapter 2, "Migrating Files, Templates, and Custom Solutions." See also *Converting Files Between Different Versions of Office Software: A File Format Matrix White Paper*, "Upgrading to Office 2000" in the *Microsoft Office 2000 Resource Kit*, and "Switching from Other Applications" in the *Microsoft Office 97 Resource Kit*.

Macros, Templates, and Custom Solutions Conversion

Detail the plan to migrate, retire, or update existing macros and templates. Include testing, methods, logistics, and escalation paths.

Template and macro conversion methods also depend on the existing version of Office. If you are moving from Office 4.*x*, you should test all macros and templates; test any that make 16-bit DLL or API calls and migrate them to 32-bit DLL or API calls. To accommodate the Word 2000 change from WordBasic to Visual Basic for Applications (VBA) there is a compatibility layer, but there may be some issues. Simple macros such as those that are recorded should encounter few problems, but you may have to work on more complex templates or macros to achieve proper operation in Office 2000. Creating new templates may be easier than revamping existing ones. New Word features may supersede some macros, but conversion is worthwhile for those you want to retain: VBA is more efficient than WordBasic for some operations and VBA programmers far outnumber WordBasic programmers, so converted items will be easier to maintain over the long run.

Migrating from a 32-bit version of Office should not present any 16-bit issues. Office 95 may require dealing with WordBasic to VBA problems and some related to object model changes in the other applications. Office 97 should present very few issues, but you should test mission- or business-critical applications.

The file format for Access has changed in each version, so you must test all converted databases thoroughly before retiring previous versions.

While you look for custom solutions to test and redevelop, assess them carefully to determine whether they should be retained. You might as well discard custom solutions that enforce obsolete business rules, that provide functionality now inherent in Office 2000, or that were cobbled together and should be redeveloped correctly. Make sure that solutions are indeed mission-critical, then test them.

 To create a usable inventory, list all line-of-business solutions, identify which software they use or depend on (Word, Visual Basic for Applications, ODBC, Internet Explorer, and so on), then list them in order of importance. Use the categories listed on the next page.

Mission Critical. Failure of these applications would significantly decrease revenue, increase expense, and cause customer or partner dissatisfaction. The organization can tolerate little or no risk of failure.

Business Critical. Failure of these applications would create significant but bearable cost and impact. The organization can tolerate low risk of failure.

Required. Failure of these applications can slightly reduce revenue, increase expenses, and cause customer or partner dissatisfaction.

Other. Failure of these applications should have negligible impact.

Macros and templates based on non-Microsoft software will need to be reengineered in Microsoft Office. Retire any items that are no longer used. Before redeveloping candidates in Office, make sure they are not simply mimicking old software. Use Office features to increase productivity and generate user enthusiasm.

For more information, see Chapter 2, "Migrating Files, Templates, and Custom Solutions," and the Office Developer Web site at http://www.microsoft.com /officedev.

Coexistence Plan

If you are not upgrading all users who share files to Office 2000, you need a plan that allows users of different versions to work together during implementation. Except for Access, Office 2000 files have the same format as Office 97, so a coexistence plan for these two versions needs to address only Access and file sharing with users outside the organization.

If your environment includes earlier versions of Office, you will have more issues *and* more options for dealing with them: 32-bit Windows viewers (for Word, Excel, and PowerPoint), 16-bit Windows viewers (for Word and PowerPoint), and installable converters (for earlier versions of Word and PowerPoint). Viewers allow previous-version users to open Office 2000 files without requiring any Office software. Converters allow users of previous versions to open Office 2000 files in their version of Office. All viewers and converters are included in a package in the *Microsoft Office 2000 Resource Kit.*

All Office 2000 applications can save files in earlier formats, and some even have a *dual* option that stores the Office 2000 format and the previous version format in one file that both versions can open without converters.

Detail how coexistence issues should be handled, including whether converters or viewers will be deployed, whether a default file format will be imposed, and how these things will be accomplished. To create the plan you need to understand how users share files and with whom. During the needs assessment for each rollout unit, make sure you understand interoperability:

- Within each organizational unit
- Between organizational units
- With partners such as customers, vendors, and regulatory agencies

You should also assess:

- How long users will coexist
- The Office versions involved
- If your organization uses system policies to enforce and change user settings
- If converters or viewers that allow users to open or view Office 97 files have already been deployed to previous-version users
- If non-Office 2000 users need to edit files, or simply view and print them

Some file types, such as Word documents, are shared across more organization borders than others and may require different treatment. Users generally share files mostly within their workgroup, although volumes and extents can differ depending on job role, application, and workgroup. If migrating an entire workgroup or business unit will take too much time or effort now, consider implementing a coexistence strategy that allows users to save files in earlier formats or provides converters to previous-version users.

Figure 1.3 shows a sample decision tree for forming a coexistence plan.

For more information, see Chapter 3, "Coexisting with Previous Versions of Office." You can also consult the *File Sharing in a Heterogeneous Office Environment* white paper, and "Upgrading to Office 2000" in the *Microsoft Office 2000 Resource Kit.*

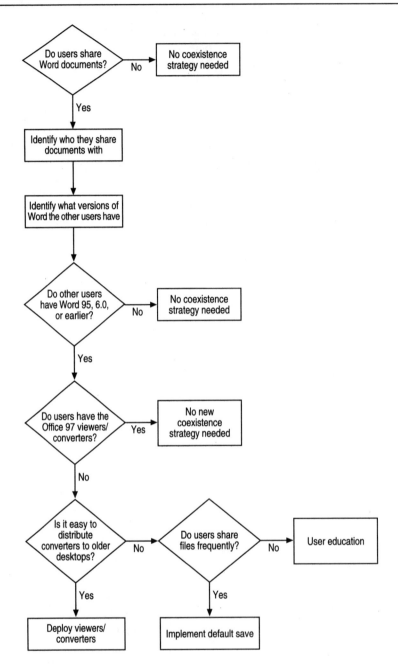

Figure 1.3   Sample decision tree.

Support Plan

⬦ What is the model for support, including user and developer support? Include steady-state support policies and levels, escalation paths, third-party involvement, and how to reduce the need for helpdesk support.

⬦ Can current staffing level handle the desktop migration? If not, consider augmenting staff by, for example, reassigning current staff to higher profile assignments such as floor support and using contractors for call handling.

⬦ Do you have any statistical information from past migrations that you can use to project needs, not only in terms of volume, but also in terms of what users will have problems with?

⬦ Can you avoid user problems by changing the custom configuration? You can install some components to the local computer (rather than on first use) so line-of-business solutions work properly, can customize Help to deal with foreseeable problems, and so on.

⬦ Do current personnel have the necessary skills and knowledge? If not, develop training for them, or hire contract personnel.

Create a specific plan for the helpdesk. Include staffing, training, hiring contractors, steps for dealing with known issues; and consider the use of Office 2000 customizable Help and alerts, escalation paths, and end-user self-help such as intranet content, cheat sheets, and the Office Assistant. Some organizations use helpdesk personnel to help deploy the software because they understand user needs. During the deployment they provide good field input on issues; afterwards they can use what they learned about the configuration to broaden their support skills.

Users often rate a migration a success or failure based on support level and quality. Even though most realize that problems are to be expected they tend to be intolerant of an unprepared or poorly staffed helpdesk. It is better to overstaff than to be caught shorthanded. You can cut back or reassign staff later.

For more information on adequately planning for and preparing the support environment, see *The Sourcebook for the Helpdesk* by Microsoft Press.

From the Trenches:
Designing a Support Plan for an Upgrade on a Deadline

Experience has shown that a good support plan is key to a successful deployment. The following real-life example describes one enterprise's aggressive support plan—designed to minimize deployment issues and to help users become productive in the Office 2000 environment as soon as possible.

The customer, a financial institution, is planning a fast-paced upgrade to Office 2000 Professional from Office 95. The customer aims to complete the upgrade of all desktops prior to a scheduled freeze of desktops later this summer due to Year 2000 issues. The Internal Technology group, which is the customer's internal technical support department, will handle all aspects of deployment. One of the main issues for the Internal Technology group is coexistence, as the rest of the financial institution will still be using Office 97.

The Internal Technology group will be both deploying and supporting Office 2000. End User Support Services (EUSS) handles first-level support calls in the call center. In addition, there are support managers that are responsible for the individual departments. These managers are very familiar with the user needs in their departments and are responsible for determining and creating the custom installation for that department (the involvement of the support managers will also make it easier for them to support installation issues after deployment).

The steady-state goal is that EUSS calls will be answered by the call center and resolved within 10 minutes or escalated to a level-two technician. The level-two technicians work for the support managers in the department and are familiar with those users. The goal for level-two technicians is to resolve an issue within 20 minutes.

Support technicians will learn about Office 2000 by attending a few informational sessions and by using the software themselves well in advance of end users. Technicians will support the pilots as well.

On the Friday before the first deployment, the technicians assisting in the rollout will attend a meeting where they watch the supervisor step through the entire installation process.

On the first business day after deployment, the helpdesk will be overstaffed so that technicians are available on the floors, making sure users are comfortable and not experiencing problems. By developing a solid plan for support before the actual deployment starts, this customer is working to minimize the impact of user issues and provide a successful implementation.

Training Plan

Document training policies and methods for users and support personnel. Assess the various methods and pick those that best fit your needs: instructor-led training, brown-bag sessions, computer-based training (CBT), intranet sites, and books. Microsoft Press offers books for all types of users and a CBT series.

The plan should address different user products (that they are migrating from), roles, and abilities. Detail training schedule and duration, and all resources. If you need third-party resources, evaluate vendors, then contact candidates as early as possible so they will be ready when you need them.

Train helpdesk personnel on the use of the new products, migration tools and strategies, how you are planning to deploy the software, their role in supporting that deployment, and coexistence strategies.

Here is a sample table for categorizing users:

Job Description	Microsoft Office Experience	Training Requirements

Figure 1.4   Table format for categorizing users.

Communication Plan

This plan is very important. It needs to address communication within the project staff and communication between project personnel and users. It should help maintain visibility, inform, create enthusiasm, foster cooperation, and communicate status and news about the project.

To prepare the plan, answer these questions:

◇ How do the various IT groups communicate regarding a planned deployment?

◇ Have there been previous deployments? How were user communications handled?

◇ Which previous strategies have effectively educated and informed users, while encouraging them to accept the change?

◇ Which previous strategies were unsuccessful and should be avoided?

◇ What materials were used?

Consider creating a team Web with Office Server Extensions (OSE) where all team members can comment on the plan, their progress, and any issues. It's a useful way to learn how to use OSE. For more information, see Chapter 13, "Deploying and Managing Office Server Extensions."

Subject to Communicate	Medium	Audience	Schedule
General News			
Project Status			
Migration Schedule			
Service Level Agreement			

Test Plan

Include information here about how you plan to test your new desktop configurations, Office-based line-of-business solutions, and distribution scenarios. Pertinent information would include any test lab resources or third parties that will assist in testing.

◇ Are there sufficient lab resources hardware, software, connectivity, and personnel to fully test this deployment? If not, how can you obtain these resources?

◇ Will you be using any special tools in your testing effort? Have all personnel been trained in the use of these tools?

◇ What are the criteria to determine whether an application gets tested?

◇ What are the criteria to determine whether a test suite passes or not?

◇ Who has ownership for the different components of the test plan?

Your test plan should include testing of at least the following:

- All possible desktop deployment scenarios
- Server test scenarios
- Migration of files, templates, macros, and custom solutions
- Third-party interoperability
- File coexistence scenarios
- Implementation of new features
- Restoring the desktop to its previous condition

Describe the test environment that will be in place to support the planning for Office 2000 implementation, including personnel, hours of operation, and third-party involvement.

Component	Configuration (Hardware & Software)
Client Computers	
Server Computer(s)	

Personnel	
Internal	Role
External	Role

Office 2000 Deployment Development Plan

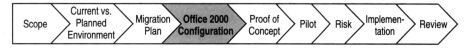

Using this section as a guide, document each rollout unit's configuration in the build worksheets in Appendix B (on the CD), creating a new set of worksheets for each rollout unit.

Hardware

Specify how existing users will get from their current configuration to the proposed configuration. Detail whether computers are being replaced or receiving component upgrades, and the exact method of doing that, including procurement and logistics. Include a hardware upgrade for each of these components.

- Desktop hardware
- Distribution servers
- Office Server Extensions servers

Operating System

Detail any changes that need to be implemented to move the users from their current operating system environment to the proposed one.

User Settings

In this section, document plans to implement pre-defined user settings including the method you will use.

Use the tables in Appendix B (on the CD) to document each setting. For more information about user settings, please see Chapter 5, "User Settings."

Microsoft Office 2000 Configuration

Office 2000 Feature Implementation

Prior to creating a custom configuration of Office 2000, your organization should understand the capabilities of Office 2000 to have a more efficient deployment that takes advantage of everything Office 2000 has to offer. Many of these decisions are not required in order to deploy Office 2000 but can help you decrease the number of times you touch the desktop, lowering your costs and the inconvenience to your end users. This section covers the main features for which you may want to plan, pointers to white papers or other additional information about these features, and decisions you may want to make prior to deploying Office 2000. Document your decisions in Appendix B (on the CD). You might, however, replace the existing text in these sections with a high-level discussion of your plans.

Specific Applications and Features

Different user communities often have different needs. Office 2000 contains different sets of applications in editions ranging from Office Standard to Office Premium. For example, users who are making quick financial decisions in Excel will not want to wait to install a feature the first time it's used—rather, they will expect immediate access to all functionality. On the other hand, some users may not know whether they need the Excel Analysis ToolPak and may want to delay loading it to conserve hard disk space.

Decisions

- Which edition(s) of Office will you deploy?
- How many editions of Office do you want to deploy?
- What is the base configuration for all users?
- What is the process for determining variations from the base configuration?

For more information on all of the features in Office 2000, see the *Office 2000 Product Enhancement Guide.* For more information on customizing the installation of Office 2000 features, see Chapter 4, "Customizing an Office 2000 Installation," and "Customizing Your Office 2000 Installation" in the *Microsoft Office 2000 Resource Kit.*

Deployment Features

Before you deploy Office 2000, you need to understand its new deployment features. Setup has been reengineered using the Windows Installer. You can now run the software from the local computer, from the source, or in a combined approach. Also included are the ability to install features the first time they are used, self-repairing applications that can fix missing files, and wizards for customizing and automating deployment.

Decisions

- Which feature set will you provide to users?

- Will you use the *Install on First Use* feature for some applications or features? This requires updating to the Windows Desktop Update for application-level Install on First Use before you deploy, or by using the Windows Installer Shortcuts transforms. For more information, see Chapter 4, "Customizing an Office 2000 Installation."

- Will some applications or features be unavailable to users?

Note   The needs assessment for each rollout unit will help you resolve these three items.

- Will the software run from the local computer, the source, or both? Each approach has pros and cons. Running software from the local computer requires more hard disk space and takes a little longer to install; running it from the server requires more network resources and a stable networking environment.

- Will you implement the Windows Desktop Update so that the self-repairing feature works for the Office 2000 application executables? This improves reliability and reduces the helpdesk burden, but it requires more planning up front.

- Which customizations to user settings will you deploy? If you plan these in advance you can deploy them with Office 2000.

For more information on the Windows Desktop Update, see the section below or Chapter 4, "Customizing an Office 2000 Installation."

To learn more about deployment features, see the *Office Deployment and Maintenance* white paper or "Installing Office 2000 in Your Organization" in the *Microsoft Office 2000 Resource Kit*.

Windows Desktop Update

Active Desktop (a feature of Microsoft Internet Explorer since version 4.01) has a two-layer interface:

- A transparent *icon layer* that displays the users' existing desktop shortcuts

- A background *HTML layer* that hosts any HTML-based items, including ActiveX controls and scripts

The HTML layer offers a customizable space for creating dynamic links to Web content, so you can use Active Desktop as a home base for launching programs, switching between files, and staying informed about what's happening on the Internet or an intranet.

The new shortcuts work with the Windows Installer by using a GUID for each application rather than a hard-coded path to the executable. The Windows Installer intercepts the GUID, checks the installation state, and then takes the appropriate action: start up the application, install it, or repair it.

Decisions

- Do you want to be able to take advantage of Install on First Use for applications?
- Do you want to be able to support the self-repairing applications feature to automatically repair a critical executable or dynamic-link library (DLL)?
- Do you have roaming users who may access computers that do not have Office 2000 on them?

If the answer to any of these is *yes*, you should deploy the Windows Desktop Update to users before Office 2000. Windows 98 and Windows 2000 already have it. For Windows NT Workstation 4.0 and Windows 95 user, install it with Internet Explorer 4.01 SP1 or later. With Internet Explorer 4.01 SP1, install the Active Desktop, which enables the shortcuts that the Office 2000 Windows Installer uses to install entire applications on demand, to repair applications that are missing critical files, and to provide Office 2000 to roaming users who access computers that don't have Office 2000 as well as their custom settings. For Internet Explorer 5, choose to install the Windows Desktop Update. The Windows Installer needs the new shortcuts but doesn't require the Active Desktop to be enabled. You can disable the Active Desktop by right-clicking on the desktop and turning it off, or, an administrator can customize Internet Explorer 5 with the Internet Explorer Administration Kit (IEAK) and disable the Active Desktop.

For more information, see Chapter 4, "Customizing an Office 2000 Installation," and the *Office 2000 Deployment and Maintenance* white paper.

Internet Explorer 5

Internet Explorer 5 is provided with Office 2000 and is integrated with its Web-based functionality to provide a development and solutions environment that simplifies Web publishing. If you are currently using an earlier version of Internet Explorer, consider upgrading. If you are installing Internet Explorer for the first time, test it fully before deploying it. Create policies and standard methods of deploying and implementing Internet Explorer 5, just as you do for Office. Use the Internet Explorer Administration Kit (IEAK) to control installation and user settings. The IEAK is integrated into the Custom Installation Wizard, the main tool for customizing Office 2000 setup. If you've already created a custom installation for Internet Explorer 5, you can use it. Internet Explorer 5 also includes the Windows Desktop Update.

Decisions

- Do users need to publish Web content?
- Do users need to access or work with Web content even when offline?
- Are you deploying Office Server Extensions and taking advantage of the Web Discussions feature?
- Are you deploying the Windows Desktop Update to take advantage of application-level Installed on First Use or self-repairing applications?

If the answer to any of these is *yes*, use Internet Explorer 5 for the highest functionality and the most efficient deployment.

- Are you deploying Internet Explorer 5 with Office 2000 or separately?
- Will it be the standard browser, or supplemental?

For more information see Chapter 4, "Customizing an Office 2000 Installation," and the *Microsoft Internet Explorer Corporate Deployment Guide.*

International Use

Office 2000 has been engineered for simplified multinational deployment. You can combine a single-language version with a MultiLanguage Pack to provide a language interface utilizing most of the Office 2000-supported languages, or you can use one of the single-language versions of Office 2000, which sometimes have more localized content than the MultiLanguage Pack. To decide which is the best solution for your environment, answer these questions:

Decisions

- Will you be creating all worldwide custom installations, or will the local IT organizations be responsible for that?
- Will you deploy Office 2000 and the MultiLanguage Pack all at one time, or will you deploy the English version worldwide before all languages are available?
- Will users have a connection to the installation source so languages can Install on First Use, or do you plan to customize Office 2000 installation for each language?

For more information, see Chapter 9, "Multinational Deployment," the white paper *Office 2000 in a Multinational Organization*, and "Deploying Office in a Multinational Setting" in the *Microsoft Office 2000 Resource Kit.*

Year 2000 Planning

Office 2000 has year 2000-compliant features. It uses 2029 as its default cutoff year, as does Office 97. Two-digit year entries between 30 and 99 are automatically resolved as 1930–1999, while two-digit year entries between 0 and 29 are automatically resolved as 2000–2029. The setting is customizable, so you can change these cutoff points. Finally, Access has a setting that forces the use of four-digit year formats for all date fields.

Excel year 2000-compliance features include:

- New date formats that display four digits for the year regardless of whether the user enters two or four digits.
- Automatic date formatting to match the system short date (which can be changed to four digits).
- Additional Excel-based tools on the *Microsoft Office 2000 Resource Kit* CD that search for and help fix two-digit year formats in existing files. You can deploy these tools with Office 2000.

Decisions

- Do you plan to institute a four-digit year format for the system short date?
- Are you going to change the default date format so Excel always displays four-digit dates?
- Do you need to customize the cutoff year for two-digit year entry in Excel?
- Do you have users who have existing files with date-dependent information?
- Do you plan to use the Access setting to force the use of four-digit year formats?

If the answer to any of these is *yes*, plan to distribute these settings. You can do this before or with Office 2000.

For more information, see the *Microsoft Office 2000 and the Year 2000* white paper and "Meeting the Year 2000 Challenge" in the *Microsoft Office 2000 Resource Kit.*

For year 2000 information regarding Microsoft products see http://www.microsoft.com/year2000 or contact your local subsidiary.

Macro Protection

Several Office 2000 features help protect against macro viruses. Office 2000 applications now allow virus protection software to scan files when they are selected and before they are opened. Check your virus protection software to see if it offers this feature or will in a future version. For more protection you can set three user security levels: **high**, which requires that macros are installed with the product or from a trusted source; **medium**, which prompts the user to disable macros; or **low**, which performs no macro checking at all. The default setting in Word is **high**, and in Excel and PowerPoint it is **medium**. A trusted source is a macro that is digitally signed or has a certificate managed by Internet Explorer. You can deploy Office with a pre-defined list of trusted sources.

Decisions

- Does your environment require the highest security for macro protection or are users allowed to share macros easily with each other? You may want to change the default settings based on environment or application.

- Is there a list of known trusted sources that you can deploy with Office 2000? If so, include it in the configuration documentation.

- Are you currently using Internet Explorer or Certificate Manager to manage certificates? If not, are you planning to do so?

- Does your current virus protection software use the Office 2000's new virus-checking capability? Is there a new version of your current virus protection software that can make use of this capability? Are you planning to upgrade?

For more information, see the *Microsoft Office 2000 Macro Security* white paper and "Managing Security" in the *Microsoft Office 2000 Resource Kit.*

Office 2000 Feature Customization

Customizable Help

You can use the Answer Wizard Builder (in the *Microsoft Office 2000 Resource Kit*) to customize the Office 2000 Answer Wizard so that users can perform natural language queries on existing Help topics, custom Help topics, and live Web site information. This supports Office 2000 custom solutions and allows users to ask questions with specialized terminology such as legal or accounting terms. You can create a help topic that lists internal helpdesk phone numbers or intranet sources, or that explains the file coexistence strategy, providing users with recommended file sharing methods rather than information on every possibility.

Decisions

- Does the helpdesk already have documentation on common user issues?

- Can you easily put this content into HTML so it can be distributed as additional help with Office 2000?

- Are in-house Office developers aware of this capability so they can use it when deploying Office 2000 custom solutions?

For more information, see Chapter 11, "Customizing Alerts and Help," and "Helping Users Help Themselves" in the *Microsoft Office 2000 Resource Kit.*

Customizable Alerts

Several Office 2000 alert dialog boxes allow users to go to the Microsoft Office Web site for information. You can customize the **Web Help** button in these dialog boxes so that it directs users to internal information instead. For example, users trying to print Word documents through an offline printer usually get a generic *printer unavailable* error message. You can customize the alert to go to an intranet page that gives current printer status and lists other potential printers, so users can solve the problem without calling the helpdesk.

Decisions

- Does the helpdesk already have an intranet site with additional help for users? If yes, take advantage of that site by using customizable alerts.

- Can existing documentation be converted easily to Web content with Word 2000?

- Are there any plans to create an intranet site with help for users in the next six months? If yes, consider creating a home page that explains plans, and including a pointer to this site in Office 2000 when you deploy it.

For more information, see Chapter 11, "Customizing Alerts and Help," and "Helping Users Help Themselves" in the *Microsoft Office 2000 Resource Kit.*

System Policies/Desktop Lockdown

System policies are a Windows 95/98 and Windows NT Workstation feature you can use to set and enforce policies on a local computer. Use them to disable Windows features that can be misused, such as the ability to change the desktop or use the Control Panel, or to create custom settings without having to touch the desktop. In Office 2000, use them to implement file coexistence strategies, customizable Help, and alerts, to enforce macro virus and year 2000 settings, and to create custom settings such as template and file locations.

Decisions

- Do you currently use system policies? If so, examine the Office 2000 templates to determine which settings you want to set for users and the organization.

- Do you have a coexistence, security (macro virus), or year 2000 plan that you want to enforce? If so, you should use system policies to do it.

For more information, see Chapter 5, "User Settings," the *Office 2000 Deployment and Maintenance* white paper, and "Ongoing Configuration of Office on Users' Computers" in the *Microsoft Office 2000 Resource Kit.*

Roaming Users

Windows 95/98 and Windows NT Workstation 4.0 allow users to call up their user profiles on different computers. Office 2000 and its user settings can be implemented to support this feature.

Decisions

- Do you have any users who roam from one computer to another and need their custom settings to follow them?

For more information, see Chapter 5, "User Settings," the *Office 2000 Deployment and Maintenance* white paper, and "Supporting Users Who Travel Between Computers" in the *Microsoft Office 2000 Resource Kit*.

Office 2000 Custom Solutions Development

Office architecture is based on the industry-standard Component Object Model (COM) specification, which allows developers to reuse and build on Office services. You can use Office 2000 to create custom solutions for publishing (Web and print), data access and reporting, business intelligence, collaboration, and data analysis and tracking. Custom solutions use tools that are already familiar to users to simplify tasks and functionality. You can deploy them with Office 2000.

Decisions

- Do you have solutions you can deploy with Office 2000? If so, make sure you also deploy any required Office functionality. Deploying solutions with Office reduces implementation costs.

- Do you want to educate business units on the development capabilities of Office 2000? If so, build information on this effort into the rollout schedule.

For more information, see the Office Developer Web site at http://www.microsoft.com/officedev.

Office Server Extensions

The Office Server Extensions (OSE) help you use in-place Web technology to foster collaboration via the intranet. OSE makes it easy for users to publish documents to the Web (by saving them to a file server) and to find, view, annotate, or retrieve Web documents.

The extensions require a server running Windows NT Workstation 4.0 with Personal Web Server, or one running Windows NT Server 4.0 with Service Pack 4 and its built-in Web server, Microsoft Internet Information Server (IIS) 4.0 or higher. OSE uses the Windows NT domain security infrastructure.

Web publishing and collaboration features are also supported by Internet Explorer 5 and by SMTP mail servers, such as Microsoft Exchange. OSE also provides a Microsoft SQL Server-compatible database.

Decisions

- Do users frequently create content such as documents, spreadsheets, or presentations that need to be reviewed by other users?

- Do users need to stay current on Web content that is frequently updated?

- Do users create and publish content for print publication and the Web?
- Are any of these users on different operating system platforms?
- Do you have a server running Windows NT Server with Service Pack 4 and IIS 4.0 on which you can run the Office Server Extensions?

If the answer to any of these is *yes*, consider using OSE.

For more information, see Chapter 13, "Deploying and Managing Office Server Extensions," the *Office Server Extensions* white paper, the *Workgroup Web* white paper, and "Using Office Server Extensions" in the *Microsoft Office 2000 Resource Kit*.

Staged Deployment of Office

You may need to deploy Outlook before the rest of Office, or the English version to international users before the corresponding MultiLanguage Pack. Staged deployment requires you to plan configuration carefully and to test all stages before deploying the first stage, if only to avoid overwriting custom settings.

If you plan a staged deployment, you can install individual applications first, then perform the Office 2000 setup later. For example, you can use the individual Outlook application setup first, then use the Office 2000 setup later but not install Outlook or any Outlook settings.

Staged deployments sometimes are unplanned: you do not install an application to a user or group of users, then find out that they need it. The new Custom Maintenance Wizard (in the *Microsoft Office 2000 Resource Kit*) allows you to edit the Windows Installer database on the local computer to change the installation state of any given feature, thereby adding or removing a feature without doing a new installation.

For more information, see the *Microsoft Office 2000 Resource Kit*.

Removing Previous Versions of Office

When installation is complete, Office 2000 setup by default removes previous versions of Office safely, leaving any components that other software may still use. You can customize the removal process. You can also run the Office Removal Wizard in stand-alone mode *before* installing Office 2000 to remove previous versions and free up hard drive space—but this makes it impossible to rollback if the Office 2000 installation encounters a problem.

For more information, see Chapter 4, "Customizing an Office 2000 Installation," and "Removal Wizard" in the *Microsoft Office 2000 Resource Kit*.

Third-Party Software Updates

List any third-party software that is integrated with Office and needs updating to run properly in Office 2000. Detail all configuration issues and plans.

Other Standard Software

If the implementation includes new computers, detail their configuration and software requirements.

Browser Upgrade Plan

Do you plan to upgrade the system browser? If so, specify the configuration, including the use of the Internet Explorer Administration Kit (IEAK), and its possible effect on Web administration, custom Web solutions, and interoperability with Office 2000.

This plan should include:

- Automatic browser configuration options
- Browser security settings
- Internet mail and news options
- Windows Desktop Update

Messaging Platform Considerations

◈ What is the existing messaging infrastructure? How does it affect the desktop? What are the existing client policies? Who supports messaging? How will the Office 2000 deployment team communicate and work with the messaging group?

◈ Does the current messaging infrastructure support Outlook as a client?

◈ Who needs to be involved in deploying the Outlook messaging and collaboration client with Office 2000?

◈ What are the deployment logistics?

◈ Do users require new profiles, or will most users migrate their existing ones? You cannot do both.

Most large organizations have separate groups for managing desktop applications and the messaging system, so this effort may require more coordination or a phased deployment (perhaps deploying Outlook along with a messaging server upgrade).

For more information, see Chapter 8, "Deploying Outlook 2000."

Distribution Infrastructure Considerations

Detail any user desktop changes needed to support the Office 2000 distribution, including installing client-side distribution software.

Database Architecture

Outline back-end database issues such as the need for ODBC drivers, restoring connections, or features to install with Office 2000.

New Configuration Build Process

Appendix B (on the CD) contains a worksheet for configuring Office 2000 clients and distribution or solution servers. Fill one out for each rollout unit (department, business unit, and so on) and use the completed sheets for testing and for the rollout. Add rows if you need more room.

For more information, see Chapter 4, "Customizing an Office 2000 Installation."

Office Profile Wizard

Document the steps for creating custom user settings and capturing them with the Office Profile Wizard. List each setting separately. Also list the user interface option for creating each setting so it can be checked after installation.

Additional Registry Settings

Document any registry settings to be deployed with Office 2000 that you can't create with the Office Profile Wizard. One example is the system short date for year 2000 compliance. A method for creating these settings is to use the user interface to create the setting on a test computer, export the necessary key(s) to a .REG file, then import the keys with the Custom Installation Wizard.

Office Removal Wizard

Document any changes to the .OPC file, which the Office Removal Wizard uses to remove previous versions of Office. The default method is a very safe one that preserves compatibility but does leave a lot of old software installed.

Custom Installation Wizard

Document the steps for using the Custom Installation Wizard to create each custom build of Office you will need. Identify which user community each custom build is for, the transform file name (*.MST) and location, and the associated .OPS file.

IEAK Customization Wizard

Document the steps for using the IEAK Customization Wizard to set up Internet Explorer 5 for your environment. Use the tables in Appendix C (on the CD) to document all settings.

Language Settings Tool

Use this *Microsoft Office 2000 Resource Kit* tool to configure the default language when coupling a MultiLanguage Pack with the English (U.S.) version of Office 2000. Use the language settings tool to customize language versions for international use.

Customization Process Flow Chart

Here is a sample flow chart for the customization process. You may not use all steps included here, you may want to add some steps, or you may want to change their order for your environment.

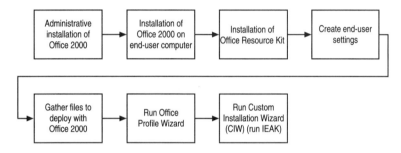

Figure 1.5   A sample customization flow chart.

Distribution Plan

Once new software is accepted, how will you distribute it to users? This section concentrates specifically on the technologies and methods available for distributing software to the desktop. Which method or combination of methods you use depends on hardware, operating system, geography, and connectivity.

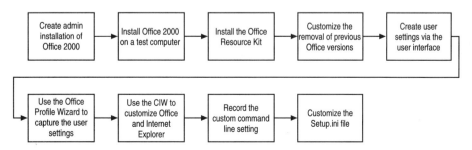

Figure 1.6   A sample distribution flow chart.

It is cheaper to use an automation tool such as Microsoft Systems Management Server than to send a technician to each desktop. The more you automated, however, the more you must plan and test to ensure a successful deployment. Listed below are the most common methods for distributing software, in ascending order of distribution cost.

- If you are upgrading hardware, specify how the vendor should deliver the computers, including all Office 2000 configuration settings. Or you can set up a build lab where computers are swapped in, built, then swapped back out to users. If you are building computers yourself, investigate tools such as SYSPREP for Windows NT Workstation or third-party tools for creating disk images.
- Deploy Office with existing software distribution tools, such as Systems Management Server.
- Implement new distribution tools to deploy Office. This cost may be high, but it may be recouped if you are deploying Office to many desktops. This complicates implementation, so stage the changes to minimize problems and improve troubleshooting.
- Use logon scripts to trigger an automated Office installation.
- Distribute specially built CDs to remote users or laptop users.
- Send technicians to each desktop.

There are other methods: e-mailing shortcuts that trigger an automated installation, Internet/intranet downloads, and so on, but each method has risks, especially methods that cannot be enforced.

◈ Do you want users to be able to interact with Setup? If not, then use the tools provided in the *Microsoft Office 2000 Resource Kit* to customize and automate Setup, making it silent. You can still customize settings or disable specific options while allowing users to run Setup interactively.

◈ Is there a system in place for distributing software? If not, is there a plan for one soon? Would it delay deployment too much to put a system in place? How do these factors affect overall costs and planning?

◈ Are there computers that cannot be reached with that system (for example, laptops, remote users, or home computers)? If so, develop plans to upgrade them.

Office 2000 Server Setup

List the servers and shares that will house the administrative installations of Office 2000, the local edition (Standard, Professional, Developer, Premium), any customization files (.OPS and .MST) that should be contained there, and user group and drive mappings associated with those shares.

MultiLanguage Pack Server Setup

List the servers and shares that will house the administrative installations of the Office 2000 MultiLanguage Pack, the edition of MultiLanguage Pack and associated languages installed there, any customization files (.OPS and .MST) that should be contained there, and user group and drive mappings associated with those shares.

Distribution Package Configurations

If you use a software distribution system, detail all steps necessary to create the installation packages. The basic steps for distributing software to clients with a Systems Management Server Package Definition File are:

- Create the package source directory
- Use the Create Package from Definition Wizard to create a package for the application
- Specify distribution servers for the package
- Specify access accounts for the package
- Advertise one or more of the package's programs to clients

Here is an overview of how to use Systems Management Server to distribute packages and deploy Office 2000:

1. Distribute the Office 2000 files to a server that has been designed to service a set of users.
2. Customize installations by creating .MST files with the Custom Installation Wizard in the Microsoft Office 2000 Resource Kit.
3. In the Systems Management Server Administration program, create a package using the Office 2000 .PDF file. See the Systems Management Server Administrator's Guide for more information on package creation.
4. Instruct Systems Management Server to distribute the package to selected end-user computers.
5. Systems Management Server picks up all the files from the specified installation point and copies them to one or more Systems Management Server distribution servers that service users.
6. When users run the package on their computers, Systems Management Server runs Setup from the copy of Office residing on the distribution server. All the main and shared Office 2000 components are accessed from this server.

For more information, see the *Deploying Microsoft Office 2000 with Systems Management Server* white paper or "Deploying Office with Systems Management Server" in the *Microsoft Office 2000 Resource Kit*.

Build-Process Flow Chart

Below is a sample build-process flow chart (Figure 1.7) for upgrading a Windows NT Workstation 4.0 client computer to Office 2000 from Office 95, using Systems Management Server as the software distribution tool. The steps illustrated would have to be completed for each workstation. The administrator does not need to log on because Systems Management Server (SMS) has elevated privileges.

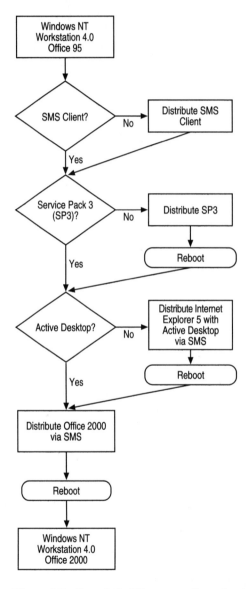

Figure 1.7   Sample build-process flow chart.

Configuration and Distribution Plan Review

Review outstanding issues, successes, failures, and lessons learned. For more information about distributing Office 2000, see Chapter 7, "Distributing Microsoft Office 2000."

Proof of Concept

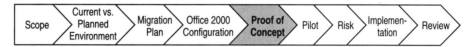

The Proof of Concept (POC) evaluates the implementation solution in a closed environment that simulates the real environment. This phase includes installation, testing, and removal of the completed Office 2000 installation(s). If necessary, it can be used as a showcase for final corporate approval. The POC allows you to gather feedback and refine the process, and you may have refer some items back to previous phases for additional work. The IT group is often used for the POC, but when you evaluate their results, remember that they may not represent the average user.

Pilot

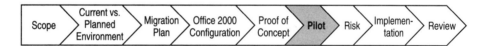

The Pilot phase focuses on production-environment proof of the entire implementation. The pilot group—a representative sample of enterprise users—follows the entire implementation process to validate assumptions and development for a sample population, and to evaluate the readiness of the team and support organization. Lessons learned validate the proposed solution and are used to further refine the process.

Note   The IT group is rarely representative of the general user. Don't use it as the pilot group.

Implementation

If you are going to alter any specifics of the deployment process or the execution of the deployment plan for the pilot, document it here. Otherwise, follow the plan as is.

Testing Procedures

Use the Pilot Testing Checklist in Appendix D (on the CD). Use the deployment project plan to perform testing, then use the results to modify the project plan.

Procedures

Use the Pilot Checklist in Appendix D (on the CD) to make sure you execute all pilot activities.

Pilot Review

When the pilot is complete, evaluate and document issues, successes, failures, and lessons learned.

Risk Assessment

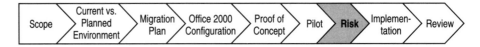

The risk assessment increases the probability of a successful implementation by decreasing project risk. The analysis quantifies the elements of risk as they relate to the project, prioritizes them according to implementation impact, and devises scenarios to alleviate specific risks. Use the questions below to isolate potential risks.

Risk Assessment Checklist

Envisioning

◇ Are there conflicting or competing projects?

◇ What are the *real* deadlines?

◇ Do members of various sponsoring organizations have differing visions of project methods and outcomes?

◇ Are there other business or political considerations that might affect deployment? For example, other environment upgrades, a merger, and so on.

Budget

◇ Has the budget been signed off at the appropriate customer level?

◇ What factors could cause cost overruns? How will overruns be handled?

Human Resources

◈ Does the project have appropriate resources? If not, identify:

- How this could affect deployment.

- A plan to obtain needed resources, including time.

◈ Are people with the appropriate technical skills available? If not, identify:

- Which areas need additional technical skills.

- How to provide technical training or hire/contract people with adequate skills. Microsoft Solution Providers are a possibility.

◈ Are project workers assigned full- or part-time?

Technology

- Are new technologies other than Office 2000 being put in place?

- What risks do these pose to a successful Office 2000 deployment?

- How do you plan to remove or mitigate those risks?

Risk Assessment Matrix

Use the matrix below to rate *Impact* and *Probability* as **high**, **medium**, or **low**.

Impact	Probability	Risk Description and Date of Identification	Mitigation Plan and Date of Formulation	Risk Owner

Figure 1.8   A sample risk assessment matrix.

Implementation

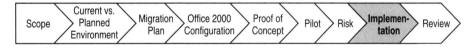

The implementation phase is derived by adjusting the pilot phase with elements from the risk assessment. Before you start implementation, complete the rollout schedule and the logistics plan. Detail these tasks:

- Communicate with users

- Conduct user training

- Migrate files, templates, macros, and custom solutions

- Ensure support organization is prepared and in place
- Create the custom configurations
- Distribute the software
- Obtain user feedback

Use the Microsoft Project plan developed earlier in this chapter to refine the rollout schedule and logistics plan. The logistics plan may require additional flow charts.

Post Implementation Review

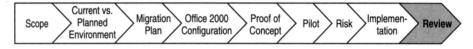

Review how things went—you may have to do this again someday. Include future software or development needs that were discovered during implementation. In addition to a critical review of the overall process, team, and results, you should focus on how to take advantage of the new Office 2000 features. When implementation is under way, use this section to review the process. Be sure to get user feedback. Review and evaluate:

- Communication
- Migration
- Software distribution
- Coexistence
- Support
- Training
- Future directions

Assess and document issues, successes, failures, and lessons learned.

CHAPTER 2

Migrating Files,
Templates, and Custom Solutions

*By Chris Kunicki,
Micro Modeling
Associates, Inc.*

Many organizations rely on Microsoft Office documents in day-to-day operations. To migrate efficiently and painlessly to Office 2000, you have to understand the value of these documents so that you can create a migration plan that meets users' needs, allays their concerns, and protects essential business documents. To help you protect existing files, templates, and custom solutions, this chapter discusses the common issues, provides suggestions for managing them, and explains file conversion methods.

What You'll Find in This Chapter:

- A definition of migration

- How to prepare for migration—including how to categorize the files in your system to create a workable inventory and a table of file classification criteria

- How to migrate data files that you have selected for conversion

- Real-life scenarios that demonstrate how to support users through deployment

- Custom solutions to common problems related to the migration of templates

- How to deal with year 2000 issues in all Office 2000 applications

Understanding Migration

For users, a primary concern when migrating to Office 2000 is converting documents from earlier versions, such as Office 4.3 or 95. This normally is handled more or less automatically: a user opens a Word 6 document in Word 2000, Word converts it to the newer format, the user saves it. Generally this proceeds smoothly, because most Office 2000 products have undergone only minor UI changes and because improvements make it easier to migrate earlier-version documents. Most users become comfortable with the new version, and go back to opening and working with the documents they use every day without interrupted productivity.

Still, there are some migration issues, specifically with documents that utilize advanced Office features that have changed from earlier versions, especially macros and the Office Object models in each of the products. With some planning, you can anticipate these issues, deal with them, and ensure a smooth migration.

Pre-Migration Work

Inventory Existing Files

The first step in developing a migration plan is to inventory the files in use in your system and categorize them as either *data* or *templates/custom solutions*.

Data files are the typical documents created by users in Word, Excel, PowerPoint, or Access—memos, employee evaluations, sales presentations, contact databases, and so on—most often used by one person or shared only within a department or business unit. These files, which usually represent 75 to 95 percent of all Office documents, tend to convert so easily that the process can be left to users. When they open an earlier-version file, Office identifies the file version and prompts for conversion to Office 2000 format. After conversion, it can be used as normal.

Allowing users to handle conversion takes advantage of the fact that users are in the best position to understand the value of their own files. They know which files they use, which have necessary data but expendable formatting, which are old enough to be archived, which are unimportant enough to be deleted, and which need closer attention because of formatting, functionality, or data.

Templates and *custom applications* often include advanced Office functionality or programmability, such as a set of templates that include standard cover letterhead, memos, or fax forms. These may require special installation or desktop configuration, and may include custom macros. Custom Access databases (to track employee training records, for example) often use programming logic based on business rules and workflow. Because these sorts of files often use custom menus, toolbars, and macros, they often require more effort by the owner, department, or IT support staff to migrate them to Office 2000.

Code is an issue because of changes to the Office programming environment and object models, especially since Office 4.3. For example, Word 6 and Word 95 use WordBasic syntax, but Word 97 and 2000 use Visual Basic for Applications (VBA) and an Object Model that helps programmers develop Word-based solutions. Most of the time Word 2000 successfully translates WordBasic commands to VBA. A migration plan has to deal with the exceptions.

Categorizing files as you inventory them shows you which files will require minimal migration effort (data files), and which will require more effort (templates or custom solutions).

Note   You may have trouble categorizing some files. Consultants find that if a file has a functional name, it probably is an application and merits some investigation. For example, a file called *Vendor Tracker* is more likely to be a custom Access-based application than a data file.

Classify Files

Inventory makes a great opportunity to *clean house*. Consider the usefulness and amount of migration effort required for the documents, templates, and macros you categorize. See how effectively these elements aid business workflow, if they aid it at all. Consider three classifications:

- **Obsolescence.** Legacy documents that have not been used for a long time or that probably will not be used again. Archive them (preferably off-line, to free up network space), so that they can be retrieved and converted if they are needed again. Don't be surprised to find files on servers that haven't been used in a long time and that aren't worth a migration effort. Encourage users to convert only necessary, useful documents.

- **User conversion.** Documents that will convert easily and simply to Office 2000 file format. For example, about 80 to 90 percent of Word files typically are three pages or less and have no complex graphics or inserts. Users can easily convert them.

- **Supported conversion and reengineering.** Important documents or databases that use advanced functionality. Converting these may require technical support and extensive testing to make sure they convert and function correctly. To save conversion, support, and maintenance effort later, review macros now to see if they are still needed. For example, if you have a custom macro that prints several pages of a document on one piece of paper, you probably don't have to convert it—the Word 2000 Zoom feature does this. Avoid converting redundant or superseded macros.

These classifications are not hard and fast, but they can save work and avoid wasted effort. As users and departments evaluate documents, make sure they understand the process and use the same criteria. Consider distributing this information:

Example File Classification Criteria

Classification	Value
Obsolescence	Not used in last 2 years
	Used once and not needed again
	No longer needed
User Conversion	File frequently used
	Legally required to retain document
	Macros – macros created by user
Supported Conversion and Reengineering	Mission critical
	Shared among multiple users
	Macros – created by power user or developer

Back Up Files Before Conversion

Back up all original files and store them in a safe location, so that if there are problems during conversion you can retrieve the original data. This takes time, but it's worth it.

Encourage Early Adoption

When users feel included and that their concerns and views are being given proper consideration, they are much more likely to help support the deployment. You can help foster this type of support by encouraging some users—perhaps power users or developers—to adopt Office 2000 before the general user population. The earlier they upgrade, the more opportunity they have to test their files and custom applications, to convert files, to discover and escalate issues, and to identify potential issues (especially ones unique to your organization).

Migrating Data Files

This section explains how to migrate data files that you have selected for conversion. In most cases, users will convert their own files by simply opening them, selecting Save, and responding to the Office prompt to save them in Office 2000 or the existing format. If you want to convert a large number of files, you can use the batch conversion process discussed in the section, "Batch File Conversion," on page 52.

Note   Converting earlier-version files to Office 2000 can sometimes lose formatting and data, and can pose compatibility issues that a migration plan should take into account. For more information, see Chapter 3, "Coexisting with Previous Versions of Office," particularly the last section, "Implementing Coexistence Strategies."

Converting Documents

You use a similar approach to migrate files for all Office applications except Access:

1. **Open** the File.
2. Choose **Save** from the **File** menu.

Office allows users to work and save files in earlier-version Office file formats, but every time you work with those files you are prompted to save in the Office 2000 format.

Converting Database Files

Access 2000 uses a slightly different approach because it requires specific conversion information. The steps are:

1. Start Access 2000.
2. From the **File** menu, select **Open Database**.
3. In the dialog, browse to the appropriate database file and click **Open**.

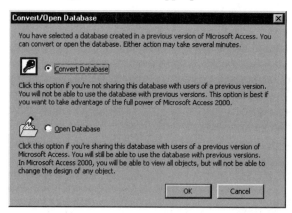

Figure 2.1   The Convert/Open Database dialog box.

4. The first time an earlier-version Access database is opened in Access 2000, the **Convert/Open Database** dialog is displayed (see Figure 2.1).

5. Click on **Convert Database** to save in Access 2000 format.

6. When prompted, select a name and location for the converted file. (Access 2000 does not allow you to overwrite the existing file, so you must provide a unique name.)

Access 2000 displays error messages if there are conversion problems.

If the file was previously opened in Access 2000 and enabled (the next section has details on enabling), you do not get the **Convert/Open Database** dialog. To convert the file to Access 2000, open it and select **Tools | Database Utilities | Convert Database** and continue with step 3 above.

Enabling Databases

Enabling a database keeps its format intact, which allows users of different Access versions to share it. When an Access 2000 user enables an earlier-version Access database, other users can browse it and add, delete, or modify records, but they cannot switch to Design view for any objects. To modify the design of existing objects or to add new objects, the database must be opened in the version of Access used to create it.

For example, Access 97 cannot read an Access 2000 database, so if users of both versions need to share a database the file must remain in Access 97 format and be enabled for Access 2000 users.

To enable a database, open it in Access 2000. The first time an earlier-version database is opened, Access 2000 displays the **Convert/Open Database** dialog box. Click **Open Database** to open the database without converting it. It is now enabled.

If the database contains forms, reports, or modules, Access 2000 creates separate copies of these objects and their Access Basic code (Access 1.*x*/2.0) or Visual Basic for Applications code (Access 95/97). This allows them to run under Access 2000 but it can increase the database size. Access 2000 does not display the **Convert/Open Database** dialog box the next time the database is opened unless the earlier version has been used to change module code, forms, or reports. If code has changed, you must enable the database again.

Batch File Conversion

Batch file conversion deals with a group of files, saving you the bother of opening and saving files one by one. Before beginning a batch conversion:

- Determine the key files to back up, if backup space is limited.
- Make sure there is enough storage space for the converted files.
- Make sure you have enough bandwidth (if converting over a network connection). Each file is downloaded locally, converted, then sent back to the server; this can use up a lot of bandwidth over a considerable time.

To run the Word Conversion Wizard:

1. From the **File** menu, choose **New**.
2. In the **Other Documents** tab, select **Batch Conversion Wizard** and click on **OK**. The wizard automates the conversion and presents a series of dialog boxes.
3. Click **Next** to continue past the first screen.
4. Select the file format from which to convert as shown in Figure 2.2, then click **Next**.

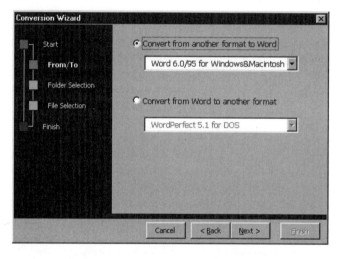

Figure 2.2   Using the Conversion Wizard.

Make sure to specify the right driver in the **Convert from another format to Word** field. If Word encounters a file format of a different type, it skips the file, stops, and prompts you to continue the process. You should monitor this process to make it sure it runs to completion.

5. Use the next screen to specify the source and target directories using the Browse buttons. Make sure the destination directory has enough storage space for the converted files and that it does not have any files with the same names as files being converted—the wizard overwrites them.

6. Use the screen shown in Figure 2.3 to select individual files:

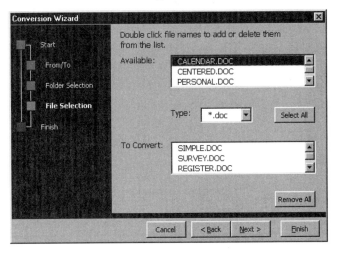

Figure 2.3   Selecting files to be converted.

7. When you have selected the files, click the **Next** button and **Finish** to begin conversion.

8. During conversion, a progress indicator is displayed (see Figure 2.4).

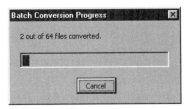

Figure 2.4   The progress bar.

9. When all files are converted, the wizard prompts for an additional batch conversion. Select **Yes** for another batch or **No** to exit the wizard.

From the Trenches: Providing a Smooth Transition for Users

Most users find that the migration process is quite easy, and that the new version of Office is not all that different from what they have been using. But it is natural to resist change. The following real-life examples provide you with some proven methods for supporting those users who need some coaxing and assistance in migrating and lead to a successful and trouble-free Office 2000 adoption within your company.

Provide brief, post-deployment support on-site. One company provided on-site helpdesk support for two hours after users received the new version of Office. One support person handled the calls, answering questions and walking users through the migration steps. Most users did not require any help, but they felt better knowing that an IT professional was standing by. By assisting users up front, the helpdesk received fewer support calls later.

Provide a brief reference card for migration. The same company gave users a card listing the conversion steps. Especially useful for the forgetful, this helped users solve problems on their own, thereby reducing the number of support calls. This information, along with a FAQ and other tips, was posted to an internal Web site.

Deploy by department or to users who work together. People who work together often use similar applications and documents and experience the same conversion problems. If you deploy to all group members at the same time, users can support each other, and the helpdesk can help numerous users at the same time.

Use IT staff members who know and work with the users. When staff members understand the business needs of users, they can more efficiently provide the assistance they need.

Implementing Data File Conversion Strategy

This section deals first with general Office 2000 issues and then discusses issues for the Office applications.

General Issues

File Size After Conversion

Conversion sometimes increases file size. To estimate how much room you need, convert a few files and compare their sizes before and after. If you have a lot of files to convert use a larger sample, and make storage requirement estimation a more formal and integral part of the conversion process.

Time to Convert

Conversion also takes time, and this can be a significant factor when dealing with large numbers of files. When you test conversion for file size, measure time as well. Remember that duration is affected by computer performance and by network bandwidth when you convert across a server.

In most cases, size and time are not significant issues, but if you have to convert a large number of files you can help things along by using a faster computer. If you have to convert across a server, you can copy files to a local hard drive, convert them, and then load them back to the server.

Microsoft Access

Default Printer

Before you can convert a database, a default printer driver must be installed on the system. For the installation procedure, use the Windows Help file (accessible on the Windows **Start** menu) and search for **printers, installation**.

External Data Sources

If an Access 1.*x* or 2.0 database application uses a 16-bit ODBC source in a code module or in a linked table definition, you have to re-create it with an identical name under the 32-bit ODBC administrator to use it in Access 95 or later versions. You can manually re-create the link in the 32-bit ODBC administrator or you can use a configuration script during installation.

Security MDA File

Access 2000 installs and sets its own default security file (SYSTEM.MDW). If an Access application provides security through a custom workgroup information file or a modified SYSTEM.MDA (Access 1.*x* and 2.0) or SYSTEM.MDW (Access 95/97) file, you must select it using the Access Workgroup Administrator before you try to convert or enable the file in Access 2000. This setting can be deployed during installation (see Chapter 5, "User Settings" for details). To convert or enable database files, the user account used when logging into Access must have:

- Open/Run and Open Exclusive permissions
- Modify Design or Administer permissions for all the tables in the database or the user must be the owner of the tables
- Read Design permissions for all objects in the database

After you address these multiple-user issues, you can convert the workgroup information file to the Access 2000 format to take advantage of new features. Search the Access 2000 Help file for **converting workgroup information files** for instructions on how to re-create the file under Access 2000. The process requires that you have all the information used to create the original security file.

Table and Query Date Literals

After Access 95, Microsoft changed the way Access interprets 2-digit date values. When dates are used in query definitions as literal values (expressed as #mm/dd/yy#), Access 2.0/95 interprets the year as 19XX. Access 97/2000 interprets 2-digit years between 0 and 29 as 20XX, and values between 30 and 99 as 19XX. Because of this, Access queries using date literals with 2-digit years may return different result sets under Access 2.0/95 and Access 97/2000.

To avoid potential problems, you should convert all literal date values with 2-digit years to the full 4-digit year equivalent. There are third-party Access add-in tools for dealing with year 2000 issues.

Note   Access uses the system-wide display default unless a field specifies another format. To set it for 4-digit date values, use the Control Panel's **Regional Settings** applet.

Tables with Many Indexes and Relationships

Access 2.0 tables could have up to 32 indexes and an unlimited number of relationships; Access 2000 limits tables to a total of 32 indexes and relationships. When you open a database that violates this restriction, Access 2000 truncates the indexes without informing the user. In most cases the database continues to function properly, but this can affect performance and cause compile errors if VBA code refers to an index. If you don't modify Access 2.0 tables with more than 32 indexes and relationships to meet Access 2000 requirements, you'll have to test VBA code to make sure that it does not refer to an index that may be deleted.

Report Margins

When Access 2.0 reports are converted to Access 2000, their margins are adjusted to the default print region as specified by the Windows default printer driver. You may need to reset margins manually after converting to Access 2000.

Forms or Reports with Excessive Controls

Each Access 2000 form or report can have no more than 754 controls, fields, and sections. A higher count causes conversion to fail, and you'll have to reduce the count and perform the conversion again.

ForceNewPage Property

In Access 2000, the **ForceNewPage** property in a report Group Header section forces a new page before every section, including the first one (unlike Access 2.0). This is default behavior and cannot be changed. You may need to modify the report layout due to this change.

SendKeys

Access 2.0 typically used **SendKeys** statements and macro actions to trigger menu items for which actions were not accessible programatically. Changes to the Access 2000 menu structure may render these inactive.

DoMenuItem

Because Access 2.0 commands are mapped to the proper equivalents in Access 2000, the **DoMenuItem** action continues to work correctly, although the action has been replaced in Access 2000 with the **RunCommand** action and it is changed automatically the first time the macro is saved in Access 2000. **DoMenuItem** methods used in code are not changed.

Microsoft Excel

Natural Language Formulas Off by Default

In Excel 2000, the default for Natural Language Formulas is **off** (they were **on** in Excel 97). If you have a column heading with the word **totals** in it and in another cell you type **=sum(totals)**, the result is a **#NAME!** error. To reset this so that Natural Language Formulas are recognized on a per-workbook basis, enable the **Accept Labels** option (under the **Calculation** tab of the **Options** dialog found in the **Tools** menu). See Chapter 5 for information on deploying this user setting during installation.

Files Saved in Earlier Version Formats Fully Calculate When Opened

To ensure that workbooks are properly calculated, Excel 2000 completely recalculates them each time they are opened, so opening an earlier-version file may take longer. If you save the workbook in Excel 2000 it will open more quickly next time.

XLM Macros

Excel 2000 supports Excel 4.0 (XLM) macros with few changes, but the Excel 4.0 macro language has not been updated to reflect the expanded object model since Excel 5.0, so you can no longer record XLM macros. The XLM macro language is no longer documented in the Excel Help files.

Lotus 123 Macros Not Supported

Unlike earlier versions, Excel 2000 does not support Lotus 123 2.3 for MS-DOS macros. You can rewrite them in VBA, but you may find their functionality has been replaced by standard Excel features, especially shortcuts to printing and navigation.

Microsoft PowerPoint

AutoShapes Change Size

When a PowerPoint 95 AutoShape is converted to the PowerPoint 2000 format, its inset pen outline is changed to a centered pen outline. You can reposition AutoShapes to look correct under PowerPoint 2000.

WordArt

In Office 95 and earlier versions, the WordArt program was used to create special text effects. In Office 2000 they can be created *in* a program by using the **Insert WordArt** tool on the **Drawing** toolbar. This feature also can be used to create 3-D effects and textured fills.

If WordArt exists on the target computer, it remains there even after Office 2000 is installed, but special text effects created with it are not converted automatically to the new WordArt drawing object. Tell users to use **Insert WordArt** to avoid this problem.

Microsoft Word

Personal Settings

Users can easily customize Word. Power users can modify toolbars, menus, shortcut keys, and accumulate AutoCorrect and AutoText entries. After upgrading to Office 2000, settings are carried forward, but they are lost if users' computers are rebuilt or replaced with new ones. It is not easy to capture the settings because they can be stored in various locations, such as the registry, NORMAL.DOT, and other templates. Most users do not mind rebuilding these settings, but it may be less trouble all around to upgrade the installation for power users with numerous customizations.

For example, in a recent migration at a health service provider, one user had accumulated 2,600 AutoCorrect entries dealing with common medical phrases and terms. She estimated that AutoCorrect cut her workload by 50 percent. Obviously, these settings had to be retained, so the IT staff upgraded her computer to bring the AutoCorrect entries into Word 2000.

Table Causes Document File Size to Increase

Documents with tables may become larger when saved in Word 2000 because it stores more information about tables with the document: 24-bit color, Text AutoFit, cell spacing, and cell padding information.

WordBasic to VBA

Macros recorded or written in versions prior to Word 97 use WordBasic code. This code is converted to VBA (using the WordBasic object) when a document is opened in Word 2000, allowing emulation of WordBasic functionality. This usually requires no additional effort, but if you encounter issues with converted code, see the Word section "Migrating Templates and Custom Solutions," below, for details.

Migrating Templates and Custom Solutions

Office solutions that automate business process and workflow often represent a significant investment that should be protected during conversion by thorough testing, and, when necessary, fixed or reengineered through coding. The rest of this section discusses migration issues you should be aware of.

Common Issues

Some migration issues are common to all Office applications. They are discussed in this section. The following sections discuss issues for individual applications.

WIN16 to WIN32 API

Office 2000 is a 32-bit application: to migrate to it you must be running a 32-bit operating system and you must convert applications that use 16-bit Windows API calls to their 32-bit equivalents.

An example of a 16-bit Windows API call:

```
Declare Function CloseClipboard Lib "User" () As Integer
```

An example of a 32-bit Windows API Call:

```
Declare Function apiCloseClipboard Lib "user32" Alias _
    "CloseClipboard" () As Long
```

Refer to the *Microsoft Office 2000 Visual Basic Programmer's Guide*, Chapter 10, "The Windows API and Other Dynamic-Link Libraries" for details on using the Windows 32-bit API.

Variable Names

Office 2000 uses Visual Basic for Applications (VBA) version 6, which aligns Office more closely with other Microsoft development tools. Some version 6 features use new keywords or function names that might conflict with names in custom solutions developed with earlier Office versions. Office 2000 cannot compile procedures that use these keywords as modules, procedures, or variable names:

- Application
- Friend
- CommandBars
- Enum
- Event

CommandBar Indexes Different Than in Office 97

When you run a Visual Basic macro that adds or manipulates toolbar buttons or menu commands for the CommandBars object, the controls may be added to a different CommandBar or you may see an error message similar to this:

```
Run-time error '5':
Invalid procedure call or argument
```

This is caused by using the CommandBars object and referring to a control index by something other than its name—for example, referring to the index for the worksheet shortcut menu instead of its name **Cell**. To fix this you have to correct the CommandBar code by adding the proper index value or the toolbar name. The name is preferable because it simplifies migration during future upgrades.

Microsoft Access

Custom Menus

In Access 2000 you can create custom menus with the CommandBar object provided by the shared Office library. Access 2.0 menus created with macros should work as expected. If you want to convert them, use **Create Menu from Macro** in the Access 2000 **Tools** menu. There are also selections to **Create Toolbar from Macro** and **Create Shortcut Menu from Macro**.

16-Bit OLE Custom Controls

16-bit OLE Custom Controls (primarily distributed with the Access 2.0 Developer's Kit) used on Access 2.0 forms and reports are not converted to their 32-bit equivalent in Access 95 or later. After converting the database to Access 2000, you must manually reinsert the 32-bit equivalent controls and re-create the event procedure code.

Wizard-Generated Code

Some code generated by Access 2.0/95 wizards can fail when run in later versions, including Access 2000, displaying a compile error to users who try to use the function. In particular, **Application.Run**, which calls routines in other Access databases, fails because the database names have changed. You can modify the code in Access 2000 to reference the correct file. Wizard-generated code that launches other Office applications can also fail. Delete the buttons that call this code and recreate them using the Command Button Wizard.

Programming Issues

DoCmd Statement

If Access 2000 fails to convert the Access 2.0 **DoCmd** statement to the new **DoCmd.** method syntax, it generates a code compilation error when you try to run the converted code. For example, Access may fail to convert:

```
DoCmd OpenForm "MyForm"
```

to

```
DoCmd.OpenForm "MyForm"
```

The difference is the period between DoCmd and OpenForm (DoCmd.OpenForm). To correct this problem, replace **DoCmd** with **DoCmd.** followed by the method name.

Procedure Name Scope

In Access 2000, if any modules and procedures have the same name, Access will raise the Compile Error *Expected variable or procedure, not Module.* To call a procedure that has the same name as a module correctly, you have to rewrite the code to call the procedure as ModuleName.ProcedureName.

Error Codes

Access 2000 generates some new error codes for invalid database and COM component actions. If earlier-version database applications check for specific error codes, test their routines to ensure they still work as expected. Access 2000 returns errors in some—but not all—cases when applications do not handle errors correctly.

Transactions

Access 2000 does not place queries executed with **<QueryDef>.Execute** automatically within a transaction (as Access 2.0 did), so if there is an execution error, it will not roll back all changes made by the query.

Code in Wizards

To use code contained in a wizard, you must open the VBA editor and set a reference to the Wizard database. For features not supported by the new wizards, Access 2000 automatically adds appropriate functions to UTILITY.MDA when converting an earlier-version Access database.

Null Values

In Access 2.0, when an expression in a macro comparison operator evaluates to Null, a True or a False is returned. In Access 2000, VBA returns a Null value in these cases. Use the **IsNull** function to determine which expressions evaluate to Null.

TransferText and TransferSpreadsheet Actions

Access 2000 does not support the use of Structured Query Language (SQL) to specify the data to export when using these actions. Instead, you have to create a query definition to define the export data, then refer to this query in the TableName argument of the TransferSpreadsheet action.

Dot (.) Operator

Access Basic statements use the dot (.) operator to refer to a field of a recordset object or a member of a collection; Access 2000 does not use this operator. If earlier-version code uses the dot (.) operator, replace it with the VBA bang (!) operator. For example: *Forms!Employee* or *rstEmployees!Employee*.

Compilation

Syntax errors in Access 2.0 code cause compilation errors in Access 2000. Compile all the modules in an Access 2.0 application before converting or enabling the database in Access 2000.

Microsoft Excel

Modules Now Reside in the Visual Basic Editor

Office 97 and 2000 use the VBA programming-integrated development environment. To view modules, open the Visual Basic Editor (on the **Tools** menu, select **Macro** then **Visual Basic Editor**) and look in the Project Explorer. If custom applications were developed with Excel 5.0/95, code is no longer accessible in worksheets.

CommandBars Replace MenuBars and ToolBars

The MenuBars and ToolBars used in previous versions of Excel have been upgraded to the CommandBars object (common to all Office 2000 applications) which allows you to include menus and buttons on the same bar. This new feature should not break existing code, but it will have an impact on future development because ToolBars and MenuBars are both modified using the CommandBar object model.

Eliminated MenuBars

A number of menu bars have been eliminated from Excel 97/2000 to make Excel more consistent with the rest of Office. If code refers to MenuBars or MenuItems that no longer exist, Excel provides a non-error return value. This means the code can run without generating errors, but it also means that you are not informed that Excel does not support the functionality. Changes made to eliminated menu bars (listed below) will, of course, not appear:

- Worksheet (XL4)
- Chart (XL4)
- No Docs Open
- Info
- Worksheet (XL4, short)
- Chart (XL4, short)
- Visual Basic Module

Object Model and Type Library

Each new version of Excel contains new objects and functionality, and refines the type library so that it is stricter about enforcing variable declarations around objects. Most VBA code from prior versions functions properly, but code developed in versions earlier than Excel 97 can report Type Mismatch Errors. You can usually fix this by changing the code from a variant data type to the Excel-specific object specified in the type library.

Methods Returning Worksheets

In Excel 95 you could return a **Worksheet** object by using the class **Excel.Sheet** as an argument to the **CreateObject** function, the **GetObject** function, or the **CreateLink** method. In versions since Excel 97, using this argument with one of these methods returns a **Workbook** object, so you must change code that uses these methods. Customized applications (such as Word or Access) that control Excel through OLE Automation are affected by changes to **CreateObject** and **GetObject**. For example, the Excel 95 code:

```
Set MySheet = CreateObject("Excel.Sheet")
```

becomes in Excel 2000:

```
Set MyBook = CreateObject("Excel.Sheet")
Set MySheet = MyBook.Sheets(1)
```

The **Style** object's parent property displays similar behavior. In Excel 5.0/95 it returns the application object; in Excel 97/2000 it returns Workbook objects.

These are subtle changes in the object model, and they reinforce the need to test mission critical code thoroughly before migration.

Range.PasteSpecial Changes Selection

If you use a line of code in a VBA macro such as

```
Range(<cell address>).PasteSpecial
```

where *<cell address>* is a range of cells, the active selection changes to that range. Versions of Excel earlier than Excel 97 *do not* change the selection when this line is executed, so macros written in those versions may not produce the desired results if the selection must remain unchanged after the macro executes the PasteSpecial method. Instead, the macro may insert data in a wrong location, or, if values are retrieved from the active location after the PasteSpecial method call, it can return wrong values to the procedure. This happens because Excel is expecting a different location when retrieving the values.

Disabling and Enabling Shortcut Menus

When you run a VBA macro that attempts to enable or disable shortcut menus, it can fail without an error message. In Excel 97/2000, shortcut menus no longer belong to their own collection of objects (ShortcutMenus) but are part of the CommandBars collection, which also includes menubars and toolbars. To promote VBA compatibility for macros created in earlier versions of Excel, you can still use the ShortcutMenus method in Excel 97/2000 to add and delete menu items on shortcut menus, but you have to use the CommandBars method to enable or disable shortcut menus.

ParamArray Arguments Are Always Base 0

ParamArray is an optional argument type that allows you to pass a variant array to a function or subroutine. In Microsoft Excel 95, a function with a ParamArray argument may return different results depending on whether it is called from a worksheet or Visual Basic code. In Visual Basic-to-Visual Basic function calls, ParamArrays are base 0 (the index number of the first element is zero); called from a worksheet cell ParamArrays are base 1. Programmers use the **LBound** method to determine the index number of the first element.

In Excel 97/2000, Visual Basic packages all ParamArrays as base 0, and this affects function calls with ParamArray arguments that should be base 1. If this happens, you have to modify the spreadsheet functions to work with base 0 ParamArrays.

Close Command Halts Code Execution

In Excel 95, Visual Basic runs code after a **Close** method is called from within the workbook, and it does not close the workbook until the code has executed. In Excel 2000, the workbook referenced in the macro closes as soon as the **Close** command executes, halting any macros it contains. You will have to modify the code to take this behavior into account.

Comparing a String to a Boolean

In Excel 2000, a macro that runs successfully in Excel 95 or earlier can return the error message *Run-time error '13': Type Mismatch* if it compares a string variable to the Boolean values True or False. To work around this, define the string variable as *variant*; it can be compared to a Boolean variable without generating an error. For example, if the macro contains the line:

```
Dim S As String
```

replace it with:

```
Dim S As Variant
```

Microsoft PowerPoint

VBA Support

PowerPoint 97/2000 supports VBA and, like all Office applications, the VBA editor. PowerPoint 2000 improves on the existing object model, but none of the modifications will prevent a PowerPoint 97 solution from functioning correctly under PowerPoint 2000. Review the "Variable Names" section of "Common Issues" on page 60 for a list of new keywords that cause compilation problems if used in a PowerPoint 97 solution.

PowerPoint 95 Automation Solutions

Unlike PowerPoint 97/2000, PowerPoint 95 does not have built-in support for VBA, but it does have an automation library that allows programmatic control of PowerPoint 95 applications developed in Visual Basic or Access that support OLE Automation. In general, you will have to reengineer these solutions to bring them completely within the PowerPoint 2000 VBA environment, because the object model was modified significantly in PowerPoint 97 to make it more consistent with the object models in other Office applications.

Microsoft Word

Custom applications written in versions of Word prior to Word 97 used WordBasic macros, and these are converted to VBA when you open a document or template in Word 2000. In most cases, converted macros execute properly, although translating one programming syntax to another can cause the issues explained below, some of which you will have to fix, and some of which will affect logic flow without reporting errors. These issues are rare, but their possibility emphasizes the need to test mission-critical applications thoroughly before deploying Office 2000.

Syntax Errors

WordBasic is an interpreted language (it does not compile or verify code that is not executed) so a WordBasic macro can have syntax errors that are not reported if the code containing them is never executed. Word 2000 compiles code before execution, reports syntax errors, and does not execute until the code is fixed or removed. You can use the error information to repair the code.

On Error Statement May Fail

Some WordBasic macros contain error trapping, and when these are converted to VBA the error trap may be ignored. VBA does not clear the On Error statement when an error occurs; WordBasic clears it, resets the error trap, and continues running the code. WordBasic macros that rely on errors being cleared will not perform with the same logic in VBA and will need to be rewritten to conform to the new error handling method.

Run-Time Error 1042

WordBasic macros converted to VBA can return this message:

```
Run-time error '1042': Settings you chose for the left and right
margins, column spacing, or paragraph indents are too large for the page
in some sections.
```

This often is the result of setting the PageWidth and PageHeight parameters with WordBasic.FilePageSetup. Up to Word 97, Word uses **points** for the PageWidth and PageHeight arguments; Word 2000 uses **twips**, and the value specified may be too small.

AddShape with Tables

When you run a VBA macro that creates and anchors a shape to a Word table selection, the position of the shape may appear in a different location from where it appeared in earlier versions of Word. This behavior is by design. In Word 2000, shapes can anchor inside table cells. In earlier versions they cannot. For example, in Word 97 the anchor of the object is forced outside the table cell, and the anchor position measures distance relative to the page. In Word 2000, the anchor remains inside the cell and measures distance from the edge of the table cell.

Shell Command

When you use the VBA Shell function to run Word, earlier versions of Word launch another instance; Word 2000, because of its Single Document Interface (SDI), does not. If you need to run a separate instance of Word 2000, use the command-line switch, **/w** to open a blank document in another instance. For example:

```
Shell "C:\Program Files\Microsoft Office\Office\Winword.exe /w"
```

Performance Considerations

WordBasic code that is converted and executed in Word 2000 may run slower than under earlier versions—another argument for converting WordBasic macros to VBA.

Year 2000

As the year 2000 approaches, there has been speculation, rumors, and suppositions. There are, however, some authentic and serious issues facing users and developers of computer applications and software.

While relatively minor compared to the issues facing legacy systems, a few Microsoft products require year 2000 adjustments. This section reviews the Office issues. For comprehensive information on year 2000 issues, see http://www.microsoft.com/y2k.

Access

Changes in date handling between Access 2.0/95 and Access 97/2000 can affect the importing of date data and the construction of queries.

When importing data, Access 2.0/95 converts 2-digit year dates to the form 19XX; Access 97/2000 converts 2-digit year dates between 0 and 29 to 20XX, and values between 30 and 99 to 19XX.

This *windowing* scheme can create issues for Access 2.0/95 queries that express date values as 2-digit literals. For more information, see the section "Table and Query Date Literals" in "Implementing Data File Conversion Strategy" on page 56.

Excel

Versions of Excel differ in how they store values in cells and handle dates. Here is how different versions handle dates:

Conversion of Directly Entered Two-Digit Years by Version

Two-digit year typed	Four-digit year used	
	Excel 97 (8.x) and Excel 2000	**Excel 95 (7.x), 5.x, 4.x**
00-19	2000-2019	2000-2019
20-29	2020-2029	1920-1929
30-99	1930-1999	1930-1999

To help you assess and fix year 2000 Excel issues, Microsoft has developed three date migration add-in tools you can use with Excel 97/2000 to prepare dates in Excel workbooks so that you can migrate them from earlier versions or audit them for the year 2000.

- **Date Fix Wizard.** Use this to change 2-digit year formats or to modify serial number dates so that they fall within a specified century.

- **Date Migration Wizard.** Use this to scan workbooks for worksheet functions that accept text dates as arguments. In Excel 97/2000, dates entered as text may produce different results than they did in earlier versions.

- **Date Watch Wizard.** Use this to check for year-ambiguous dates and formats.

You can find these tools in the *Microsoft Office 2000 Resource Kit* Toolbox at http://www.microsoft.com/office/ork/. To add them to a standard installation, see Chapter 4, "Customizing an Office 2000 Installation."

PowerPoint

PowerPoint presents few Y2K issues, but you should check presentations that include embedded OLE data (such as Excel charts) to make sure they are compliant.

Word

While Word allows you to pull in data from database systems, it does not validate that dates are year 2000 compliant. You have to do this. Word allows calculations with field codes, and you will have to verify that any field codes used to perform date calculations work as expected.

Security

Office 2000 enhances security to protect users and organizations from viruses and the execution of unauthorized macros. New features include:

- Ability to configure security modes for users
- Ability to digitally sign VBA solutions
- An antivirus API that allows third-party vendors to integrate with Office

To migrate custom solutions you have to consider Office 2000 environment security settings. For details, see the *Microsoft Office 2000 Resource Kit*, Chapter 9, "Managing Security" and the *Microsoft Office 2000/Visual Basic Programmer's Guide*, Chapter 17, "Securing Office Documents and Visual Basic For Applications Code."

A few migration security issues stand out. If a macro has a **High** security setting, all VBA code in Word, Excel, and PowerPoint must be digitally signed. If it is not, the macro will not execute, although the user will be permitted to open the file. To correct this, you will have to review all custom applications that use VBA.

You cannot digitally sign Excel 4.0 macros (XLM): they will not execute (and cannot even be loaded) if the Office 2000 security mode is set to **High**. You can avoid this with a registry setting, but this option bypasses only XLM, not VBA. To bypass XLM in high security mode, deploy this registry key:

```
[HKEY_LOCAL_MACHINE\SOFTWARE\Microsoft\Office\9.0\Excel\Security]
    XLM 1 - dword
```

Summary

Always check the online version of the *Microsoft Office 2000 Resource Kit* at www.microsoft.com/office/ork for the most current information on file conversion issues.

CHAPTER 3

Coexisting with Previous Versions of Office

When migrating to Office 2000, large companies often need to find a way to allow previous versions of Office to coexist. The goal is to allow users of *all* Office versions to work together with minimal problems until the deployment of Office 2000 is complete. Coexistence is complicated, often requiring tactical trade-offs, special implementation efforts, and contingency plans for users who may not be covered by the basic migration plan. There is no single best method, and to pick the one most suited to your circumstances, you have to assess your organization's configuration and infrastructure—particularly file sharing. This chapter shows how to do this, how to pick the best strategy for your environment, and how to implement it. It begins by assessing the features and coexistence potential of the Office applications.

What You'll Find in This Chapter

- How to effectively operate and manage different versions of Office within one company

- How to plan your deployment according to the specific coexistence capabilities of each Office application—including tables of the read and write capabilities for Word and Access

- How to conduct an in-depth analysis of your users' and company's needs to determine the best coexistence plan—including a table of common user issues

- How to assess different strategies and choose the strategy that best suits the needs of your organization—including descriptions of proven successful strategies

- How to deploy your strategy—describing both the big picture and detailed steps and procedures

Coexistence Capabilities

Strategy decisions are easier to make once you understand the coexistence capabilities of each Office application, particularly file sharing. This makes it possible to make informed decisions about which capabilities to implement.

Microsoft Word

Word 2000 Coexistence Features

Word 2000 has several coexistence capabilities.

- It uses the same file format as Word 97. No file format coexistence strategy is needed for users of these versions.

- It can open and edit files created in previous versions going back to Word for Windows 2.0, including Macintosh versions, and back to Word 3.*x* for DOS.

- It can save files in formats going back to Word for Windows 2.0 (you can even select one format as a default) without additional tools.

- It allows you to disable features not supported by Word 97, which can prevent loss of formatting if a Word 97 user saves changes to a Word 2000 file.

- It can save files in .RTF format, which can be read by all previous versions going back to Word 95 and Word for Windows 6.0 without additional tools.

- It can save to HTML format (with good fidelity) so that any user with a browser can view (but not necessarily edit) content.

- It allows you to set the Default Save to any valid format, including previous versions of Word. Although this may lose some formatting, it alleviates the need for users to know how to set formats when saving a file.

Saving to other version formats is useful, but it must be used carefully. Except when saving to .RTF, this can lose formatting, macro code, or information the Versions feature stores. Even with .RTF, when users of earlier versions save changes to a file, their version cannot save elements it does not recognize.

Earlier Version Coexistence Features

Earlier versions also have features that help with coexistence. Versions back to Word for Windows 2.0 allow you to install additional converters that allow Word 2.0 to read Word for Windows 6.0 file, and or allow Word 6.0/95 to read Word 97/2000 files. The converter made available for Word 97 also works for Word 2000 because both versions use the same file format—a fact that also allows Word 97 to read Word 2000 files.

Viewers

Viewers are available so that users who are not running any version of Word can read and print documents with full fidelity. Because the file format hasn't changed since Word 97, the existing viewers can read Word 2000 files. Viewers are available in 16-bit and 32-bit Windows versions.

See the *Microsoft Office 2000 Resource Kit* for details on features that do not convert between versions of Word.

Word and Read/Write Capability

Here are the file formats each version of Word for Windows can read or write. As you read the application and version name down the left hand column, read across to see which formats that version can read and/or write.

Format Application	Word 6 / Word 95 Format		Word 97 / Word 2000 Format	
Word 6 for Windows	Read Write	Read Write	Read with converter	Read with converter
Word for Windows 95	Read Write	Read Write	Read with converter	Read with converter
Word 97	Read Write	Read Write	Read Write	Read Write
Word 2000	Read Write	Read Write	Read Write	Read Write

Microsoft Outlook

Outlook presents a simpler coexistence case than the other applications because it does not have to contend with archives of old data files: it uses the same .PST format as earlier versions of Outlook and the Microsoft Exchange Client. If all users are at least running Outlook, you will have very little coexistence planning to do. Users running the Microsoft Exchange Client or Schedule+ may have trouble reading each other's free/busy times or assigning delegates to their accounts. Details on how to deal with this are covered in the "Strategies" section on page 82.

Microsoft Excel

Earlier versions of Excel cannot add converters, so they cannot read Excel 2000 files. You will need to plan accordingly.

Excel 2000 Coexistence Features

Like Word 2000, Excel 2000 can open and save files in several formats.

- Excel 2000 and Excel 97 use the same file format, so no file format coexistence plan is needed for these users.

- Excel 2000 can read files created from earlier versions of Excel going back to Excel 2.1.

- Excel 2000 can save files in formats going back to Excel 4.0. If Excel 2000 users know that other users have an earlier version of Excel, or if the default has been changed, they can save to the earlier format without additional tools.

- Excel 2000 can create high-fidelity HTML files that any user with a browser can read, although editing capabilities are limited.

- Excel 2000 has a dual-format feature allowing you to store Excel 97/2000 and Excel 5.0/95 formats into one file. This file is almost twice the size of a standard file and takes almost twice as long to open and save, but users of all of these versions can open this file and the Excel 2000 user doesn't lose any information or formatting. Users of earlier versions are prompted to open the file read-only; they can override that prompt and open it read/write. If they try to save changes, Excel 5.0/95 can't write the Excel 97/2000 data stream and it is lost. Because this can alter the file without the author's knowledge, it is safer to write-protect these files (using the file system) before distributing them.

Saving to an earlier version format can lose data, features, or formatting. Data loss is by far the most troublesome. Excel 2000 worksheets can have up to 65,536 rows; previous versions could only have 16,565. Excel 2000 worksheet cells can store up to 32,000 characters; previous versions could store only 254. The converters in Excel 2000 truncate cells or sheets at the Excel 5/95 limits and do not preserve the data. Granted, spreadsheets this large are less common, but they can reach this size, especially when database queries insert thousands of records in a spreadsheet file or when complex forms exceed the character/cell limit.

Earlier Version Coexistence Features

Excel 97 can read Excel 2000 files (both versions use the same format) but earlier versions cannot install additional converters and have no coexistence features.

Viewers

A 32-bit viewer allows Excel 97/2000 users to read and print documents with full fidelity. It is a handy tool, especially when the Excel 2000 user cannot take the chance of losing any data or formatting.

Some third-party 16-bit viewers do a reasonable job of converting files, although they also can lose macro code or formatting.

See the *Microsoft Office 2000 Resource Kit* for details on features that do not convert between versions of Excel.

Excel and Read/Write Capability

Here are the file formats each version of Excel for Windows can read or write. As you read the application and version name down the left hand column, read across to see which formats that version can read and/or write.

Format Application	Excel 5 / Excel Format		Excel 97 / Excel 20 Format	
Excel 5 for Windows	Read Write	Read Write		
Excel for Windows 95	Read Write	Read Write		
Excel 97	Read Write	Read Write	Read Write	Read Write
Excel 2000	Read Write	Read Write	Read Write	Read Write

Microsoft PowerPoint

The goal of the coexistence features of PowerPoint has always been to preserve the look of the presentation, regardless of what the presenter is using to display it. Because it is common to use someone else's computer to make a presentation, PowerPoint has always included features that enable users of different versions to edit a presentation and show it on almost any personal computer.

PowerPoint 2000 Coexistence Features

PowerPoint 2000 can read and write to most PowerPoint formats because of these coexistence features:

- File format has not changed since PowerPoint 97, so no file format coexistence strategy is needed for these users.

- You can add converters to earlier versions (from PowerPoint 4.0 forward) that allow users to open and edit PowerPoint 2000 files.

- PowerPoint 2000 can save to formats back to version 4.0, allowing users of earlier versions to read and write files without additional software (although some formatting may be lost).

- A dual-file format allows the PowerPoint 2000 or PowerPoint 97 user to store both the PowerPoint 97/2000 and PowerPoint 95 formats in one file. This file is much larger than the compressed PowerPoint 97/2000 file, and thus takes longer to load and save, but it preserves the newer features and allows users to open the file without additional software. Although the default for PowerPoint 95 users is read-only, they can choose read/write but will lose the PowerPoint 97/2000 information if they change and save the file.

- The Pack and Go feature allows PowerPoint 2000 users to save a presentation and a viewer, then present on a Windows computer without the same (or any) version of PowerPoint.

- Web publishing capability allows wide read-only distribution of PowerPoint content that preserves much of the presentation's look and feel. Any users with an Internet browser can view the content.

Earlier Version Coexistence Features

Users of earlier PowerPoint versions can add new converters that allow PowerPoint 95 users to read and edit PowerPoint 97/2000 files or allow PowerPoint 4.0 users to edit and open PowerPoint 95/97/2000 files. If you deployed these converters for Office 4.*x*/95 users, they are already compatible with Office 2000.

Converters preserve the look of presentations, sometimes at the cost of editability because objects without an equivalent feature in the earlier version are stored as pictures.

Viewers

Viewers allow you to give presentations with full fidelity, including animation, on computers without PowerPoint loaded. Because file format hasn't changed since PowerPoint 97, the existing viewers can read PowerPoint 2000 files as well. There are 16-bit and 32-bit Windows versions.

See the *Microsoft Office 2000 Resource Kit* for details on features that do not convert between versions of PowerPoint.

PowerPoint and Read/Write Capability

Here are the file formats each version of PowerPoint can read or write to.

Format Application	PowerPoint 4 Format	PowerPoint 95 Format	PowerPoint 97 / PowerPoint 20 Format	
PowerPoint 4 for Windows	Read Write	Read with converter	Read with converter	Read with converter
PowerPoint for Windows 95	Read Write	Read Write	Read with converter	Read with converter
PowerPoint 97	Read Write	Read Write	Read Write	Read Write
PowerPoint 2000	Read Write	Read Write	Read Write	Read Write

Microsoft Access

Now based on Unicode so that users of different language versions can share files, Access 2000 is the only Office 2000 application with a new file format (each version since Access 2.0 has had a different format).

Access 2000 Coexistence Features

Access 2000 has more coexistence features than previous versions.

- You can open files back to version 2.0 without converting. You can't edit objects such as forms, reports, modules. or table definitions, but you can add, change, or delete data and run any compatible objects.
- You can save an Access 2000 database file in Access 97 format. (Security is not converted. See the *Microsoft Office 2000 Resource Kit* for details.)
- You can create Data Access Pages—HTML front-ends to an Access database—if you have Internet Explorer 5.0 or higher.

Earlier Version Coexistence Features

Earlier versions cannot read Access 2000 files, so users must keep files in the earliest version format to coexist.

Snapshot Viewer

You can create an Access 2000 database report and distribute it, along with Snapshot Viewer, to users without any version of Access. Users who don't need Access can still receive and read reports.

Access 2000 and MSDE Run-Time

With Office 2000 Developer, you can create a complete Access 2000 solution and distribute it royalty-free using either the Access 2000 or MSDE run-time, even to users without Access. Users can add, edit, or delete records, run queries and reports, and so on, but cannot make any changes to the solution or create objects.

Access and Read/Write Capability

Here are the file formats each version of Access can read or write:

Format Application	Access 2.0 Format	Access 95 Format	Access 97 Format	Access 2000 Format
Access 2 for Windows	Read Write			
Access for Windows 95	Read Write Data	Read Write		
Access 97	Read Write Data	Read Write Data	Read Write	
Access 2000	Read Write Data	Read Write Data	Read Write	Read Write

See the Office Developer Web site (www.microsoft.com/officedev) for more details on Office 2000 Developer, and the *Microsoft Office 2000 Resource Kit* for details on features that do not convert between versions of Access.

Coexistence Analysis

How Users Share Files

Once you understand how versions of Office applications share files, you need to understand how users in your environment share them so that you can balance capabilities and usage patterns to develop the right coexistence strategy. Who do users share files with? Do recipients need to edit files or simply view them? Can you control who receives files? How long will the migration to Office 2000 take? The table below lays these issues out so that you can research and record the answers. Once you have the answers, you are on your way to building the best coexistence strategy for your organization:

Coexistence Questions	Result
Do users share files with other users outside of their business unit (or rollout unit—the people who will be upgraded at the same time) but within the organization?	
Which types of files do they share? Word, Access, Excel, PowerPoint?	
Are shared files very large? Very complex? Do they contain macros?	
When files are sent outside the business unit, do recipients need to edit them or merely read them?	
How frequently do users share documents outside of their business unit?	

Coexistence Questions	Result
How are files sent? Over e-mail, on workgroup file shares with limited permissions, or public file shares where all users in the organization can read and write files?	
Are documents sent outside of your organization? Answer the same questions as above for this case as well.	
How flexible are receiving organizations? For instance, can recipients install converters, or will senders need to ensure compatibility?	

Answering these questions may lead you to ask others about the file sharing relationship, such as which features are in use and how they will be affected by saving files in other formats. Consider helping certain users or groups test their file sharing methods to see if features, formatting, or data are lost. For example, the layout of Web pages developed in Word with nested tables is lost if those files are saved in any other format.

There are a number of ways to gather the information you need:

- Utilize software inventory tools:
  - To see what versions are in use, and what percentage of users have each version.
  - To list how many computers are incapable of running Office 2000—this shows how long you can expect these users to be incompatible.

> **Note**   See Chapter 6, "Preparing for Office 2000 Distribution," for more information on using SMS to create a software inventory.

- Interview departmental IT and helpdesk resources familiar with how users share files.
- Get a contact in each business unit to determine how users share files.
- Formal surveys. This method is costly, time consuming, and usually garners a low response, but it may be the only option in large, completely centralized organizations. An HTML form that gets answers to some of the questions listed above is probably the simplest way to conduct a formal survey.

Coexistence Time Frame

The factor with the highest impact on your strategy might be the simplest: how long will you take to move the organization to Office 2000? If all or most of the users who share files will be migrated quickly, say within three months, then you may not want to implement a coexistence strategy that you'll soon have to undo. Or you can create a plan for just one or two applications. If Word documents are commonly shared outside of business units but Excel and PowerPoint files are not, you can implement a coexistence strategy just for Word.

Longer coexistence timeframes usually require more strategies—for insurance. For instance, you can set the default save format for Word files to the earlier version and distribute converters to users who don't have Office 97 or 2000. Now if Word 2000 users change the default format back to Word 2000, users of earlier versions can still open the file because they have the appropriate converter. This strategy requires more resources because you have to install software on old desktops as well as new ones, but it helps to avoid helpdesk calls from users who can't open files. If you can automate software installation, this extra insurance is generally considered cheap protection; if you can't, then you need to decide which is easier to bear: the costs of deploying converters and viewers or the costs of helpdesk support and business interruption.

Existing Versions of Microsoft Office

Your strategy also depends on how many versions of Office you have in your organization, and the percentage of users for each. A software inventory is the best way to get accurate information. Large organizations with a central IT organization and business unit IT groups sometimes are surprised by the number of Office versions that show up in an automated inventory.

If the use is fairly evenly distributed across versions since Office 4.x, the simplest solution for Word, Excel, and PowerPoint is to distribute the Office Converter Pack to all users. For Access, which has a different file format in Office 2000, you have to encourage solution owners to upgrade their solutions by the business unit rollover date. If use is not evenly distributed, you may want to leave small groups of users to their own devices to avoid the cost of developing and implementing a strategy for them. This sounds harsh, but the point is to migrate users to a consistent software platform; you have to control the costs of catering to tiny groups that are falling further and further behind.

System Policies

Administrators can use system policies (a Windows feature) to set and enforce user desktop settings. You use the System Policy Editor to create a policy and store it on the server: when users log on, the policy's registry settings are brought down to the desktop and override any customized settings. To change a policy, use the System Policy Editor to find and change settings. Users receive the updated registry settings the next time they log on.

Because they are easy to deploy and change, system policies can greatly simplify a coexistence strategy. For instance, suppose you want to have the first several groups of upgraders save their files in an earlier-version format, and then allow them to move up to the Office 2000 formats when it is running on most desktops. With system policies, you can simply change one policy setting per application.

Suppose that after a group upgrades you find that its members underestimated how many files they share outside of the organization with users who run earlier versions of Office. With system policies you can change the strategy in midstream by opening the existing policy file and changing the default save setting back to the earlier format.

Deployment Methods

A coexistence strategy is also influenced by the deployment methods available to you. Automated software distribution tools such as Tivoli or Microsoft Systems Management Server can simplify the task and reduce costs by distributing the Office Converter Pack and making the distribution mandatory to insure it is installed on desktops.

Without automation, you have to rely on users to install the Office Converter Pack, and this may require an additional, if temporary, strategy that forces the first several groups of upgraders to save files in an earlier-version format until most users are up to speed. The savings of this method often outweigh the benefits (and cost) of sending a technician to each desktop.

Very Large Organizations

A final factor affecting a coexistence strategy is the size of the organization and its in-place IT structure. Very large organizations usually have too many desktops to allow a rapid deployment. Sometimes their IT structure is hierarchical, with a central group handling decisions that affect all users, and subgroups handling issues within business units. If business units have a lot of custom solutions, you may choose to boost compatibility by leaving the desktop version decision up to business unit IT groups. If file sharing is complex or widespread, a simple rollout may be impractical, and the central IT group may have to rely on business unit IT groups to create localized strategies. Even when general decisions are controlled by the central IT group, business unit groups still may have influence over scheduling.

When organizational complexity increases the coexistence timeframe and the cost and time needed to accurately assess the situation, it may be best to go with the safest strategy: set the default save for upgraded users to the older format, then distribute converters and viewers. If you do this using system policies, you can switch users over to the new format when all desktops have been upgraded.

Strategies

The guidelines in this section can help you decide which strategies are best for your organization.

General Strategies

User Education

Because there is no *one size fits all* coexistence solution, adaptable user education is often the most important component of your strategy. How you accomplish it depends on what works best in your environment: information distributed after installation, customizable Help, an intranet site, *brown-bag* informational sessions, instructor-led training, or a combination of these. Generally, you will have an education effort tied to your overall upgrade plan, and you can include coexistence material in that, rather than implementing any of these just for coexistence. One exception is an intranet PC support site, which can provide cheap, easily maintained user education, especially if the user desktop includes a shortcut to it. In addition to technical information, the site can include links to converter packs, viewers, registry settings for default save choices, and other tools that support coexistence.

Customizable Help

With Office 2000 you can customize Help topics, link keywords to the Answer Wizard, and deploy this content with the Office 2000 image to make sure that Office Assistant users see specific recommendations on file sharing and coexistence, rather than generic information. For instance, if you plan to deploy in the U.S. this year, but internationally next year, you can customize a Help file that instructs users to save files in previous-version formats or HTML when distributing them internationally. For more information, see the *Microsoft Office 2000 Resource Kit*: Chapter 8, "Helping Users Help Themselves."

Default Save

The default save feature (available since Office 97) allows administrators and users to set which format an Office application uses each time it saves a file. You can select any valid file format for that application—Office 95, HTML, or non-Microsoft formats such as Lotus 1-2-3 version 5. The system default is the equivalent format for that version. The end user can change the format each time she saves a file; however, the default will be reset each time she accesses the Save feature.

Users can change the default through the **Tools, Options** dialog box. Administrators can change it through a registry setting, using the methods detailed in Chapter 5, "User Settings." System policies make it easy to change the default and to inform users with messages displayed during the save. For instance, a message can state the default save format is set to Word 6.0/95 until date *X*, at which time the business unit migration will be complete and the default will be reset it to Word 2000.

Office Converter Pack

The Microsoft Office Converter Pack (available on the *Microsoft Office 2000 Resource Kit* CD or from the Office Resource Kit Web site) makes it possible for users of earlier versions of Office to read and edit files from Office 2000 and from some non-Microsoft applications such as Lotus Ami Pro. You may not need all the converters, and you can install only those you need by editing the CONVPACK.INI file and changing the installation state of individual converters to **NO**. To install the pack without user interaction, use the **Setup.exe –s** command.

For more information on the Office Converter Pack, see the section "New Tools for the Conversion Process" in Chapter 10 of the *Microsoft Office 2000 Resource Kit*.

HTML Format

Office 2000 elevates HTML to almost the same level as the native, or binary, file formats: almost everything converts and is represented properly in HTML versions. The HTML files include information that the original applications can use so that the content behaves properly. For example, an Excel spreadsheet saved in HTML is not interactive when viewed with a browser because the browser cannot update formulas or charts as numbers change. But when the same spreadsheet is opened in Excel, formulas and charts update, and you can do just about anything you could do if the file had remained in Excel format.

This makes HTML a good format for distributing information. Most users on most platforms have access to a Web browser and thus can display the material; users with Internet Explorer version 5 (or a compatible browser) will have the fullest experience. The file's owner can keep a copy and use the original Office application to make changes that are reflected in the Web version. This does not make HTML a good format for co-authoring documents, however. Users with earlier versions of the application won't be able to convert the file properly, and the file will not be able use the special information that allows it to behave like a binary-format file in Office 2000.

Office Server Extensions

The Office Server Extensions add numerous server-based features to a Windows NT Server 4.0/IIS 4.0 Web server. All of these features are documented in white papers available at www.microsoft.com/Office and in the *Microsoft Office 2000 Resource Kit*, but the feature most useful to a coexistence strategy is Web Discussions. This allows users with Netscape Navigator 3.0 or higher, Internet Explorer 3.0 or higher, or any of the Office 2000 applications to view and comment on (but not edit) HTML documents, Word documents, Excel spreadsheets, or PowerPoint presentations. (The best experience is with Internet Explorer 5.0 or Office 2000.) The Office Server Extensions store the comments in a database but displays them with the document, allowing users with recent browsers to collaborate even though they are on different platforms or running different applications.

For more information on the Office Server Extensions, see Chapter 13, "Deploying and Managing Office Server Extensions," as well as "Using Office Server Extensions" in the *Microsoft Office 2000 Resource Kit.*

Microsoft Outlook

Outlook 2000 uses the same file format as previous versions of Outlook and the Microsoft Exchange Client, removing most coexistence or migration issues. You may, however, need to plan for HTML-based e-mail, electronic forms, Schedule+ users, and the use of delegates.

HTML-Based E-Mail

Outlook 2000 allows users to create HTML e-mail messages. Users of Outlook 98 and 97 can read HTML e-mail (because a plain-text version is always available) but will lose some formatting and layout. You can't disable this feature without disabling all of the user customization capabilities, so you should educate users on this issue.

Coexisting with the Microsoft Exchange Client

Some new features in the standard Outlook 2000 e-mail message form (such as **expiration date**) cannot be translated by Exchange Clients. If an Outlook user creates a view on a public folder without checking the option for Exchange Client compatibility, Exchange Clients may not be able to use the view. Nor can they use forms created only for the Outlook environment. Environments running both clients should use the Exchange Forms Designer, which works for both.

Coexisting with Schedule+

Both Outlook and Schedule+ allow users to assign calendar delegates that can create and accept meeting requests on behalf of the user, but user and delegate must be on the same calendaring program (Outlook or Schedule+).

Outlook 2000 users can direct book appointments for Outlook 2000 and Schedule+ calendars, and can view free/busy status and details; Schedule+ users can view only free/busy status for Outlook users.

If there are Schedule+ users in your environment, you can minimize disruption by moving all close calendaring user relationships (such as delegates) to Outlook 2000 at the same time and moving resource accounts (such as conference rooms) last so that all users can continue to view details for these accounts.

For complete details, see the section "Upgrading to Outlook 2000" in Chapter 11 of the *Microsoft Office 2000 Resource Kit.*

Specific Strategies

This section discusses strategies for the entire Office 2000 suite, explains their benefits and issues, and outlines how to evaluate and choose between them. These are the most common strategies used since Office 97; you may decide to create a hybrid by incorporating pieces of them.

The Middle Road Strategy

Relying heavily on the Office Converter Pack, this strategy employs some of the methods described in this chapter, but not all. It preserves most Office 2000 functionality, provides coexistence, and simplifies helpdesk chores by distributing converters and viewers for older software versions, but it may prove costly if you can't automate software distribution. Generally, however, the Office Converter Pack is small enough to distribute in a logon script. This strategy works best for environments with these characteristics:

- A reasonably cost-effective method of distributing the Office Converter Pack to older-version desktops.
- A deployment span of about six months.
- Sharing of Word files throughout the organization.
- Sharing of Excel spreadsheets and PowerPoint presentations primarily within workgroups.
- Use of Web components for Excel solutions that require interactivity by users with different versions of Excel.
- Use of HTML as the preferred publishing format.

To implement this strategy you must:

- Create an intranet site that explains the implementation and allows users to help themselves in situations not covered by the plan. Users need to know exactly what capabilities other users will have, and what document features may be lost when saving to earlier formats. Include instructions for changing the default format, procedures for changing formats on a per-file basis, and hyperlinks for installing the Office Converter Pack and the various viewers.
- Upgrade all users in the same department together.
- Set the default save format to Word 6.0/95 until the entire organization has migrated to Word 2000. System policies make it easy to change the policy once all users are upgraded; if you don't use policies, use push methods such as SMS or adding the registry setting to users' logon scripts.
- Distribute the Office Converter Pack to older desktops so that users can read Word 97/2000 files, view and print Excel files, and either read or view/show/print PowerPoint files.

- Educate helpdesk personnel on the plan. They may have to help users install the Office Converter Pack and save files in an earlier version format.

- Leave all shared Access databases in their earliest-version formats until all users have upgraded to Access 2000. Add a dialog box that warns Access 2000 users not to convert the database. Make sure all databases upgraded to Access 2000 are tested before they are distributed.

The Safety Net Strategy

This minimizes business interruption while maximizing users' ability to open files. It is the simplest method for the helpdesk to support because it implements coexistence for users of all Office versions, although it can be the most costly if you cannot automate software distribution. It works best for organizations that:

- Want users of all Office versions to be able to open files for editing.

- Have an effective software distribution process in place.

- Are less concerned about data loss than about compatibility.

- Share all types of files across business units or frequently share files with users in other organizations with different software.

- Plan to take a year or more to deploy.

To implement this strategy you must:

- Educate users on features lost by saving to earlier-version formats, provide them with hyperlinks for installing converters and viewers, and make sure they know that HTML is the preferred format for widespread publishing.

- Set the default save format for each Office application to the version with the most users.

- Distribute the Office Converter Pack to all users of older versions.

- Make sure the helpdesk has tools that help users install the Office Converter Pack and reset Office 2000 file formats to older or newer formats, depending on need.

- Leave all shared Access databases in their earliest-version formats until all users have upgraded to Access 2000. Add a dialog box that warns Access 2000 users not to convert the database. Make sure all databases upgraded to Access 2000 are tested before they are distributed.

The Low Cost Strategy

This saves money by changing the default save formats, eliminating the need to deploy converters or viewers to earlier version users. You can change the defaults before you deploy Office 2000 or use system policies, which usually take less than an hour to implement. If you don't use system policies, users can reset their defaults and may end up sharing files with users who can't read them.

A more significant issue is that Excel or PowerPoint users may lose a lot of work when they save files to an earlier version, so you must research usage carefully to find the best default format for your organization. The dual file formats preserve more information but require more storage space; single version formats are more efficient but lose more formatting. HTML is widely compatible, but non-Office 2000 users may not be able to edit files.

Not surprisingly, this method can be the most difficult for the helpdesk to support, particularly if the default save setting cannot be enforced.

This strategy works best for organizations that:

- Have no cost effective way to deploy the Office Converter Pack to older desktops.
- Can't enforce installation of the Office Converter Pack.
- Seldom use spreadsheets that exceed the cell/row size limitations of Excel 5/95.
- Commonly share all types of files across departments.
- Seldom use complex forms or complex formatting that must be preserved exactly.
- Can use system policies to enforce default save settings during coexistence and to change them to Office 2000 formats after everyone has upgraded.
- Will take more than six months to deploy.

To implement this method you must:

- Educate Office 2000 users on why they should save files in earlier-version formats, and explain the features, formatting, or data that may be lost; educate users of previous versions on what to do if they receive an Office 2000 file that they cannot open.
- Use system policies to set the default save format or use the Office Profile Wizard to deploy new default settings with Office 2000.
- Make sure the helpdesk is prepared to help users install the Office Converter Pack and reset default save settings.
- Leave all shared Access databases in their earliest-version formats until all users have upgraded to Access 2000. Add a dialog box that warns Access 2000 users not to convert the database. Make sure all databases upgraded to Access 2000 are tested before they are distributed.

Implementing Coexistence Strategies

There are four steps in implementing coexistence strategies:

1. Install software (converters, viewers).
2. Create user settings, such as default save, to ease coexistence. These settings are generally stored in the registry.
3. Educate users on the issues and help them make choices. File sharing methods are determined by sharing patterns, so users need to know how to deal with situations not covered by the plan.
4. Schedule the rollout to help coexistence by simultaneously upgrading groups that work together.

Deploying Converters and Viewers

The *Microsoft Office 2000 Resource Kit* CD and Web site include the Office Converter Pack (\PFiles\ORKTools\ToolBox\Tools\OCP\ folder) and PowerPoint viewer. Use **Setup.exe –s** to install the pack without user interaction. To **customize** it, open the file CONVPACK.INI using Notepad to see a list of all converters. To exclude individual converters change their installation state to **NO** in this list. Save the file in **Text Only** format.

Use the regular **Setup.exe** without the **–s** command line switch to allow users to install interactively.

Use any distribution method to deploy. The Office Converter Pack is small enough that you can even deploy it by temporarily adding the command line to users' network logon scripts.

Implementing Default Save

Applications' default save format is simply a registry setting. Chapter 5, "User Settings," explains how to create specific Office 2000 registry settings, but here is how to implement a default save setting for all users.

The method you choose depends on your infrastructure, what level of effort you can support, and how strongly you want to enforce settings.

Using System Policies to Implement Default Save

System policies are the preferred method: they are fairly simple to set up in a Windows NT Server environment, are enforceable, and are simple to change—which is particularly important for default saves because you probably will want to change the setting later. For more information on system policies, see Chapter 5, "User Settings," the *Guide to Microsoft Windows NT 4.0 Profiles and Policies* white paper on the Microsoft Windows NT Workstation 4.0 Web site, the Windows NT 4.0 Workstation and Server Resource Kits, or the *Notes from the Field* volume *Managing a Microsoft Windows NT Network* from Microsoft Press.

1. To create a system policy, you must use the operating system you are creating the policy for. If you have both Windows 98/95 and Windows NT Workstation 4.0 in your environment, you'll need a system policy file for each. Due to differences in the registries for these operating systems, system policies are not operating system independent.

2. Start the System Policy Editor that is installed from the *Microsoft Office 2000 Resource Kit* CD You should find it at **Start | Programs | Microsoft Office Tools | Microsoft Office 2000 Resource Kit Tools.** If you haven't installed it yet, do so now. This is the latest System Policy Editor and has the features and loads the templates you'll need.

3. Click on **Options, Policy, Template** to make sure the Office 2000 template (.ADM) files are loaded. You should see all of them; if you don't, you may not be using the System Policy Editor from the *Microsoft Office 2000 Resource Kit*. Browse the \\Windows\Inf folder on the computer where you installed the System Policy Editor.

4. If you have a policy file in place, open it; if you don't, click on the **New** button to create one using this screen (see Figure 3.1):

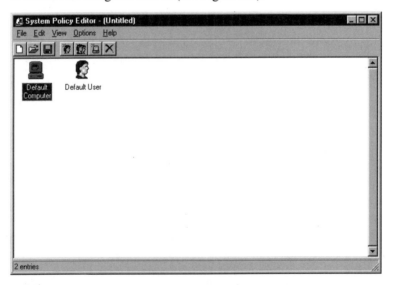

Figure 3.1   The System Policy Editor.

5. Most of the settings you need are in Default User. Double-click on it.

6. First, edit the message users get when saving files to a pre-determined, non-Office 2000 format. You'll find this setting at: Microsoft Office 2000\Customizable error messages\Default save prompt text.

7. Click on the box until it shows a check mark. If you decide not to change this setting, click on the box until it is gray (user's setting), not blank (no setting).

8. Add a message that explains why users are saving in the earlier format, as shown in Figure 3.2, and then click **OK**.

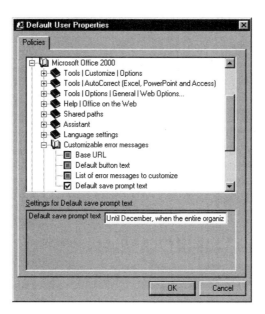

Figure 3.2   Configuring the default save prompt.

Note   When users choose **Save,** the default is set in the dialog box, but they can override in any instance to change the format. Users need this capability if they are sharing with someone who needs a different format, are publishing Web content, or are using features that don't convert and don't need to share the file.

9. Create save settings for each of the applications:
Microsoft Excel 2000\Tools\Options\Transition\Save Excel files as
Microsoft PowerPoint 2000\Tools\Options\Save\Save PowerPoint files as
Microsoft Word 2000\Tools\Options\Save\Save Word files as

10. Put a check mark in each setting, then at the bottom of the dialog box use the drop down to choose the preferred file format, as shown in Figure 3.3.

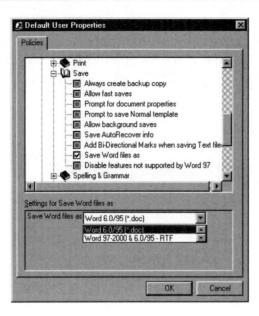

Figure 3.3   Configuring the default save format.

11. Save the file when you are done. If you opened a pre-existing file, save it under the same name and location. If this is a new system policy file, you must name it **config.pol** for Windows 9*x* users or **ntconfig.pol** for Windows NT Workstation users, and store it in the logon directory on the server. For a Windows NT Server:
\\<primary domain controller>\netlogon\config.pol
For a NetWare server:
\\<preferred server>\sys\public\config.pol

Deploying Default Save Settings with Office 2000

If you don't have system policies implemented and can't get them implemented in time for Office 2000, there are five ways to deploy registry settings as part of the installation:

- **Use the Office Profile Wizard.** Install Office 2000 on a test computer, change the settings through the user interface, run the Office Profile Wizard to capture those settings to an .OPS file, then include the file in a custom installation by using the Custom Installation Wizard.

- **Import registry settings with the Custom Installation Wizard (CIW).** Create a registry setting with the user interface, use the Registry Editor (**Regedit.exe**) to export the key to a .REG file, then use the Custom Installation Wizard to import it. Do this only for settings that the Office Profile Wizard doesn't capture.

- **Add registry settings with the CIW.** Enter the key manually in the same pane of the CIW used in the method above. This is not recommended, because it is too easy to make a mistake.

- **Use simulated system policies.** Use these if you have not implemented system policies but need to enforce settings more strongly than is possible with the Office Profile Wizard. Open the System Policy Editor and click on **Open Registry** in the **File** menu. This opens the registry on the test computer and allows you to make changes using the Office templates. Use the System Policy Editor and templates to create settings in the \\HKEY_CURRENT_USER \Software\Microsoft\Policies\Microsoft\Office\9.0 branch of the registry. When you are done, use the Registry Editor to export this branch of the registry, and then use the Custom Installation Wizard to import the keys into the transform file. These policies are enforced each time the user starts up an Office 2000 application. The drawback is that there is no easy way to change settings back.

- **Add a registry file to the CIW Add Installations Pane.** This runs the registry setting after setup is complete and all other files have been copied and the settings written.

The first three of these methods store settings in the database created on the local computer after Setup completes. This database is referenced any time users want to make a change to their installation, or when another user logs onto the computer for the first time. It allows you to enforce which settings users start out with. Registry settings you add after installing Office 2000 are not stored in this database, so they affect only the user who is logged on when Setup is run.

Other Methods for Deploying User Settings

You can also create a registry file by exporting a key from the Registry Editor (Regedit.exe), then distribute the file through e-mail, a Web page hyperlink, SMS, and so on.

User Education

When you enforce an earlier-version default save, be sure to tell users why you chose this setting, what features may be lost during save, how long the setting will be in force, and how (and under what circumstances) they can change the setting. Guidelines help users do the right thing.

Users should also understand the overall coexistence strategy, which versions of Office your files can be shared in, and how to share with users of previous versions inside and outside the organization.

Preparing the Helpdesk

Make sure helpdesk members understand the coexistence strategy and its implementation method completely. They probably will have to distribute to the Office Converter Pack and any necessary registry files, so make sure they have access.

Helpdesk technicians also have to understand each possible file format for each application, their benefits and possible problems, procedures for saving to other formats, and what sort of features, formatting, or data may be lost when doing so.

The helpdesk is pivotal to a successful coexistence strategy—from helping you understand your organization's file sharing dynamics to helping users deal with situations not covered by the coexistence plan. A thoroughly prepared and competent helpdesk improves users' experience and saves time and money.

C H A P T E R 4

Customizing an Office 2000 Installation

You can customize an Office 2000 installation to provide users with the tools they need, minimize installation effort at the desktop, tailor the software environment, and reduce helpdesk burden. This chapter discusses the Windows Installer, and then explains how to use it and *Microsoft Office 2000 Resource Kit* tools to customize installation, adjust the amount of user interactivity, remove previous versions of Office, and deploy different parts of Office 2000 at different times.

What You'll Find in This Chapter

- An overview of the features and benefits of Windows Installer

- How to best prepare for and customize Setup—including a list of the features and functionality that are customizable

- Overviews of the Custom Installation Wizard and the Internet Explorer Administration Kit—including functionality and troubleshooting tips

- How to use the Office Profile Wizard to customize user settings

- How to customize the Office Removal Wizard using one of three possible methods—including a reference table of switches and their functionality

- How to use the SETUP.INI file to supply commands during Setup

- How to implement a staged deployment

The Windows Installer

The Windows Installer service replaces the Acme Setup and the .STF files of Office 4.*x* – Office 97. It improves on the old Setup program, which did not allow Office administrators to:

- Manage shared resources adequately.
- Enforce installation rules consistently.
- Customize easily.
- Install only the components users need, while simplifying adding components later.
- Diagnose and repair configuration problems at application run time.

The Windows Installer is provided as an operating system service because these needs are common to all desktop applications (not just Office 2000). It is included with Office 2000 and Windows 2000, and it also works on the Microsoft Windows 95/98 and Windows NT Workstation 4.0 operating systems. It is also provided in the Windows 2000 Software Development Kit, so that software developers can use it to deploy and maintain Windows software.

Standard Format for Component Management

The Windows Installer service views all applications as consisting of three logical entities: components, features, and products. Components are collected into features, and features are collected into products.

Components are collections of files, registry keys, and other resources that are installed as a unit. They are not exposed to the user, but they allow developers to ensure that mutually dependent files are installed or uninstalled together. This simplifies design, deployment, and administration. The Windows Installer verifies that each component exists and is properly installed; it also tracks files, registry keys, and shortcuts that are shared by applications, and does not allow them to be removed if other applications on the system are using them. This prevents two common desktop maintenance problems: unwanted removal of necessary resources and unwanted retention of unnecessary ones.

Features are groups of components (pieces of an application) that a user can choose to install or omit.

Products are entities such as Office 2000 or Word 2000, consisting of one or more features. Each product is described to the Windows Installer with a package file (.MSI)—a database that optimizes installation performance by describing the relationships between features and components for a given product. At installation, the Windows Installer service uses the product's package file to determine which operations to perform.

Windows Installer Shortcuts

The new Windows Installer shortcuts (supported by the Windows Desktop Update) offer an improvement over hard-coded shortcuts, which run an application's executable when they are accessed. The Windows Installer shortcuts include a globally unique identifier (GUID) that the Windows Installer uses to identify the application and check the application's installation state (explained in the next section) when the shortcut is accessed. The Windows Installer can then install an application appropriately on first use, and check that the critical files and settings are correct. The Windows Installer requires the new shortcuts for application-level Install on First Use and self-repairing applications: it has no way to intervene when a user accesses an application through a hard-coded shortcut.

As part of the Windows Desktop Update, the new shortcuts are supported on Windows 98 and Windows 2000. If you are running Windows 95 or Windows NT Workstation 4.0, you have to install the Active Desktop option with Internet Explorer 4.01 (SP-1 or greater) or the Windows Desktop Update with Internet Explorer 5.0. This includes the Active Desktop, but you can disable it; and you can hide Internet Explorer from users if you use version 5 of Internet Explorer and the Internet Explorer Administration Kit (IEAK). The new shortcuts are required only for application-level self-repairing applications and install on first use—the applications themselves handle these operations for individual features. For details on deploying this correctly and efficiently, see "Adding the Windows Desktop Update" in the "Internet Explorer Administration Kit (IEAK)" section later in this chapter.

Installation States

The Windows Installer recognizes an installation state for each feature. Possibilities are:

- **Run from My Computer.** The feature is installed to the local computer. At the application level, this is similar to the old *typical* installation: the most commonly used components install to the local computer, while others install on first use or are unavailable.

- **Run from Network (Source).** The feature or application runs from the network or CD.

- **Installed on First Use.** A feature or entire application appears in the user interface but is not installed until the first time it is accessed. For example, if Word is given the installation state **Installed on First Use**, users see the Word shortcut on the **Programs** menu but the software is not loaded onto their computers until they access the shortcut for the first time. To install an entire application this way, you must use the new Windows Installer shortcuts; you don't need them to install individual features of a locally installed application.

- **Not Available.** The feature or application is not installed and no shortcut is presented to the user.

Self-Repairing Applications

Each time the Office 2000 applications start up, the Windows Installer checks to see that all *critical* files are present and valid, and repairs problems with key files that will prevent the application from starting properly. For instance, if a user uses the shortcut to Word 2000 but the Winword.exe file is missing the Windows Installer automatically reinstalls the file, and then starts Word. While the repair is underway, this dialog box is displayed (Figure 4.1):

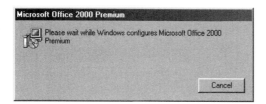

Figure 4.1   The Office 2000 Premium Detect and Repair dialog box.

Each Office 2000 application can also repair non-critical files. Users can access this feature through the **Detect and Repair** command on the **Help** menu or through the Control Panel's Add/Remove Programs applet.

Customizing Windows Installer Packages

To customize a package, the administrator creates an .MST (transform) file. The Windows Installer reads the .MSI (original installation state) then uses the .MST file values to transform the package, overriding the .MSI file values.

A transform is a record of the difference between two .MSI files. Tools such as the Custom Installation Wizard (CIW), which creates transforms, provide a convenient user interface for doing so. The user is actually modifying a copy of the original .MSI. When the transform is written at the end of the session it is created by using an Installer API that compares the original and updated .MSIs, saving a record of the changes in an .MST file.

Preparing to Customize Setup

Before you customize Setup, you need to understand the Office 2000 applications, their features, and which functionality you can enable for all users through a custom installation. Specifically:

- The applications available in each edition of Office 2000.

- Deployment features to implement.
- Upgrading to Internet Explorer 5.
- Multinational functionality.
- Macro virus protection.
- Customizable Help.
- Customizable alerts.
- Custom solutions capabilities.
- System policies/desktop lockdown.
- Support for roaming users.
- Office Server Extensions.

Next, prepare the software so that you can begin customization:

- Perform an administrative installation of Office 2000 to the server, using the command **Setup.exe /a**.
- Install the *Microsoft Office 2000 Resource Kit* CD Toolbox on the desktop computer you are using to create the customizations.
- Perform a regular user installation on a test computer to create user settings. Options are discussed in Chapter 5, "User Settings."

Tip   Rather than rerunning the administrative installation of Office 2000, you can copy it to other distribution servers. Create a subfolder (under the main directory) that contains all additional and customized files to make it easier to ensure that all files get to each distribution server. For more information on distribution, see Chapter 8, "Distributing Outlook 2000."

The SETUPREF.XLS spreadsheet is a valuable resource when you customize Office 2000. It is installed with the *Microsoft Office 2000 Resource Kit* under **Start | Programs | Microsoft Office Tools | Microsoft Office 2000 Resource Kit Documents | Office Information.** It contains three reference sheets:

- The Setup Command-Line Options
- The Setup Settings File Format
- Customizable Properties

Use these when you create a command line for installing Office 2000 properly, edit the SETUP.INI file, and modify or add options in the Custom Installation Wizard.

Custom Installation Wizard

The Custom Installation Wizard (CIW) is the primary tool for customizing Office 2000 Setup. This section discusses how it works, what you can customize with it, and some tips about what actually happens when you make certain choices. After a brief explanation of the .MST file, this section works through CIW functionality in the order you would use it. The CIW is in the *Microsoft Office 2000 Resource Kit* Toolbox at **Programs | Microsoft Office Tools | Microsoft Office Resource Kit Tools | Custom Installation Wizard.** When you open the CIW, you see this screen (Figure 4.2):

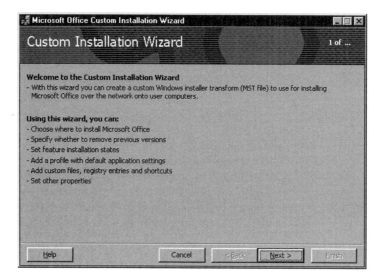

Figure 4.2   Welcome screen for the Custom Installation Wizard.

The .MST (Transform) File

The .MST file transforms the Office 2000 package into the custom installation you design. In the past, you used the CIW (the NIW in Office 95 and 97) to edit the Office package setup table (.STF) file. With Office 2000 and the new Windows Installer technology, you never change the package instruction file (now called the .MSI file). Instead, you use the CIW to create an .MST file that is used in combination with the original package file to create a set of instructions for the Windows Installer. The .MST is a database of all customizations, and if you deploy a lot of additional files with Office, it can get quite large.

Open the .MSI File

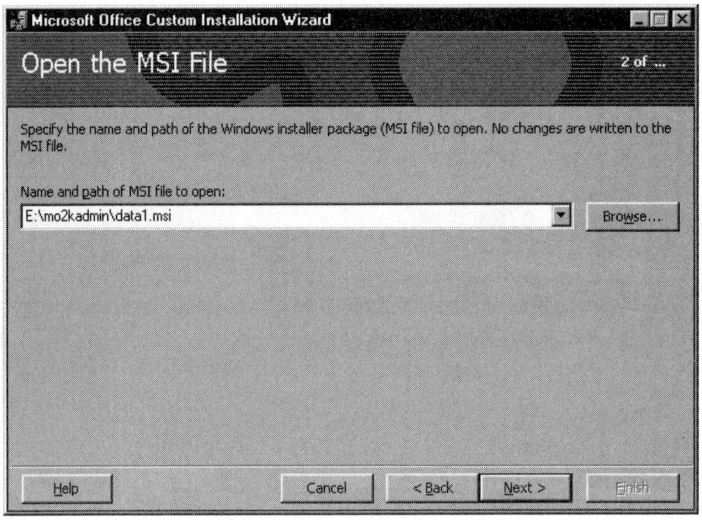

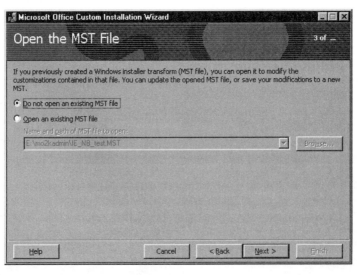

Figure 4.3   Opening an .MSI file to edit with the CIW.

The CIW first prompts you to specify which .MSI file to open (Figure 4.3). Use the **Browse** button to find the .MSI file you want. If you have several administrative installations on one server for the different Office editions, be sure you've located the correct one. The .MSI you use determines the options you see in the CIW.

Open the .MST File

Figure 4.4   Opening an .MST file to edit with the CIW.

In the next pane, specify the .MST file (figure 4.4). Select **Open an Existing MST file** (then select its path name) if you want to change an existing file or check its content and use it as a baseline. If you plan to use the Windows Installer Shortcuts transforms for adding the Windows Desktop Update described in the "Distributing Office 2000 User Settings" topic in the IEAK section later in this chapter, you need to open the appropriate .MST file here. Otherwise, create a new .MST using the default option.

Select the .MST File to Save

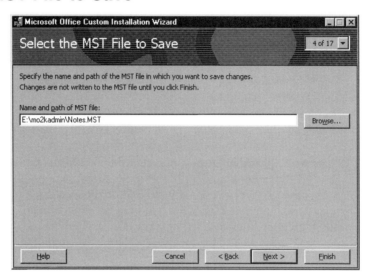

Figure 4.5   Saving your .MST file.

Choose a valid location for the new .MST file and a name that describes the file's purpose (Figure 4.5). You can use long file names and spaces, but if you plan to use batch files for distribution, 8.3 names without spaces are easier to use. The best place to store the .MST is in a folder off the root of the administrative installation that contains all customization files. If you change an existing .MST file, the CIW suggests storing the new version under the previous name and location, so be careful not to overwrite the original file if you don't intend to.

Tip   The drop-down list in the upper right-hand corner of the screen lets you move to a specific pane, which is handy when you are simply making a few modifications.

Specify Default Path and Organization

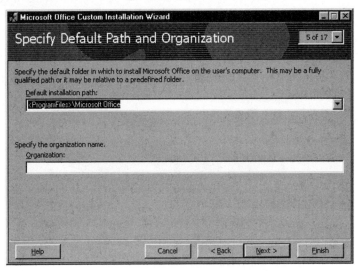

Figure 4.6   Specifying the default path in which to install Office.

In this pane (Figure 4.6), specify the path on the local computer that Office 2000 should install into, and the organization name. The default is \\Program Files\Microsoft Office, and this usually is the best place to put the software. This was also the location for Office 97, so if you are leaving any Office 97 components on the computer, choose a different location for Office 2000 to avoid overwriting any files with the same name or causing other conflicts. For example, you may decide to leave Access 97 on desktops until all databases are tested and converted. Because Office 97 and Office 2000 applications cannot coexist in the same directory, you must use a different installation path. Outlook 97/98 and Outlook 2000 cannot coexist *on the same computer*, even in different directories, however, Outlook 97/98 can coexist with the rest of Office 2000, and Outlook 2000 can coexist with the rest of Office 97.

The organization name is used automatically for all installations that use this .MST file.

Remove Previous Versions

With the screen shown in Figure 4.7, you can customize (in basic ways) how previous versions of Office are removed from the computer. The "Office Removal Wizard" section later in this chapter covers more complex customization.

Choose **Default Setup behavior** to safely remove *all* earlier versions of the Office 2000 applications that you are installing. *Safe* means that it retains common files, shared applications, and user modifiable files such as templates. Choose this option to run a customized removal routine.

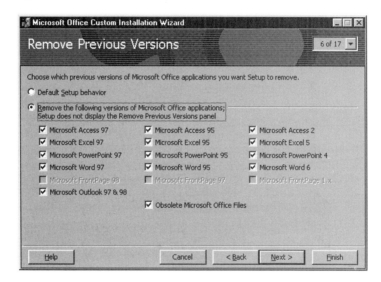

Figure 4.7   Configuring the removal of previous versions of Office.

If the general process for removing the earlier versions of Office fits your needs but you want to leave some applications on user computers, clear their check boxes to prevent Setup from removing them.

Set Feature Installation States

Each Office 2000 feature can have any of the various installation states discussed previously. If you install Office 2000 without changing any feature installation states, the result is something close to the *Typical* installation, and the most commonly used features are installed on the local computer. With Office 2000, however, most remaining features are set to **Installed on First Use** and a few are set to **Not Available**.

The Set Feature Installation States screen shows the possible states (Figure 4.8):

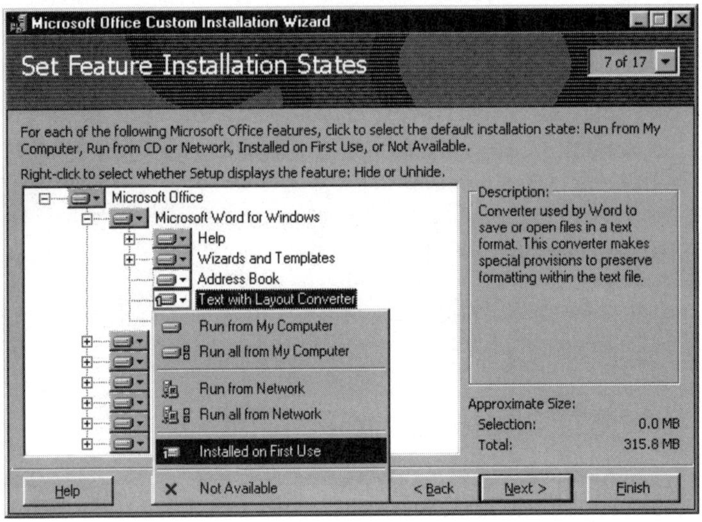

Figure 4.8   Setting feature installation states for Office applications.

- **Run from My Computer.** If you choose this for the top level feature of an application, some of its sub-features may still have an **Installed on First Use** or **Not Available** installation state.

- **Run all from My Computer.** Choose this to install the selected feature and all sub-features to the local computer.

- **Run from Network.** Choose this to install the selected feature to run from the network. All sub-features that were previously set to **Run from My Computer** or **Installed on First Use** are set to **Run from Network.** Sub-features marked **Not Available** are not changed.

- **Run all from Network.** Choose this to run the selected feature and all of its sub-features from the network. Most of Office 2000 runs from the network, however, a few features cannot be run from the source and will have the **Not Available** installation state.

- **Installed on First Use.** Choose this to install a feature or an entire application the first time it is used. To use this to install an entire application, client computers must have the Windows Desktop Update. You do not need it to install individual features on first use if the application is already installed.

- **Not Available.** Choose this to prevent installing a feature.

All installation states are stored in Installer specific Registry entries that are created after Office 2000 installs and are used in the Add/Remove Programs applet in the Control Panel. Once Office is installed, any state changes made by the user, either through Add/Remove or by triggering the **Installed on First Use** of a feature, are reflected by the Registry settings and in the Add/Remove Programs applet.

Tip   For mobile or laptop users or those who usually connect over slow links, it is better to install all necessary files to the local computer and avoid using **Installed on First Use or Run From Network**. Further, if you install an application on first use, the first time the user accesses the application, the Windows Installer installs only those files necessary to start up the application. All other files are installed when the user accesses the feature that is dependent on that file. Users can become annoyed if too many features are installed on first use.

If you right-click on a feature or application and choose **Hide**, you conceal it from users running the Control Panel Add/Remove Programs applet. This does not change the installation state—it simply hides the user interface so that the user can't change it. Once a feature is hidden, it cannot be unhidden.

Customizing Default Application Settings

Use the pane shown in Figure 4.9 to add customized user settings captured by the Office Profile Wizard (and stored in an .OPS file). When you choose **Get values from an existing settings profile**, the Custom Installation Wizard automatically disables the option to migrate user settings from a previous version of Office. You can click on the check box to migrate settings from a previous version, but they overwrite the settings in the .OPS file. Settings included with the CIW are written when Office 2000 Setup runs; migrated settings are written when the application runs for the first time.

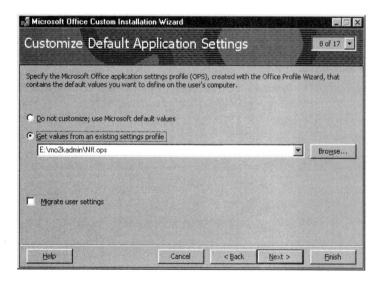

Figure 4.9   Customizing default application settings.

For more information, see Chapter 5, "User Settings."

Adding Files to the Installation

Use this pane to add files to the .MST file. These can be any sort of files but they usually pertain to Office 2000—templates, Help files, clip art, or custom solutions. When you add a file, the dialog prompts for an installation location. You can select it from a drop-down list of folders that Office Setup creates, or type in a folder location.

The example shown in Figure 4.10 adds Excel tools (part of the *Microsoft Office 2000 Resource Kit* for recovering corrupted Excel files and for fixing year 2000 date problems) to the installation by putting them in the \Addins folder.

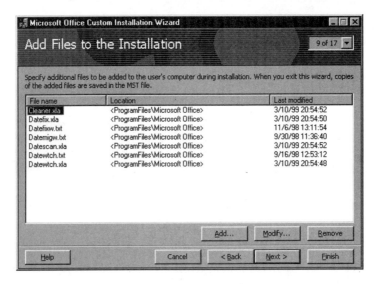

Figure 4.10   Adding files to the default Office installation.

Adding Registry Entries

Although the Office Profile Wizard is the preferred tool for capturing and distributing custom user settings, you can also add registry settings by importing a .REG file or by manually entering a key. Registry keys are complex, and entering them by hand introduces the possibility of mistakes. Hand-entered keys overwrite imported registry entries, which overwrite entries added through an .OPS file. The screen shown in Figure 4.11 allows you to add registry keys to the Office installation.

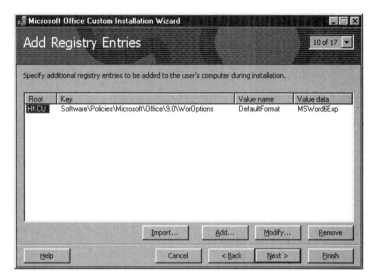

Figure 4.11   Adding registry entries to the Office installation.

For more information, see Chapter 5, "User Settings."

Managing Shortcuts

By default, a shortcut to each Office 2000 application is placed in the root of the **Start, Programs** menu, a shortcut to Outlook is placed on the desktop and in the **Quick List** toolbar, and the remaining shortcuts are placed in the **Programs, Microsoft Office Tools** menu. Use the dialog box shown in Figure 4.12 to add shortcuts or modify or remove the defaults. Shortcuts for absent applications are not displayed.

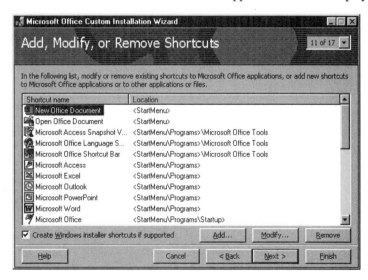

Figure 4.12   Add, modify, or remove shortcuts in this pane of the CIW.

Check **Create Windows installer shortcuts if supported** at the bottom of the dialog if you want the Windows Installer to manage the shortcuts and provide the **Detect and Repair** and **Installed on First Use** features (described earlier in this chapter).

Identifying Additional Servers

In order to work, the **Installed on First Use, Detect and Repair,** and Add/Remove components features must be able to connect to an administrative installation of Office 2000. You can add servers in this dialog (Figure 4.13) to provide the Windows Installer with additional locations to use for failover (this *does not* provide load balancing). If a valid location isn't available, due to network problems or a server that is no longer available, a dialog box prompts the user to enter or browse for a valid path. A valid location is one that the user has rights to with the correct .MSI file.

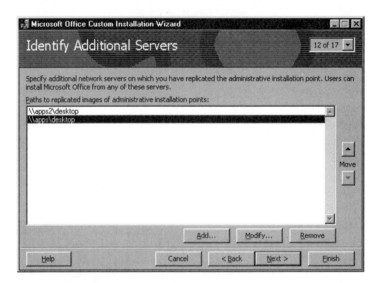

Figure 4.13   Specifying additional installation servers.

There are other benefits to identifying additional servers. You can use them as part of a distribution strategy. For instance, most organizations have multiple distribution servers and map each user to only one server (for load balancing purposes), while giving their IT technicians access to all distribution servers. By including all distribution servers in the Identify Additional Servers list, a technician can use any server to install Office 2000 for a user; the list would still include a valid server for the user to add or remove components, or install features on first use. Another potential use for adding additional installation servers is as follows. You can upgrade all laptops when users are in the office, provide a CD with additional components, then add the CD drive path in the

Identify Additional Servers pane. When users put the CD in the drive the Windows Installer will find it.

Add Installations and Run Programs

Use this dialog (Figure 4.14) to add installations, programs, or post-installation scripts to the Office 2000 Setup. For example, you can arrange to update virus checking software as you deploy Office 2000. Anything you add in this dialog box runs after the Office 2000 installation completes.

Note   These applications install after Office 2000 successfully reboots the computer. If you use an automated process to initiate the Office 2000 installation, but do not log on as the user and complete the process, users logging on for the first time are going to have to wait while the additional software installs.

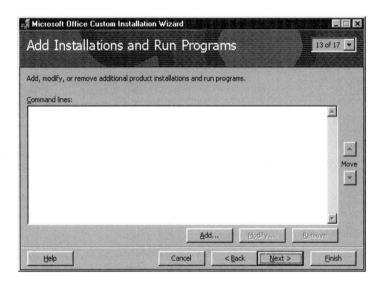

Figure 4.14   Add, modify, or remove other programs in this pane.

The first version of the Windows Installer that shipped with Office 2000 did not allow you to add other Windows Installer programs such as Microsoft Publisher, Microsoft PhotoDraw, or the MultiLanguage Packs to Office Setup and chain them together into one installation process. The CIW displays a warning (Figure 4.15) when you click on the **Add** button:

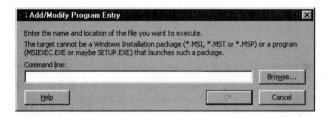

Figure 4.15   This warning describes the limitations of the Add/Modify Program Entry feature.

A new Setup.exe (found on the *Microsoft Office 2000 Resource Kit* CD and Web site) allows you to add a single Installer package Setup, which is installed after the first installation is completed. To chain applications:

1. Replace the Setup.exe in the root of the administrative installation of the software that you want to run immediately after the software you are customizing. For example, to chain a MultiLanguage Pack installation to Office 2000, replace the Setup.exe in the root directory of the MultiLanguage Pack administrative installation by copying the special *Microsoft Office 2000 Resource Kit* version of Setup.exe to this location.

2. In the dialog box above, add the command line for the MultiLanguage pack Setup with the **/chained** switch immediately following Setup.exe:

```
\\ServerName\ShareName\setup.exe /chained TRANSFORMS=lpk.mst
```

where *lpk.mst* represents the name of the .MST file created to customize the MultiLanguage Pack. You can use any of the other setup switches as well.

For more information, see Chapter 9, "Multinational Deployment."

Outlook Installation Options

There are a number of options for customizing your Outlook 2000 installation. In the Customize Outlook Installation Options pane (Figure 4.16), you can choose **Do not customize Outlook profile and account information** to either prompt the user for information or leverage a .prf file. Since a user or automated process would have to modify the registry, this option is unavailable if the workstation is locked down to prevent registry changes. Alternatively, you can choose **Customize Outlook profile and account information**, which forces you to set default profile information for the user. During initial installation, the setup file will install the relevant information. If there is an existing profile, Outlook will not remove or change it.

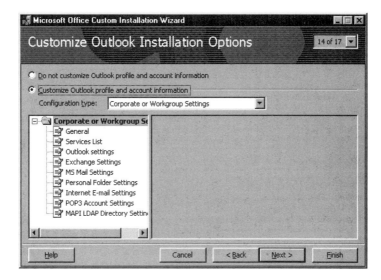

Figure 4.16   Customizing Outlook installation options.

For detailed information on customizing your Outlook 2000 installation, see Chapter 8, "Deploying Outlook 2000."

Internet Explorer 5.0

Internet Explorer 5.0 is included with Office 2000 but is not installed by the Windows Installer or required by your Office 2000 installation. Office Setup uses an internal command line to launch Internet Explorer Setup. Figure 4.17 shows how to configure this.

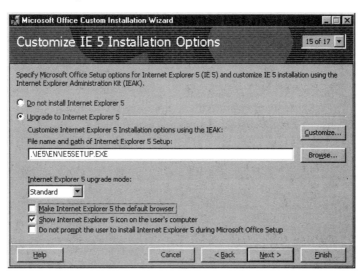

Figure 4.17   Customizing Internet Explorer 5.

Use this dialog box to make Internet Explorer the default browser, display the Internet Explorer icon on the user's computer, or disable installation.

Warning   Using this dialog alone *does not* install the Windows Desktop Update. You will have to customize the setup in order to include it. Please see the "Adding the Windows Desktop Update" section for more details.

For more complete customization such as choosing specific features or creating settings and restrictions, click on the **Customize** button to launch the Internet Explorer Administration Kit (IEAK). Launching the IEAK from the Custom Installation Wizard imposes certain settings (described below) that you cannot change. If your requirements differ, run the IEAK outside of the CIW and choose from the complete list, and then point the CIW to that location in this pane.

Note   Customized builds of Internet Explorer 5 contain two copies of IE5Setup.exe: one in the original location in the language folder (EN by default) and one at the bottom of the added \Ins subtree. You must reference the original location in the language folder in order to install Internet Explorer 5 with Office.

When you launch the IEAK from the CIW:

- You do not have to supply an IEAK customization code.

- You are seen as a *Corporate Administrator* that is creating a flat build (installing all necessary Internet Explorer components into a folder on a network share) of the customized Internet Explorer 5.

- Outlook Express and NetMeeting are always installed because Office 2000 functionality requires them: Outlook Express for Outlook 2000's newsreader, NetMeeting to schedule and to automatically start or join online meetings.

More information on the IEAK is included later in this chapter; complete information is in the *Internet Explorer 5.0 Resource Kit*.

Modify Setup Properties

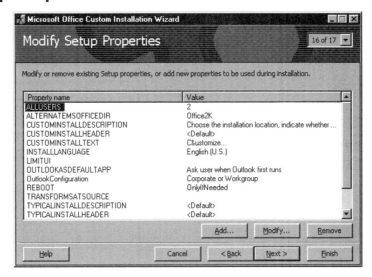

Figure 4.18   Modifying Setup properties.

Use these ways to modify Setup properties:

1. The SETUP.INI file (for all computers in the organization).
2. The .MST file through the CIW (for all computers the .MST is used for).
3. The Setup.exe command line (for any others—this overrides SETUP.INI and .MST settings).

The SETUPREF.XLS spreadsheet (in the *Microsoft Office 2000 Resource Kit Toolbox*) documents the properties in this dialog and others. The SETUP.INI file is documented in the "SETUP.INI" section beginning on page 130.

Finish

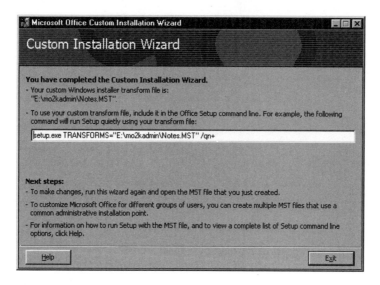

Figure 4.19   Completing the CIW.

When the CIW finishes creating the .MST file, it presents a screen similar to this sample command line (Figure 4.19), which runs Setup with the .MST file you just created, uses the **/qn** switch to run it with no user interaction or interface, and uses the + to prompt for a reboot or display a **Setup completed successfully** dialog box if Office doesn't require a reboot. The sample shows correct syntax. Other switches are documented in the SETUPREF.xls spreadsheet included on the *Microsoft Office 2000 Resource Kit CD*.

Internet Explorer Administration Kit (IEAK)

The *Internet Explorer 5.0 Resource Kit* explains the Internet Explorer Administration Kit (IEAK) and how to use it to customize Internet Explorer 5.0. You can purchase the resource kit through Microsoft Press at http://mspress.microsoft.com/reslink.

Adding the Windows Desktop Update

You can install the Windows Desktop Update with either Internet Explorer 4.0 or Internet Explorer 5.0. Windows 98 and Windows 2000 include the updated shell already and do not need to have it added. If the Active Desktop has already been installed with Internet Explorer 4.01 (SP1 or greater), a user installation of Internet Explorer 5.0 includes the Windows Desktop Update. If not, the Windows Desktop Update is not installed with Internet Explorer 5.0, and the user is not given the choice to install it during a standard interactive installation. Instead, you must use the IEAK to add the Windows Desktop Update to Internet Explorer 5.0 Setup. Although Internet Explorer 4.01 (SP1 or greater) lets you deploy the Windows Desktop Update by installing the Active Desktop, it does not allow you to disable the Active Desktop through the Internet Explorer Administration Kit 4.

The Office 2000 Setup program determines whether the Windows Desktop Update is installed at the beginning of the installation process. If it is present, Office Setup creates the new Windows Installer shortcuts and can install applications on first use. If Setup does not detect the update, it cannot create the Windows Installer shortcuts. If a transform is being applied that changes the feature installation state for an application to Installed on First Use, then Office Setup installs the core components for that application locally and creates a normal shortcut that points to the .EXE file. Office 2000 Setup was designed this way to prevent broken installations in a mixed environment.

Until recently, the documented process to provide the Installer shortcuts for a computer without the Windows Desktop Update was to perform separate installations of Internet Explorer 5 (configured to add the Windows Desktop Update) and Office, with reboots for each install. After Office 2000 became commercially available, the development team created a set of special transforms included in the Windows Installer Shortcuts Update so that Office 2000 and Internet Explorer 5.0 could install together with one reboot. This enables the new shortcuts and Windows Installer features of **Installed on First Use** and self-repairing applications.

To use these transforms to add the Windows Shell Update:

1. In pane #3, "Open the MST File," shown in Figure 4.4, open one of the transforms contained in this Update: O9WIS_1.MST for customization of any Office 2000 CD1 (Office Premium, Office Standard, Word), and O9WIS_2.MST for any Office 2000 CD2. These transforms contain commands (that you cannot see or edit) that solve the issue described above, but nothing else.

Note   You must use an updated version of the CIW (Microsoft Office Custom Installation Wizard Update (Add Installations)) to modify the supplied .MSTs. Both updates are included on the accompanying CD.

2. Create all other customizations.

3. In pane #15, "Customize Internet Explorer 5 Installation Options," shown in Figure 4.17, click on the **Customize** button. This launches the IEAK Customization Wizard.

4. On pane #10, "Corporate Install Options," select "Internet Explorer is not set as the default browser" if you do not want Internet Explorer 5 to become the default browser. Clearing the checkbox on pane #15, "Customize Internet Explorer 5 Installation Options," will *not* prevent Internet Explorer 5 from becoming the default browser.

5. After finishing the IEAK session and returning to the CIW, in pane #13, "Add Installations and Run Programs," shown in figure 4.14, add the following command:

    ```
    .\Setup.exe /fs data1.msi /chained
    ```

    This relative path runs the same Setup again in the special reinstall mode that changes the shortcuts to Windows Installer Shortcuts after Office 2000 *and* the Windows Desktop Update are installed and the computer has rebooted.

Note   This example assumes that a CD1 related product is being installed. If not, the name of the .MSI will be different.

---

6. If you are installing Internet Explorer 5 separately from Office, use the IEAK to include the Windows Desktop Update by clicking on **Yes** in the **Windows Desktop Update** dialog (Figure 4.20).

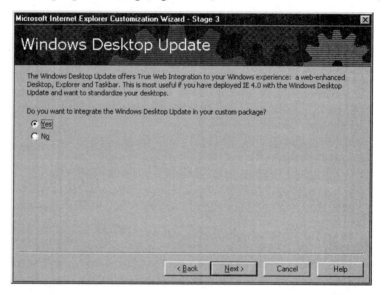

Figure 4.20   Including the Windows Desktop Update in the Office installation.

7. To disable the Active Desktop, Channels, or Outlook Express icons, see the next section.

8. Replace the Setup.exe in the root of the administrative installation of Office 2000 with the updated version supplied with the *Microsoft Office 2000 Resource Kit*. This updated Setup.exe is available on the accompanying CD. The updated Setup.exe allows you to run another Windows Installer operation after Office 2000 installs, such as the command you added above to fix the shortcuts. It also allows you to *chain* installations such as the Microsoft Publisher installation on CD2 to Office 2000 Premium CD1.

Disabling Internet Explorer 5.0 Default Features

Disabling the Active Desktop

The Active Desktop (part of the Windows Desktop Update) does not need to be enabled for the new Windows shortcuts to work, and some organizations prefer to disable it. There are a several ways to do this:

- The IEAK Customization Wizard Active Desktop dialog in the Desktop Customization section.
- The IEAK Customization Wizard Policies and Restrictions section.
- The IEAK Profile Manager.
- System policies.

Using the IEAK Customization Wizard Active Desktop Dialog

1. On a test computer, right-click on the desktop and turn off the Active Desktop.

2. Run the IEAK Customization Wizard on that computer.

3. In the **Active Desktop** dialog (Figure 4.21), click on **Import the current Active Desktop components**. Check that the settings are correct by clicking on the **Modify Settings** button, then the **Web** tab; the **View my Active Desktop as a Web page** check box should be cleared.

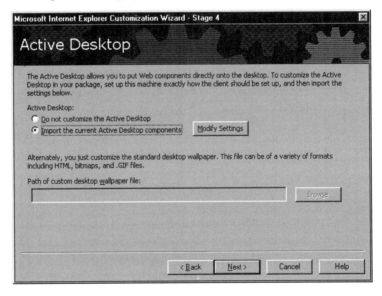

Figure 4.21   Configuring Active Desktop.

Click on **Next** to display a dialog box with which you can import the toolbar settings on the current computer. You can customize this area to remove the

Channels button from the **Quick List** toolbar that is part of the Windows Desktop Update or add or remove other buttons.

Using the IEAK Policies and Restrictions Section

The last section of the IEAK deals with policies and restrictions. If you use the Custom Installation Wizard to launch the IEAK, you are assigned the role of *Corporate Administrator*. If you run the IEAK outside of the CIW, you must choose that role to expose the settings you need to disable the Active Desktop. The restrictions function as simulated system policies (deployed with Internet Explorer 5.0) that disable a user's ability to change certain policies.

1. In the **System Policies and Restrictions** dialog (Figure 4.22), click on the plus sign (+) to expand the **Web Desktop** folder.

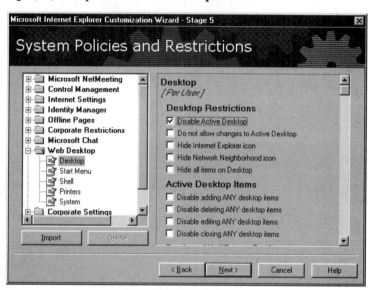

Figure 4.22   Configuring Policy to disable Active Desktop.

2. Click on the **Desktop** category, then click on the **Disable Active Desktop** check box.

3. To conceal the menu choice to enable Active Desktop from users, click on the **Start Menu** category (as shown in Figure 4.23), then click on the **Remove the Active Desktop item from the Settings menu** check box.

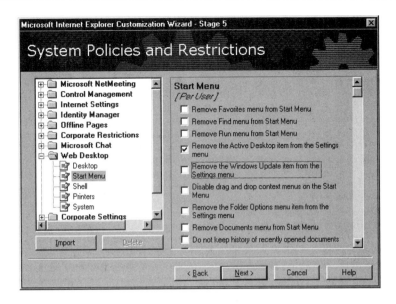

Figure 4.23   Configuring Policy to remove the Active Desktop item from the Settings menu.

Tip   Take some time to explore all of the settings in this dialog box. Some that aren't specific to Internet Explorer 5.0, such as hiding hard drives on My Computer, are useful in controlling desktops, particularly if you are not using system policies.

Using the IEAK Profile Manager

You can use the IEAK Profile Manager to create Internet Explorer 5.0 policies and restrictions during and after deployment. It looks like the **Policies and Restrictions** dialog, but its settings are stored in a configuration script instead of being distributed with Internet Explorer 5.0. You can deploy the script to user desktops or you can store it on a server and provide an Internet Explorer pointer, which allows you to make changes without having to redeploy to user desktops.

The setting for the configuration script is in **Tools | Internet Options | Connections | LAN Settings | Use automatic configuration script**. Supply a URL address in the form of **http://** or **file:**. If you want to deploy this setting with Internet Explorer 5.0, make sure it is on the test computer before using the IEAK to import the Connections from the test computer.

Using System Policies

You can also create system policies by using the settings policy files exposed in the IEAK Profile Manager:

1. Start the System Policy Editor.
2. Choose **Options**, **Policy** template.
3. Click on the **Add** button and add the templates with the settings you need.
4. Browse to the \\Program Files\IEAK\Policies\en folder to see all of the policy templates. (Templates and their uses are explained in the "Office Policy Templates" section of Chapter 5, "User Settings.") To disable the Active Desktop, add the SP1SHELL.ADM template.
5. If you have enabled system policies, open an existing policy file; if you have not enabled them, create a new file.
6. Double-click on **Default User**.
7. Click on the plus sign (+) to expand **Desktop**.
8. Click on **Desktop Restrictions**.
9. Click on **Disable Active Desktop**.

Disabling the Channels Bar

Disabling the Active Desktop does not necessarily suppress the Channels Bar. You can use the same methods you use to disable Active Desktop to disable the Channels Bar. The setting for the Channels Bar is in the **Offline Pages** branch, and the **Offline Pages** item. In the right-hand pane, check the box for **Disable channel user interface completely**.

Disabling Outlook Express

Outlook Express automatically installs if you install Internet Explorer 5.0 with Office 2000. This is because Outlook 2000 relies on Outlook Express to provide the newsreader feature. If you don't want Outlook Express because you won't be installing Microsoft Outlook, use the IEAK from outside of the CIW and remove it as a feature.

Hiding Internet Explorer 5.0

If you want to use another browser, disable browsing for certain user groups, or use the **Installed on First Use** and self-repairing features but not show users that Internet Explorer 5.0 is installed on their computers, you can use the Policies and Restrictions section to hide Internet Explorer 5.0:

1. In the **System Policies and Restrictions** dialog (shown in Figure 4.24), click on the plus sign (+) to expand the **Web Desktop** folder.

2. Click on the **Desktop** category, then click on the **Hide Internet Explorer icon** check box.

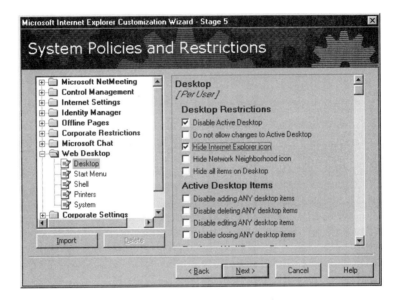

Figure 4.24   Hiding the Internet Explorer icon.

Note   The IEAK Profile Manager and the System Policy Editor both create this setting. To disable the setting in these locations, use the procedure for disabling the Active Desktop.

Using Automatic Configuration and Proxy at the Same Time

If you use Automatic Configuration for desktops, you can configure Proxy settings as a backup:

1. In the Automatic Configuration pane (Figure 4.25), check **Automatically detect configuration settings**.

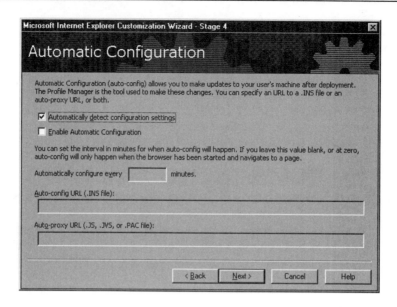

Figure 4.25   Configuring Internet Explorer to automatically detect configuration settings.

2. In the Proxy Settings pane (Figure 4.26) specify the proxy server name and port.

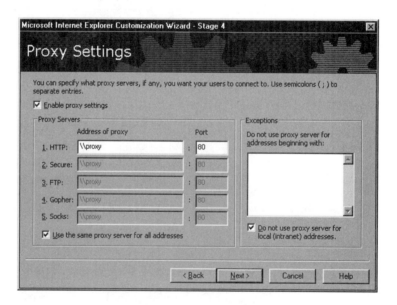

Figure 4.26   Configuring Proxy settings.

Office Profile Wizard

The Office Profile Wizard (part of the *Microsoft Office 2000 Resource Kit Toolbox*) captures custom user settings. It is explained fully in Chapter 5, "User Settings," but here is a recap of how to use it to customize configuration. Install Office 2000 on a test computer and use the user interface to customize the settings, such as those created in the **Tools**, **Options** dialog box. Then run the Office Profile Wizard to capture the Office settings and store them in an .OPS file.

It is simpler to do this before working with the Custom Installation Wizard, but you don't have to. You can use both wizards at the same time and create the .OPS file while the CIW is still running, although you cannot run the Office Profile Wizard while an Office 2000 application is running.

Office Removal Wizard

Use the Office Removal Wizard (in the *Microsoft Office 2000 Resource Kit Toolbox*) to remove previous versions of Office, individual applications, or Office 2000 itself.

Default Removal Options

The Office Removal Wizard runs as part of Office Setup. It removes previous-version applications safely, leaving files that are customized or are being used by another application—shared Office code, shared components such as Spelling and Organization Chart, sample files and templates, and so on. In an interactive setup, it lists all previous versions and allows you to select which to remove; in a non-interactive (quiet) installation, it automatically removes all previous versions in a safe manner.

To allow for rollback, Office Setup does not remove anything until Office 2000 installs successfully. If the installation fails or is interrupted, users can continue using their current software. When you calculate hard disk space requirements for the installation, remember that the existing software *and* Office 2000 are stored until the installation is complete and the old software is removed.

The Windows Installer, which has elevated privileges on Windows NT Workstation and Windows 2000, starts the Office Removal Wizard when it runs as part of Office 2000 Setup. The privilege level lets you use the Wizard to remove previous versions of Office even if the user does not have administrator rights.

Customizing the Office Removal Wizard

There are three ways to customize the Office Removal Wizard:

- Through the CIW (covered in the CIW section beginning on page 101).
- With command-line switches.

■ Editing the OFFCLN9.OPC file.

Using Command-Line Switches

To customize with this method, you have to run the Wizard outside of Office 2000 Setup—you can't edit the command line used within Office Setup.

To see the switches, go to the Office Removal Wizard directory (usually \\Program Files\ORKTools\ToolBox\Tools\Office Removal Wizard), and use the **Setup.exe /?** command to display the dialog box shown in Figure 4.27:

Figure 4.27   Command-line switches for the Office Removal Wizard.

Switch	Setting	Explanation
/A	Aggressive	Removes everything, including all files in the \\Windows\Temp directory.
/S	Safe	Removes nothing that could be in use by another application or that could have been modified by the user, such as templates and samples.
/Q	Quiet	No user interface and no interaction with the Office Removal Wizard.
/R	Restart	Restarts the system if needed. For example, if a common DLL such as OLEAUT32.DLL is removed.
/L	Log file	Generates a log file while removing applications.
/L!	Log only	Performs no clean up operations.
<log file>	Log file name	Specifies a name other than the default for the log file. The default is Offcln9.log.
<opc file>	.OPC file name	Specifies a name other than the default for the .OPC file. If you plan to customize the removal process for different user groups, name the .OPC files appropriately and use this switch to point to them.

If you want the Office Removal Wizard to run non-interactively, you must specify either **Safe** or **Aggressive** mode (/S or /A) *and* any other switches, or nothing will happen.

Editing the .OPC File

OFFCLN9.OPC is a long text file containing all of the instructions for the Office Removal Wizard. You can edit it to fine tune previous-version removal; for instance, to remove more software than Safe mode but less than Aggressive mode. Before you edit, back up the original file. Open OFFCLN9.OPC with WordPad or Word (it is too large to open with Notepad) and be careful to maintain its original *text* format when you save it.

There are two sections: a short top section listing which applications to detect, and a long second section containing the removal logic for each of these applications. Files are grouped by application, feature, and whether it is safe or risky to remove them. Semicolons are used to insert remark lines.

The OPC.DOC file that installs with the *Microsoft Office 2000 Resource Kit* Toolbox contains detailed information on the file.

DETECT, REMOVE, KEEP

In the top section of the file, which handles the detection logic, applications are tagged DETECT, REMOVE, or KEEP. When you run the Office Removal Wizard either interactively or as part of the Office 2000 Setup process, DETECT finds which Office applications are on the computer and allows you to KEEP or REMOVE them. When you run the Office Removal Wizard without interaction and outside of Office 2000 Setup, you must tell the wizard which applications to remove. Typos can break the file, so make only necessary changes.

SAFE versus RISKY

The rest of the file has bracketed sections that list whether it is safe or risky to remove items in that section, followed by the names of the applications that use those items. To customize this section you must be familiar with the applications being removed, files that store settings for previous versions (such as NORMAL.DOT for Word and GALLERY.XLS for Excel), and shared applications such as Spelling that are used by Microsoft Project or third-party solutions you might not be removing. You also have to know which features have changed. For instance, Office 2000 has new clip art and if you remove the old art you may upset users that rely on the previous selection. Sections marked *safe* are removed, those marked *risky* remain on the computer. To remove more items, change their setting to *safe*. If you want to remove most of a section, change its status to *safe* but put a semicolon in front of any files you want to retain.

User Modifiable Files

USER_MODIFIABLE_FILE= marks files that a user *can* modify—template and sample files, for example. A safe removal leaves these files. Removing the USER_MODIFIABLE_FILE= tag can free up a lot of disk space, although it can also delete user changes.

Tip   The OFFCLN9.OPC file is long and its syntax is very sensitive. An easy way to document changes you make to it is to create a Word copy of the file and format changes so they are easy to see—in bold red type, for example. Then you can search for the formatting to find changes quickly.

If you are using Word, you can also enter changes with the Track Changes feature turned on. This shows changes and the original text, and makes a handy record. You can Track Changes in the original file, save an alternate copy for a record, then accept all changes in the original, and save it as plain text. The working file *must have changes accepted and be in plain text* for the Removal Wizard to use it.

Running the Removal Wizard before Installing Office 2000

Office 2000 Setup does not remove previous copies of Office applications until it completes successfully. This enables rollback (restoring users with a working desktop) if the new applications don't install completely. While this is a good safety net, some computers don't have enough hard disk space for both versions. In this case, you can test the removal and installation processes until you are confident, then use the Office Removal Wizard to delete the previous version before installing Office 2000.

Note   When it is run outside of the Office 2000 Setup process, the Office Removal Wizard has only *user* privileges on Windows NT Workstation, so your profile must have *administrative* permissions.

For more information on the Office Removal Wizard and the .OPC file, see the *Microsoft Office 2000 Resource Kit* and the OPC.DOC in the Toolbox.

From the Trenches: Customizing an Office 2000 Installation

A large financial institution in the Northeast region of the United States wanted to deploy Office 2000 very quickly and with a number of customizations. They planned to use helpdesk personnel to distribute Office 2000 after the business day had ended so that their employees' workday would not be interrupted.

The main areas of customization they were concerned with included:

- Installing all of the features in Word, Excel, PowerPoint, and Access so users would never have to wait for a feature to install.

- Making Outlook unavailable and impossible for users to add because the company uses Lotus Notes as its e-mail system.

- Ensuring that users are storing documents on the network in their home directory.

- Taking advantage of all year 2000 tools and settings.

- Providing a fully customized version of Internet Explorer 5—complete with the Windows Shell Update to support self-repairing applications and settings to disable the Active Desktop. Also, providing a second build of Internet Explorer that prevents access to the Internet for those users who should be restricted.

To create the customized Office Setup, we first installed Office Professional and the *Microsoft Office 2000 Resource Kit* Toolbox to a test computer from the CD-ROM. We used the **Tools | Options** and **Tools | Customize** menu commands in Word to create all of the customizations in the applications—including the default document locations and year 2000 settings for Access. Then, we used the Office Profile Wizard to capture those customized settings in an .OPS file.

Next, we used the Custom Installation Wizard to change the installation states for all features to *Run All From My Computer,* and changed the installation state for Outlook to *Not Available.* We also right-clicked on **Outlook** and clicked **Hide** so that users would not see the program. The Hide option prevents users from changing Outlook's installation state in the Control Panel's Add/Remove Programs applet. The OPS file with the custom user settings was added next. We added three additional installation server locations in the CIW so technicians could install from any server, but users could still run repair or maintenance procedures from a server they have permissions for. We added a number of files to the installation—including some internal templates for Word, clip art, and the Excel year 2000 tools included on the *Microsoft Office 2000 Resource Kit* CD. Finally, we added two command lines for additional programs to install after Office 2000—an upgrade to their fax software and an upgrade to the Notes client.

The removal process was customized as well. We wanted to remove as much extraneous data as possible—including temp files. But we needed to make sure that Project 95 would still run successfully. We customized the OPC file, changing as many applications to REMOVE as possible and deleting User_Modifiable_Files. In addition, we added logic to remove the Office 97 Viewers.

For the actual upgrade procedure, we uninstalled Office 95 first—ensuring there would be no problems with hard drive space. Then we installed Internet Explorer 5 (this was prior to the Windows Installer Shortcuts Update) to get the Windows Desktop Update on the computers before Office 2000. After the reboot, we ran our customized Office 2000 Setup with the following command line:

Setup.exe TRANSFORMS="H:\Apps\Mosff2k\CustomFiles\GSL.MST" /qb-

We preferred the **/qb-** switch because it provided progress bars, which would let the technicians know when it was safe to move to the next computer, and because it would automatically reboot the computer if necessary and keep the process moving.

SETUP.INI

You can use the SETUP.INI file to supply commands during setup. Customizing the file (it is optional) offers some advantages:

- By adding content to SETUP.INI you are not subject to UI command line length limitations, which can help when you are using long paths or feature names.

Note A *new* Setup.exe avoids this limitation. It is available on the Office Resource Kit Web site, http://www.microsoft.com/office/ork.

- Using SETUP.INI helps avoid the typographical errors often made when entering complex command lines.
- You can edit SETUP.INI to create a non-interactive, customized Office 2000 Setup from a CD. For more information, see Chapter 7, "Distributing Microsoft Office 2000."
- SETUP.INI allows you to enforce specific settings, even when you allow users to run an interactive setup.

SETUP.INI is in the root directory of the administrative installation of
Office 2000. To edit it, open it with Notepad and read the text in the file. Use
SETUPREF.XLS from the *Microsoft Office 2000 Resource Kit* Toolbox as a guide
to which values you can set. Lines are commented with semicolons: to use a line,
remove its starting semi-colon, read the instructions, then add or edit the value.
For example, to add a pointer to an .MST file, remove the semicolon before the
[MST] section bracket, then remove the semicolon from in front of the first
MST1= line for a UNC path or the lower one for a drive mapping. Change the
path to point to the .MST file (see Figure 4.28).

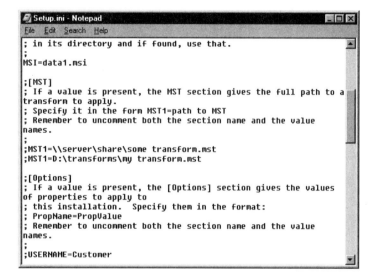

Figure 4.28   Editing SETUP.INI to point to your .MST file.

Use the [Display] section to run Setup interactively or quietly, and to display or
conceal a dialog box on completion (if Setup doesn't need to reboot). There are
several choices between no display and full display, the most popular being *basic*,
which displays progress bars but does not allow interaction.

You can use several SETUP.INI files, each with its own name and pointed to by a
command line, but this introduces the possibility of command-line typos. Since
you are likely to have multiple .MST files, use the **Modify Setup Properties** pane
in the Custom Installation Wizard to change command line settings that vary with
each rollout unit.

The Setup Command Line

This determines how Setup runs. To enforce your customizations, add an argument to point Setup to the .MST file and use one of the quiet mode switches for the user interface level. Once you have determined which command line to use, you can use any of several methods to distribute it.

Most organization use this command line:

Setup.exe TRANSFORMS="\\APPS\MSOFFICE\ACCT.MST" /qb-

Where \\APPS\MSOFFICE\ACCT.MST is the path to the .MST, **/qb** runs in quiet basic mode (which shows progress bars but runs non-interactively), and the minus sign (**-**) suppresses all modal dialog boxes, including a completion message.

The complete list of commands you can add to this line is in SETUPREF.XLS, in the *Microsoft Office 2000 Resource Kit* at **Start | Programs | Microsoft Office Tools | Microsoft Office Resource Kit Documents | Office Information**.

Tip   The minus (**-**) switch, which suppresses all modal dialog boxes, including a completion message, is not documented in the original version of SETUPREF.XLS.

Third-Party Customization Tools

In the past, many organizations used third-party tools to customize Office installations rather than using the tools that come with Office. In general, the administrator would use the tools to take a snapshot of the computer before installing Office, then install and configure Office to their specifications, and then take another snapshot. Afterwards, the administrator would deploy the snapshot that includes both files and registry settings. While this method worked reasonably well for previous versions of Office, *this is not a recommended customization method for Office 2000, or any other Windows Installer application, for upgrade situations*. There are several reasons for this:

- Windows Installer operations such as **Install on First Use** and self-repair for applications may not work.

- Office Setup evaluates the software and settings on the existing computer, which affects how installation runs. For example, if a user has Microsoft Project 95, then certain shared Office 95 code is not removed. If Microsoft Project is not on the test computer, the result could break Microsoft Project 95 installations.

- Third-party add-in tools may not work properly. These tools are usually deployed on a departmental basis rather than an organization-wide basis, and the image is likely to break their integration with the Office applications.

The most important of these reasons is the first one. If you use a third-party installation tool, you lose many of the benefits of Office 2000. The rule of thumb is to use the *Microsoft Office 2000 Resource Kit* tools to customize Office 2000, and any tool of choice to distribute it.

If you are creating an image for new computers or computers that are being wiped clean, then including Office 2000 in that image should work fine.

Staged Deployment

Staged deployment installs Office 2000 components over time. For example, you might deploy all of Office Professional except Outlook because the messaging group is preparing to migrate to Exchange in six months.

Creating Customized Staged Deployments

The simplest way to deploy an entire application after the rest of Office 2000 is to use the individual application edition in the Office 2000 edition. A Select licensing agreement allows you to use the individual editions included in the edition of Office you purchase. For example, with Office 2000 Standard you can use the individual editions of Word, Outlook, Excel, and PowerPoint. This makes deployment easier and more convenient.

Single-Language Staged Deployment

Here is an example procedure for deploying Outlook *after* Office Professional without Outlook has been deployed:

Stage 1

1. Create an administrative installation of Office 2000 Professional on a server.

2. Perform an interactive user installation of Office Professional on a test computer including all applications.

3. Create any custom settings for Office Professional, including those for Outlook.

4. Run the Office Profile Wizard to capture those settings to an .OPS file. It is not harmful to have Outlook settings on a computer that doesn't yet have Outlook.

Note   If you do not know what your Outlook settings will be, edit the Proflwiz.ini file to prevent capturing Outlook settings when you deploy Office, and deploy the Outlook settings in Stage 2 with Outlook. If you do it this way, make sure you don't deploy any Office settings with Outlook. For more information, please see Chapter 5, "User Settings."

5. Run the Custom Installation Wizard to customize Office Professional. Use the .OPS file, and choose **Not Available** for the Outlook installation state. Right-click on **Outlook** and choose **Hide** (so a user cannot install the software through the Add/Remove Programs Control Panel applet).

6. Create any other necessary customizations.

7. Deploy the customized Office Professional to users.

Stage 2

1. Create an administrative installation of Outlook on a server.

2. Run the CIW to customize Outlook. Do not add custom settings or an .OPS file as this could overwrite existing customized settings.

3. Deploy the customized Outlook to users.

Do not try to create two different .MST files for the same package (or .MSI file) and successively deploy them. The second deployment will simply put you into Maintenance Mode for the original installation, allowing you to add or remove components. For more information on creating user settings and the Office Profile Wizard, see Chapter 5, "User Settings." For more information about creating administrative installations of different versions of Office 2000 in the same network directory, see "Staging Your Deployment of Office Premium" in Chapter 3 of the *Microsoft Office 2000 Resource Kit*. For more information about staged deployment, please see individual topics in the index of this book and "How to Distribute a Standard Office User Profile in a Staged Deployment" in Chapter 6 of the *Microsoft Office 2000 Resource Kit*.

CHAPTER 5

User Settings

User settings determine how users interact with the Office 2000 applications. With some planning, you can use settings to increase users' efficiency in your environment and to decrease desktop maintenance and support costs. This chapter explains how user settings work, discusses the preferred methods for creating and changing them, and provides instructions for creating, customizing, and distributing them.

What You'll Find in This Chapter

- A description of the user setting's architecture—including how to determine the setting's order of precedence when a conflict occurs

- How your administrator can most effectively use system policies with Office 2000—including a table of policy settings and their uses

- How to best use the Office Profile Wizard (OPW) to create your company's user settings—including a table of OPW's switches and their uses

- How to successfully migrate your users' custom settings to Office 2000

- How to distribute custom user settings using different methods, including the Custom Installation Wizard, macros, and combinations of these methods to address special needs

- How to remove user settings and cautions you should be aware of

Warning   This chapter discusses changing the Windows system registry using the Registry Editor. Using the Registry Editor incorrectly can cause serious, system-wide problems that require you to reinstall Windows. Microsoft cannot guarantee that any problems resulting from use of the Registry Editor can be solved. Use this tool at your own risk.

Office 2000 User Settings Architecture

Most Office 2000 user settings are stored in the registry because this supports roaming users, multiple users of a single computer, and allows administrators to configure settings for users. The remaining settings are stored in Application Data folder files.

Some user settings are created when Office 2000 is installed, others are created when an application runs for the first time, and still others are created when the user accesses a particular feature or dialog box for the first time. The Office 2000 Setup program creates settings through the customization tools provided with the *Microsoft Office 2000 Resource Kit*, or by migrating existing settings from a previous version of Microsoft Office. Settings can also be implemented through system policies.

Precedence

Rules based on how the settings are created determine which take precedence in the event of a conflict:

1. Settings created with system policies take precedence over settings created using any other method.
2. New settings created by a user take precedence over any defaults not created with system policies.
3. Settings migrated from a previous version of Office take precedence over settings created during Setup.
4. Settings added with the Office 2000 customization tools take precedence over any defaults.
5. Office 2000 defaults take precedence if there are no customized settings.

The flowchart on the following page (Figure 5.1) shows how settings take precedence.

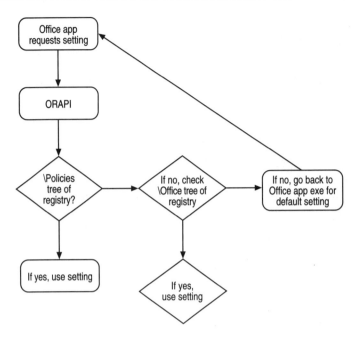

Figure 5.1   How rules are processed.

Registry API

Word, Access, Excel, PowerPoint, Outlook, FrontPage, Publisher, and ClipArt Gallery all communicate with the Windows registry through the Office Registry API (ORAPI). This provides several benefits, including:

- Applications can check registry settings each time they boot, rather than just when a setting is changed.

- Registry settings can use environment variables (such as *%username%*) to hold information that changes for each user.

To minimize Windows registry size, default settings are stored in Office application executables and written to the registry only when a user makes changes.

System Policies

A feature of Windows 95/98 and Windows NT Workstation 4.0 or higher, system policies allow administrators to create, change, and enforce settings on any client computer. When a user logs on to a domain, the operating system checks for a policy and, if one is found, imports its settings into the current user's registry.

Administrator-created settings are stored in a policy file on the logon server, which makes it easy to change and distribute them. For Office 2000 applications, registry settings created with the System Policy Editor are stored apart from user-created settings. Users can change these settings, but the next time they start the Office 2000 application, it will check the policy tree, import the administrator-created settings, and overwrite any changes from the previous session.

Note   You can prevent users from making changes by creating a setting that disables the corresponding application user interface.

Since the Office 2000 applications check this tree each time they start, the user is prevented from changing settings that are implemented with policies for more than a single application session.

For more information on system policies, see the *Guide to Microsoft Windows NT 4.0 Profiles and Policies* white paper at http://www.microsoft.com /ntworkstation/deployment/deployment/ProfPol.asp, the *Windows 98 Resource Kit* and the *Windows NT 4.0 Workstation and Server Resource Kits* at http://mspress.microsoft.com/reslink, or the book *Managing a Microsoft Windows NT Network: Notes from the Field* (Microsoft Press).

Policies Tree of the Registry

Office 2000 improves the implementation of system policies over previous versions. In the past, user changes to system policy settings remained in force until the next time they logged on to the network; some users stay logged on, thus enforcing the changes for long periods. In Office 2000, the applications check for policy settings each time they start up.

A new system policy feature for Office 2000 is rollback (the ability to restore a user's previous settings). In previous versions, if a policy setting caused problems for end users that weren't anticipated, there was no way to roll back to the user's settings. You could change it to the application default or to any other valid choice, but that might not be the user's previous settings.

Finally, the new implementation of system policies lets you use environment variables with Office 2000 settings.

Office 2000 settings created with the System Policy Editor do not overwrite the user's previous settings; instead, they are stored in a Policies registry tree, in HKCU\Software\Policies\Microsoft\Office\9.0, although Outlook and the Windows Installer store a few policies in HKLM\Software\Policies\Microsoft \Office\9.0. Now, if you remove a system policy setting, the Office 2000 application can roll back to the previous settings in the *regular* policy location.

System Policy Editor

The best version of System Policy Editor to use for Office 2000 is the one included on the *Microsoft Office 2000 Resource Kit* CD-ROM. This is the version that ships with Windows NT 4 SP4. It accepts environment variables and automatically loads the Office policy template files. Use it to create a policy file, or to open one that is already in use.

When you open a policy file, the System Policy Editor window displays two items: Default Computer and Default User, as shown in Figure 5.2.

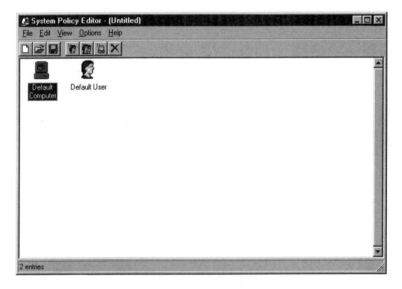

Figure 5.2   The System Policy Editor.

Settings created in Default Computer are stored in HKEY_LOCAL_MACHINE and are enforced for all users on that computer. Settings created in Default User are stored in HKEY_CURRENT_USER and are enforced for that user, independent of the computer used.

Double-click on either of these icons to display a dialog box that lists potential settings. When you select a setting, the choices valid for it appear at the bottom of the dialog box, as shown in Figure 5.3.

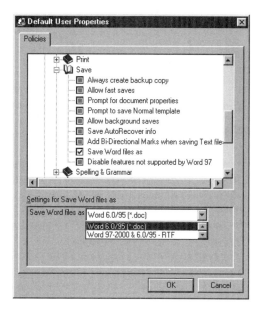

Figure 5.3   Changing settings for the default user policy.

There are three states for each setting check box:

- **Gray:** make no changes to the setting. If a setting exists, it won't be changed; if one doesn't exist, one will not be created.

- **Check:** enforce the selected setting on the user's computer.

- **Clear:** stop enforcing a policy. The user's setting reverts to its previous value. This has changed from previous versions, in which it enforced *no value* for the setting.

Tip   To enforce a setting, check the box next to the name of the setting in the top half of the dialog box *and* choose a value in the bottom half. If you don't choose a value, no setting is created.

Office Policy Templates

The best way to create a policy with Office 2000 settings is to use Office 2000 policy templates—.ADM text files that provide the System Policy Editor with information needed to create valid registry settings. There are several Office 2000 policy templates, all of which load automatically when you use the System Policy

Editor from the *Microsoft Office 2000 Resource Kit* CD-ROM. The Internet Explorer templates do not load automatically.

Template File Name	Purpose
Office Templates	
ACCESS9.ADM	Access 2000 Settings
CLIPGAL5.ADM	Disable downloading of media clips from the Internet.
EXCEL9.ADM	Excel 2000 Settings
FRONTPG4.ADM	FrontPage 2000 Settings
INSTLR1.ADM	Windows Installer Settings
OFFICE9.ADM	Common Office 2000 Settings
OUTLK9.ADM	Outlook 2000 Settings
PPOINT9.ADM	PowerPoint 2000 Settings
PUB9.ADM	Publisher 2000 Settings
WORD9.ADM	Word 2000 Settings
Internet Explorer 5.0 Templates	
AAXA.ADM	Data Binding settings
CHAT.ADM	Microsoft Chat settings
CONF.ADM	NetMeeting settings
INETCORP.ADM	Dial-up, language, and Temporary Internet Files settings
INETRES.ADM	Internet properties: including Connections, Toolbars, and Toolbar settings. Equivalent to the Tools	Internet Options… command.
INETSET.ADM	Additional Internet properties: AutoComplete, display, and some advanced settings.
OE.ADM	Outlook Express Identity Manager settings. Use this to prevent users from changing or configuring identities.
SP1SHELL.ADM	Active Desktop settings
SUBS.ADM	Offline Pages settings
WMP.ADM	Windows Media Player, Radio Toolbar, and Network Settings customizations.

Tip   Before creating policy files, load *all* template files—including Internet Explorer and the Operating System policy template files—even if you don't plan on using all of them. Adding policy templates later could potentially corrupt the policy files.

Creating Policies

To implement system policies, you must create a policy file, name it appropriately, and put it in the correct location. When creating policies, you must use the operating system for which you are creating the policy because operating system registries differ. If your environment includes Windows 9*x* and Windows NT Workstation 4.0, you need a system policy file for each.

Complete the steps below. When you are done, the client operating system will automatically detect the policy.

1. Create the policy on a computer running the same operating system users have.

2. Start the System Policy Editor included on the *Microsoft Office 2000 Resource Kit* CD-ROM. If it is not installed, install it now. This is the latest System Policy Editor and has the features and Office 2000 policy templates you'll need.

3. Click on **Start, Programs, Microsoft Office Tools, Microsoft Office 2000 Resource Kit Tools, System Policy Editor**.

4. Check that the Office 2000 template (*.ADM) files are loaded by clicking on **Options, Policy Template**. You should see all of the Office 2000 policy templates loaded. If you don't see them, browse the \\Windows\Inf folder on the computer where you installed the System Policy Editor and make sure you are using the System Policy Editor included with the *Microsoft Office 2000 Resource Kit*.

5. If you need to add Internet Explorer 5 templates, add them from: \\Program Files\Ieak\Policies\en.

6. If a policy file exists, open it. If not, click on the **New** button to create a new one. You should see this dialog box (Figure 5.4):

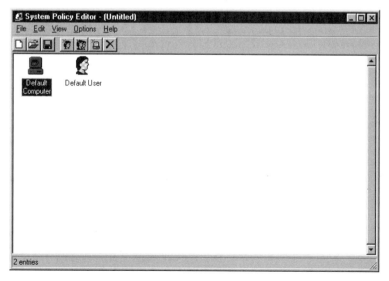

Figure 5.4   Creating a new policy.

7. Double-click on **Default User**, which contains most of the pertinent settings, arranged by application.

8. Click the plus sign (+) to expand each section.

9. To create a setting, check the box next to it. If you decide not to create a setting for this item, click on the box until it is grayed (which means the existing setting—policy or user—is used); do not leave it blank (which means the existing policy setting for this item is removed). See Figure 5.5.

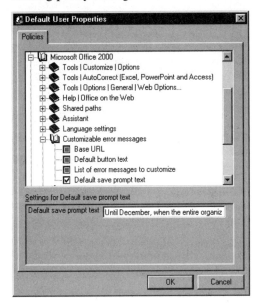

Figure 5.5   Changing settings for the new policy.

10. When all settings are created, click **OK** to save the file. If you opened a preexisting file, it should have the same name and location. If you have created a new policy for Windows 98/95 users, it must be named **config.pol**; if it is a new policy for Windows NT Workstation users, it must be named **ntconfig.pol**.

11. If this is a new system policy file, store it in the logon directory on the server. For a Windows NT Server, the location is:
\\<primary domain controller>\netlogon\config.pol
For a NetWare server, the location is:
\\<preferred server>\sys\public\config.pol

Desktop Lockdown

Many organizations lock down user settings to make Office more secure and easier to use and support. There are plusses and minuses to locking down settings, however. For example, if your organization is moving from Office 95 to Office 2000, you may elect to change the default *save* format to Word 95 until most users migrate to Office 2000. Although this may cause some formatting loss, it still is worthwhile if users frequently share Word documents through e-mail, because it allows Word 95 users to read files created by Word 2000 users. But if users don't often share files, all it does is cause occasional loss of formatting, and, probably, calls to the helpdesk.

Or suppose you want to protect users from macro virus infections. You can set each application's macro security to *High*, clear the **Trust installed templates and add-ins** check box, and disable the user interface for changing the setting. This is secure, but it prevents users from recording and running their own user productivity macros. The minus here outweighs the plus.

Obviously, it makes more sense to create effective macro protection settings. Check the key Microsoft Word 2000\Tools\Macro\Security\Security Level. Create the setting, then disable the user interface for it by checking the key Microsoft Word 2000\Disable items in user interface\Predefined\Disable command bar buttons and menu items\Tools\Macro\Security. This grays out the menu item for this setting, indicating that the user cannot choose or modify this command. Macros run only from templates and wizards installed with Microsoft Office or from Word documents or templates that have been digitally signed or certified.

For more information on macro security, see the *Microsoft Office 2000 Macro Security* white paper on the companion CD.

Settings Useful in Lockdown

You can select the amount of control you want in your environment by enabling or disabling Office settings. The list below, while not exhaustive, shows some of the more useful settings. See the next section, "Other Settings," for a list of settings not related to lockdown.

Policy Setting	Purpose
In All Applications	
Tools, Macro, Security	In each Office application, it sets the macro security level and whether to trust installed templates and add-ins.
Disable items in user interface	In each Office application, it prevents the user from changing any settings, even for one session.

(continued)

Policy Setting	Purpose
Microsoft Office	
Tools	AutoCorrect	Creates AutoCorrect settings for Excel, PowerPoint, and Access including adding words.
Shared Paths	Creates settings for the paths for templates.
Assistant	Creates settings for the Office Assistant, including the default Assistant, whether it is on, and the actions that the Assistant responds to.
Customizable error messages	Base URL	URL for the **More Help** button in Help dialog boxes.
Customizable error messages	Default save prompt text	The dialog box text users see when saving a file if the default save format is anything other than the Office 2000 Format.
Access	
Tools	Security	Prevents users from creating or changing security settings.
Tools	Miscellaneous	Do not prompt to convert older databases	Prevents users from accidentally answering the prompt and converting a database.
Excel	
Tools	Options	General	Default File Location	Sets the default location where files are saved.
Tools	Options	Transition	Save files as	Changes the default file format for saving files.
Miscellaneous	Enable four-digit display	Displays dates in four-digit year format, regardless of how many characters users enter, making it easier for users to spot incorrect dates.
PowerPoint	
Tools	Options	Save	Save PowerPoint files as...	Changes the default format files are saved in.
Tools	Options	Save	Default file location	Changes the default location where files are saved.

Policy Setting	Purpose
Word	
Tools I Options I Save I Save Word files as...	Changes the default format files are saved in.
Tools I File locations I Documents	Changes the default location where files are saved.
Tools I AutoCorrect	Changes AutoCorrect and AutoFormat defaults for Word.

Other Settings

This table shows other settings you may find useful to customize. Most of these can be created with the System Policy Editor (the few that cannot are noted). This table is not exhaustive.

Setting	Purpose
In Each Application	
Office Assistant, Options (If the Assistant is not on, click **Help, Show the Office Assistant**. Click once on the Assistant to get to Options.)	Determines options settings for the Office Assistant, including shown or hidden, the default, and the actions that trigger it.
Tools, Customize, Options, Personalized Menus and Toolbars	In Office 2000, the user interface displays the Standard and Formatting toolbars together in one row, and the menus show a shorter list of commands, with the most recently used commands displayed first. Use these settings to make the menus and toolbars work more like Office 95 and Office 97.
Access	
Tools I Options I General I Use four-digit year formatting	Forces four-digit year formatting for an individual database and/or all databases. Cannot be set with system policies.
Tools I Options I General I Default database folder	Changes the default folder for storing database files. Cannot be set with system policies.
Tools I Add-Ins I Add-In Manager	Chooses to automatically load any add-in needed in your environment. Cannot be set with system policies.
Windows Start menu I Settings I Control Panel I Regional Settings I Date	Customizes the short date to a four-digit year format to force all dates to display a four-digit year in Access and Excel.

(continued)

Setting	Purpose
Excel	
Tools | Add-ins	Pre-loads any add-in, such as AutoSave or the Analysis ToolPak.
Tools | Options | View | Windows in Taskbar	If users don't like seeing each spreadsheet on its own taskbar button, this setting reverts to the Excel 97 behavior of one Excel button, regardless of the number of open files.
Windows Start menu | Settings | Control Panel | Regional Settings | Date	Customizes the short date to four-digit year format to force all dates to display four-digit years in Excel and Access.
PowerPoint	
Tools | Add-ins	Pre-loads any add-in.
Tools | Options | View | Windows in Taskbar	If users don't like seeing each presentation on its own taskbar button, this setting reverts to the previous behavior of one PowerPoint button, regardless of the number of open presentations.
Word	
Tools | Options | Save | Disable features not supported by Word 97.	Disables the user interface for features (such as nested tables) that will not convert properly when a Word 2000 file is saved in Word 97.
Tools | Options | Save | Save AutoRecover info every:	Turns on AutoRecover and sets the amount of time between saves. If the user has to reboot the system or shut down Word without saving the document, Word recovers it to the point of the last AutoRecover save.
Tools | File locations | AutoRecover Files	Changes the default from Application Data to another location.
Tools | Options | Compatibility | Recommended options for:	Changes default settings to be more compatible with a different file format such as Word 6.0/95 or WordPerfect.

Simulating System Policies

System policies make it easy to implement, change, and restore settings. If your organization isn't ready to implement system policies or your client or network operating system can't support them, you can still use the System Policy Editor and the policy templates to simulate creating and implementing Office 2000 policy settings. The simulation procedure is outlined in the following section. It involves most of the same steps as real implementation, except that you use the System Policy Editor to open the registry and create settings on a *test* computer. Then you run the Registry Editor on the test computer, find the Policies tree, export the Office 9.0 keys to a registry file, and include those settings with the Office 2000 installation using the Custom Installation Wizard.

To Simulate System Policies:

1. Start the System Policy Editor by clicking on **Start | Programs | Microsoft Office Tools | Microsoft Office Resource Kit Tools | System Policy Editor**.

2. Make sure all Office templates are loaded by clicking **Options | Policy Template...**

3. On the test computer, open the registry by clicking **File | Open Registry**.

Note   When the local registry is open, setting check boxes have only two states: checked (creates a setting) and blank (removes a setting).

4. Create settings or make changes. Most settings can be created after double-clicking on the **Local User** icon.

5. Click on **File | Close** and choose **Yes** to save changes to the registry.

6. Start the Registry Editor by clicking on **Start | Run**. Type *regedit* and click **OK**.

7. Look for the registry's Office 2000 Policies tree. It should be at: HKCU\Software\Policies\Microsoft\ Office\9.0. Select this branch and click **Registry | Export Registry File...**

8. Enter a name for the file and click **OK**. Store the file in the folder you created for custom files in the root of the administrative installation.

9. Run the Custom Installation Wizard and import the settings in the Add Registry Settings pane.

For more information, see the "Distributing Office 2000 User Settings" section later in this chapter.

From the Trenches:
Establishing User Settings across the Organization

A large multinational organization was developing a plan for creating and implementing user settings for Office 2000. The organization included both centralized and regional IT groups, and they needed to determine which of these IT groups would be responsible for establishing user settings and their implementation. Because the organization already had implemented company-wide system policies, they had the luxury of determining which settings would be implemented as policy and which could be established only as new system defaults.

To work through these decisions, the organization came up with some criteria:

- Any settings that affected the entire organization would be created by the centralized IT group and be incorporated into the standard organization-wide build. Examples included default save file formats, year 2000 features, and macro security settings.

- The regional IT groups would implement settings that needed only to be defaults and therefore could be added to the build used in that location, as long as they didn't override any centralized settings.

- Settings that were critical to the functioning of the organization or that would help reduce helpdesk costs would be implemented through policy.

- Settings that simply helped the end user or that the user needed to be able to change would be implemented through the Office Profile Wizard.

As they went through the process, the organization decided that central IT did not have any settings that it needed to implement through the Office Profile Wizard—if the setting was important to the organization worldwide, it would be implemented through system policies. A side benefit of this decision was that this made implementation easier for the regional IT groups: they didn't have to worry about keeping track of the central IT settings, keeping track of several .OPS files for use in transforms, or overriding the central IT settings since system policies would take precedence over default settings.

After evaluating all of the possible settings, the central IT group narrowed the system policy settings to a very small set:

- The default save location was set to the user's home directory using an environment variable.

- Macro security was set to *High* for Word and to *Medium* for each of the other applications.

- A setting was established to disable the Access prompt to convert databases to Access 2000 format, which is used to prevent accidental conversion of older databases still in use by non-Access 2000 users. (This setting does not prevent users from actually converting databases; it just disables a prompt that appears any time a user opens an older format database.)

- A four-digit date display was enabled in Excel so users who enter two-digit year dates can easily see if the date is evaluated for the wrong century.

Since the organization already had a sizable installation base of Office 97 users, they decided not to force users to save their files in earlier version formats on an organization-wide basis. Some of the regional IT groups that currently were using only Office 95 were planning to add a couple of policy settings to change the default file format for Word to Word 6.0/95 format, and for Excel to the dual 97/2000 & 5.0/95 format. Using policies for this setting made it easy to change once all users had upgraded to Office 2000. In addition, they had already implemented a policy setting for a four-digit system short date as part of year 2000 preparedness. (Both Excel and Access base their short date formats on the system format.)

Many of the regions were considering the following settings to deploy as new defaults through the Office Profile Wizard:

- Using four-digit formatting in Microsoft Access. (Unfortunately, this setting cannot be made through policy, and so must be set as a default.)

- Setting the workgroup templates location to a regional server.

- Implementing customizable Help and Alerts on an organization-wide basis, but replicating the Web site for the content worldwide for performance and load balancing. Therefore, this setting would be implemented on a regional basis.

- Reducing margins for some regions to save paper.

- Giving responsibility for all multilingual settings to the regional IT groups.

The net result of this business process was that it was relatively easy for the central IT group to create and enforce organization-wide settings while still giving the regional IT groups a lot of flexibility to customize settings for their users. In addition, it made the process of creating the standard image for Office 2000 easier since it eliminated the step of using the Office Profile Wizard for the central IT group.

Creating User Settings with the Office Profile Wizard

The Office Profile Wizard (OPW) allows you to change default user settings without preventing the user from changing them later. Often this is the best option.

For example, suppose your organization has a policy of storing all user files in individual server-based home directories (so they can be accessed and backed up). You want to prevent users from accidentally saving files to their hard drive's My Documents location, but you don't mind if they want to save some effort by pointing Excel to a subdirectory of their home directory. You can use the OPW to create a setting that causes files to be saved to the home directory by default, but still lets users change to another location. Here is how to use it.

1. Install Office 2000 or the individual application on a test computer.
2. Use the UI—usually the **Tools | Options** dialog box—to specify settings.
3. Run the Office Profile Wizard. In its dialog box, specify whether you are creating a settings file or restoring one. Enter the name and location of the new settings file in the associated text box.
4. The Profile Wizard then writes all of the pertinent Office 2000 registry keys to an .OPS file.
5. Import the .OPS file into the Transform file using the Custom Installation Wizard (CIW). This includes these settings in the custom Office 2000 installation.

Use the CIW to include the settings (rather than deploying them as part of a separate process) so that they will be included in the local database created after Office 2000 completes installation. Settings in the local database are available to any user who logs on to that computer.

 Note The .OPS file is not operating-system specific—use the same one for both Windows NT Workstation and Windows 9*x* users.

Customizing the Office Profile Wizard

The Office Profile Wizard uses an initialization file, **Proflwiz.ini**, to determine which branches and keys of the registry to include in the .OPS file it creates. This is a text-only file that defines which branches of the registry the Office Profile Wizard is supposed to capture. Most Office 2000 settings are included in the .INI file; a few non-Office 2000 settings such as the system short date are also included. Use the Proflwiz.ini file to capture other settings, such as a setting for a private ClipArt catalog, some Internet Explorer 5.0 settings, or even settings created with the System Policy Editor.

If you need to exclude settings or include some that the Office Profile Wizard does not currently capture, edit the Proflwiz.ini file. Open it with a text editor such as Notepad and add branches, keys, or sub-keys. Any time you add a registry branch or key, test the results thoroughly. Don't make branches too large or create defaults for settings that were customized on the default computer but aren't needed throughout the organization.

If you use the OPW to return all settings to their defaults, you can edit the Proflwiz.ini file to keep some from being reset. The file has many useful settings, and is commented extensively. You can un-comment any setting you want to enforce.

For example, if you are implementing Office Server Extensions or FrontPage 2000 Server Extensions and want to make it easy for users to publish to Web Folders, you can customize Proflwiz.ini to distribute the necessary settings. Simply create the Web folders on the test computer, find the line **#   <NetHood>** in Proflwiz.ini, and delete the # character to un-comment it.

For more information on customizing Proflwiz.ini, see *Customizing the Profile Wizard* in the *Microsoft Office 2000 Resource Kit.*

Using the OPW in Staged Deployment Scenarios

Staged deployments call for careful planning. Among other considerations, you particularly want to avoid re-distributing application settings that may have been changed since they were installed in an earlier phase. System policies simplify this because settings created through policies stay in effect until an administrator changes them, but it you use the Profile Wizard, you have to perform some extra steps.

For example, suppose you deploy Office 2000 without Outlook, which you want to hold back for messaging infrastructure testing. All Office editions have Outlook, so you can't simply distribute a version that doesn't include it. You can, however, distribute Office Professional without Outlook by making it unavailable with the Custom Installation Wizard, then add Outlook later using the individual edition rather than the Office edition. To simplify the staging, deploy the Outlook settings when you install Office: they will then be ready in the registry when you want to add Outlook and in the meantime won't cause any problems. This avoids customizing the Profile Wizard when you later deploy Outlook to exclude the Office settings, and the chance that any Office settings deployed with Outlook will change user settings and generate helpdesk calls.

See the *Profile Wizard* chapter in the *Microsoft Office 2000 Resource Kit* for more details on editing the Proflwiz.ini file.

Office Profile Wizard Switches

Office Profile Wizard switches allow you to customize operation in several ways, including preventing users from running the wizard interactively. You can see the switches (shown in Figure 5.6 below) by typing *Proflwiz.exe /?.*

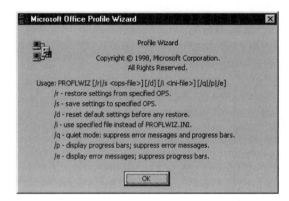

Figure 5.6   Usage parameters for the Office Profile Wizard.

Here's how to use them.

Switch / Command Line	Use
/r	Restore the settings captured in a specified .OPS, for example, when upgrading or reimaging a computer.
/s	Back up the settings on a user computer prior to an upgrade or re-image.
/i	Use a specified .INI file instead of Proflwiz.ini. This is useful if you have several .INI files, depending on user need.
/q	Quiet mode. Use this in combination with any other switch to suppress user input, error messages, and progress bars.
/p or /e	Use these switches in combination with other switches to suppress user input and control the display.

Using the OPW as a Backup Tool

When you upgrade computers, the OPW can serve as a backup tool. Run the Wizard on a user's computer to capture the settings, then store the settings file in a network location; run the Wizard on the new computer in **restore** mode to import the settings to the current configuration. To restore a profile, run the OPW on the user computer with the **/r** switch, or run it interactively and choose to restore settings (see Figure 5.7).

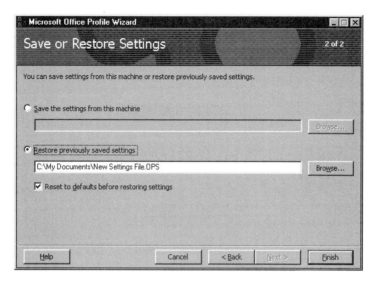

Figure 5.7   Restoring settings with the OPW.

Restoring Application Defaults with the OPW

You can also use the OPW to restore Office 2000 application settings to their factory-set defaults.

Note   This procedure defaults *all* settings, so before you do it make sure there are no custom settings you want to preserve.

Restoring defaults can be useful when you are testing different configurations, or if you are troubleshooting potential setting problems. To use the OPW in testing, create an .OPS file that captures the user settings *after* Office 2000 is installed but *before* any settings are customized. To restore settings, check **Reset to defaults before restoring settings** if you run the OPW interactively, or add the **/d** switch if you run the OPW from the command line.

Warning   Do not edit Proflwiz.ini to capture the .PST file—it can overwrite the existing .PST file with a blank one. Proflwiz.ini does not capture this setting as a default.

Using the OPW as a Helpdesk Tool

The helpdesk can also make good use of the OPW. Suppose a user calls helpdesk to report that an application is not working the way it used to. The helpdesk technician walks the user through the detect-and-repair process, but the problem persists. Since detect and repair only affects files and not user settings, it is possible that a user setting (intentional or not) is causing the problem. Users often can't remember which settings they've changed, and many helpdesks don't have application experts who can deduce the cause from the effects.

For example, after a bad experience with a macro virus, a user might change the macro protection to High and turn off trusting templates installed with Office. As mentioned earlier, this prevents the user from recording and running personal productivity macros. If this user calls helpdesk and reports that none of the personal macros are working anymore, a technician may not know enough about Office 2000 to consider the macro virus protection features as the root of the problem.

But with the Office Profile Wizard tool and the necessary .OPS files, technicians can fix the problem by helping users restore their Office 2000 settings, or the organization or system defaults. This may delete other customizations, but it gets the user back in business much more quickly than re-imaging the computer or trying to run down some hidden cause.

Migrating Custom User Settings

To migrate user settings from previous versions of Office, check the **Migrate user settings** checkbox in the Customize Default Application Settings pane of the CIW. This causes the older settings to be migrated the first time each Office 2000 application is used. The application looks for a registry settings branch from previous versions and imports them.

Customized settings created with the Office Profile Wizard or imported into the CIW are created when Office 2000 is installed, but migrated settings overwrite any customized settings. While this may be the point, you still may want to insure that your custom settings take precedence. For example, suppose you want to set the default file location to the user's home directory on the network and create some year 2000 settings. You don't care about other settings and you know that it's easier for the user to migrate the other settings than to re-create them. The year 2000 settings are new to Office 2000, so there won't be a conflict with those settings. But, if there's a conflict in the default save location, particularly if it is currently set to C:\My Documents, you need to make sure your file location settings take precedence.

Do this by changing the previous version settings to match the custom installation ones. You can do this programmatically by creating the appropriate settings on a test computer with the previous version of Office, finding the settings in the Registry Editor, exporting them to a registry file, then importing the file into the end user's computer registry. Use the Custom Installation Wizard to import these settings into the Transform, creating them with Office 2000 Setup before the Office 2000 applications run for the first time. Another option is to use real or simulated system policies (as described above) because settings in the registry \Policies tree take precedence over all other settings.

Distributing Office 2000 User Settings

The next sections describe ways to distribute custom settings with Office 2000.

Note   If you are using system policies you do not have to distribute settings.

The Custom Installation Wizard

With the Custom Installation Wizard (CIW), you can customize Office 2000 during installation by adding registry settings in any of three places:

- Customize Default Application Settings (Pane #8 in CD1 of Office—not present in the MultiLanguage Pack, Office 2000 Premium CD2, the Proofing Tools Kit, or Office Server Extensions).

- Add Registry Entries (Pane #10 in Office CD1, may vary for other Office Family products).

- Add Installations and Run Programs (Pane #13 in Office CD1, may vary for other Office Family products).

Customize Default Application Settings

Click **Browse**, then navigate to the .OPS file location, as shown in Figure 5.8. If there is no .OPS file, close all Office 2000 applications and use the OPW to create one.

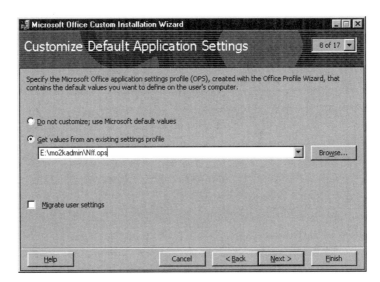

Figure 5.8   Selecting .OPS file.

When you choose **Get values from an existing settings profile**, the **Migrate user settings** check box is automatically cleared. Check it again to migrate settings. Remember: migrated settings take precedence if there are conflicts.

Settings in the profile you specify are stored inside the transform file (created with the CIW) and are included in the database created on the local computer after installing Office 2000. They are created for each user that logs on to that computer.

Changing the .OPS File

If you don't have to change a setting in the .OPS file, you can simply change the setting on the test computer and run the Office Profile Wizard again. If the CIW has already imported the .OPS file into the transform file, go back to the Customize Default Application Settings pane and browse to the new .OPS file.

Add Registry Entries

Use this pane (Figure 5.9) to import registry (.REG) files or enter registry settings manually.

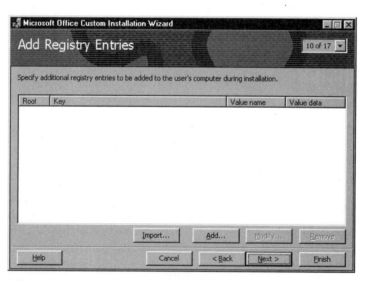

Figure 5.9   Importing registry entries with the CIW.

Typing in entries raises the risk of errors and you should avoid it, but if you have to enter some manually, click **Add** to display this dialog box (shown in Figure 5.10):

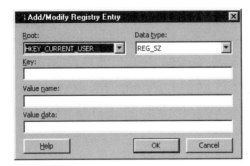

Figure 5.10   Specifying the registry entry to import.

Figure 5.11 shows an imported registry key:

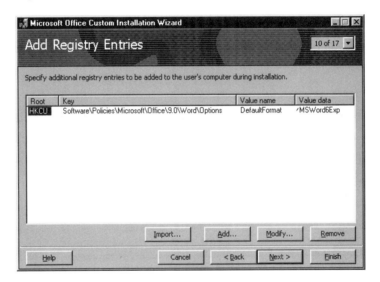

Figure 5.11   Your imported registry key.

In this case, the default save setting was created by:

- Using the System Policy Editor to open the registry on the test computer and create a custom setting in the Policies tree.

- Using the Registry editor to export the Policies tree to a registry file called Policy.reg.

This is similar to using system policies in that the setting is enforced; it is dissimilar in that there is no easy way to change or roll back this setting.

Settings created in this method, like those created with the Customize Default Application Settings pane, are stored in the transform file and in the database created on the local computer after installation. They are created for every user who logs onto that computer.

Add Installations and Run Programs

The third place you can add registry settings is in the CIW **Add Installations and Run Programs** pane (shown in Figure 5.12). To import a registry file use the command:

regedit –s *<filename>*

The **–s** switch disables the confirmation dialog, and *<filename>* is the complete path and name of the registry file you want to import. The example below selects the same registry file that was imported in the Add Registry Entries pane (above) and adds it as a program to run after installation. With this method, the settings contained in this registry file are not a part of the transform file or the local database, so they are created only for the user who is logged on when Office 2000 installs, not for the computer itself.

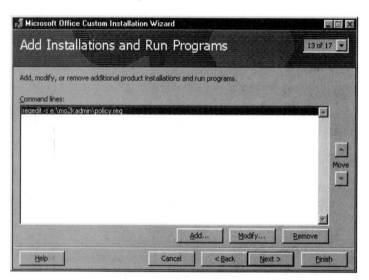

Figure 5.12   Adding registry settings through the Add Installations and Run Programs pane.

Office 2000 applications create some settings when they run the first time and these may overwrite custom settings, so you have to add registry settings *after* installation. Add a first command line to run the application then a second to run the registry file.

Conflicts

Since there are three ways to add registry settings with the CIW, you may run into conflicts such as exporting a registry setting that is already in the .OPS file. Here is how the settings take precedence:

1. Settings created in the Add Installations and Run Programs pane are written last and always take precedence.
2. Settings added manually in the Add Registry Entries pane overwrite all other settings.
3. Settings created by importing a registry file in the Add Registry Entries pane overwrite settings created by an .OPS file.
4. Settings created by using an .OPS file overwrite the Office 2000 defaults.

Other Methods of Distributing User Settings

What do you do when you need to distribute a registry setting that you didn't know about when you deployed Office 2000? This section explains how to change or fix registry settings after installation.

Non-CIW Distribution Strategies

Macros

You can access and customize most capabilities and objects in Office 2000 applications, including dialog boxes. If you can't use the System Policy Editor to create a setting or disable its interface, you can deploy a macro after Office 2000 is installed or (using the CIW Add Programs and Installations pane) run one during Setup to create settings for the logged on user.

Registry Files

You can deploy a registry file to users through logon scripts, e-mail, Web page hyperlinks, or software distribution tools such as Microsoft Systems Management Server. Create a registry file as described earlier in this chapter, then use a command line as detailed in the "Add Installations and Run Programs" section. You can then add the command line to a logon script that you send through e-mail, make it into a Web page hyperlink, or distribute it as a package. Registry file distribution requires little bandwidth, so, if the change is important, *push* it to users rather than allowing them to *pull* it.

Repairing Distributed Settings

Setting changes sometimes disrupt Office 2000 operation. These can be made by users through the UI or by applications that change default user settings. If you are using system policies, you can restore settings by having users log off the network and then log back on. If you are using simulated system policies, you can re-distribute the registry file.

If you are not using system policies, run the Office Profile Wizard in **restore** mode to re-set Office defaults to the .OPS file settings. To avoid upsetting users by overwriting custom settings you are not concerned with, customize the Proflwiz.ini file to include only certain settings.

Combining Various Distribution Methods

You can combine distribution methods if you consider when the setting needs to be written and whether it should be enforced. The summary at the end of this chapter lists the characteristics of each creation method. The list below explains timing and precedence.

1. System policies always take precedence.

2. Post-deployment methods, such as importing a registry file, running a macro in an application, or running a post-installation script, overwrite existing registry settings. If you migrate settings, make sure each application has run at least once.

3. Migrating settings from a previous version overwrites settings created during Office 2000 installation, except those created using simulated system policies.

4. Registry keys added through the CIW Add Registry Entries pane take precedence over any remaining methods in this list.

5. Registry keys imported through the CIW Add Registry Entries pane take precedence over any remaining methods in this list.

6. Using the Office Profile Wizard to capture user settings and then distributing them through the transform file created by the CIW takes precedence over the pre-set defaults created by Microsoft.

Removing Office 2000 User Settings

If you remove Office 2000, registry settings are by default not removed with it: you have to remove the registry's Office 9.0 tree. Remember: applications such as virus checkers and third party add-ins sometimes depend on registry settings—test all of the computer's applications before removing settings.

If you are using system policies and no longer need to enforce a particular setting, remove its policy. For example, if a policy sets the default save format for Word 2000 to Word 95, you no longer need that policy once all users are on Word 2000. Run the System Policy Editor to find the setting, clear its check box, and save the changes to the policy file. This returns the user to any previous custom setting if there is one, to the default otherwise.

If you have simulated system policies by distributing the Policies tree of the registry, there is no easy way to remove the key.

Summary

There are several ways to create and distribute user settings. If you need to enforce (or change) settings, use system policies; if you don't need to enforce them (as with system defaults) use the Office Profile Wizard with the Custom Installation Wizard. Test all settings first in the lab and then in a production environment to make sure that they do not disrupt applications or user productivity. This is particularly important for enforced settings.

Here is a summary of the benefits and shortcomings of each method.

Method	Create	Deploy	Enforce	Change	Re-set	Remove
System Policies	Easy	Easy on Windows NT Server, more complex on NetWare	Yes	Yes	Yes	Yes
Office Profile Settings	Easy	Easy	No	Yes, but need to run Wizard on users' computers	Yes	Yes (restore Office defaults)
Simulated System Policies	Easy	Easy with CIW	Yes	Yes, with another deployment	Yes, with another deployment	No
Registry file with CIW	Harder	Easy with CIW	No	Yes, with another deployment	Yes, with another deployment	No
Registry file without CIW	Harder	No, unless there's a software distribution system	No	Yes, with another deployment	Yes, with another deployment	No

CHAPTER 6

Preparing for Office 2000 Distribution

By Shelly M. Bird,
Consultant,
Microsoft
Consulting
Services, Federal

Efficient, cost-effective software distribution reduces total cost of ownership (TCO). To plan for it, you have to inventory essential software and hardware, and this chapter explains how to gather that information with Microsoft Systems Management Server.

What You'll Find in This Chapter

- How to accurately assess your workplace's hardware and mitigating factors when creating your inventory

- How to troubleshoot data gathering so that you don't miss hardware and software in your company—for example, skipping all of the systems that don't shut down overnight

- How to target your inventory to gather all of the data you will need for a successful deployment

- How to maximize the capabilities of Systems Management Server to capture your inventory data

- A variety of methods for gathering inventory data

- How to best work with users to collect soft data, and what soft data will be most useful to you

What Makes a Successful Inventory

To distribute software in complex networked environments, you must have a clear picture of the current network setup, including network infrastructure, server and workstation operating systems, application environment, and user needs. You need to consider physical factors such as geographical constraints or remote-user needs. The more information you can compile, the easier it will be for you to create an effective distribution plan with an efficient workflow. Figure 6.1 shows how recommended deployment decisions are influenced by software, and Figure 6.2 illustrates the same information for hardware.

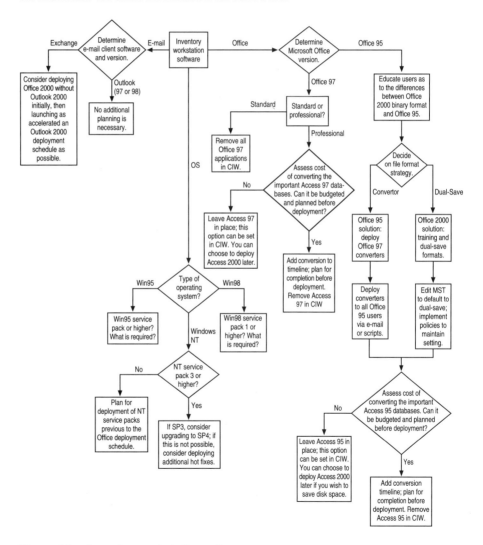

Figure 6.1   Assessing workstation software.

The software inventory should determine:

- **Operating system (including service pack level).** If you are using Windows NT, Service Pack 4 is considered a basic requirement for Office features such as the Office Server Extensions. You can also use Windows NT infrastructure for security and configuration.

- **E-mail client type.** You should migrate Exchange clients early, and you often have to perform a few more steps to take care of Personal Address Books and Schedule+ data.

- **Current installed version of Office.** This can drive coexistence requirements, which can in turn drive viewer and converter deployment, selection of default file save settings, and so on.

Figure 6.2 shows how recommended deployment decisions are influenced by hardware:

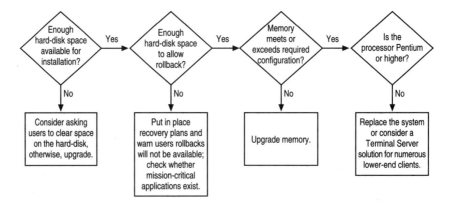

Figure 6.2   Assessing whether workstation hardware can sustain the upgrade.

The hardware inventory should determine:

- **Amount of memory.** This can determine which components you will install, your rollback options, and so on.

- **Remaining hard disk space on the system disk.** This can affect several options, including rollback, timing for removal of previous software versions, deployment of *Installed on First Use* option, and so on.

- **Processor type.** This can determine performance in several ways, especially in client-server applications.

How effectively you deal with these factors depends heavily on how accurately you inventory *and* understand the target system.

Inventory Planning

Inventory, analysis of the results, report creation, and testing in the laboratory form the bulk of the work performed before planning is finalized and scheduled. Typically, this pre-deployment work should take anywhere from 60 percent to 80 percent of the entire deployment schedule. If this work is done properly, then a successful deployment can be completed relatively quickly. The following sections describe the kinds of information you need to gather. Keep in mind that one purpose of the inventory is to determine which previous versions of Office will be upgraded, because upgrade prerequisites vary. In particular, keep a clear distinction between Office 95 and Office 97 installations.

Initial Preparations

During the inventory process, expect the unexpected. For example, in a recent deployment project for a company, Trey Research, MCS reviewed early reports (before visiting the site) and interviewed users to determine which operating systems were in place. Although the interviews showed that only Office 95 and Windows 95 were present, MCS's inventory revealed a wide range of operating systems and software.

MCS had to amend the testing plan as they discovered what software was actually running. For instance, while the group deploying Office 2000 had few Macintosh machines, a significant percentage of the rest of the company used Macintoshes, Microsoft Office 98 for the Macintosh, and Eudora Pro. Consequently, MCS had to test the compatibility of new Office 2000 configurations with the Macintosh population.

In short, be flexible when you allow for preparation time, be prepared to reorganize as new information arrives, and be ready to refocus testing plans to accommodate the unanticipated.

Accurate Inventory of Hardware and Software

Deployment success greatly depends on your ability to anticipate potential problems. You have to gather accurate data on users' software and hardware so you can prioritize time-intensive tasks such as upgrading or replacing RAM, hard disks, or CPUs for the new environment.

Unfortunately, inventory information is often unavailable and incomplete. Even when it is available, users' systems often change too rapidly to get a reliable snapshot. You frequently have to scramble to get an accurate *and* timely picture.

At Trey Research, MCS used Microsoft Systems Management Server (SMS) to gather inventory data. This simplified much of the process, but did not alleviate all problems. For example, users who leave sessions running for days remain unseen by SMS, which conducts an inventory as part of a logon.

Obtaining accurate information on the wide range of installed software (and the various versions of that software) on users' systems proved very challenging. Classic SMS software inventory required building a file, AUDIT.RUL, that compared cyclical redundancy checks (CRC) of particular files to a list that mapped the results back to particular software names and version numbers. This meant MCS had to know precisely what was being searched for—taking into account all the possible patches and upgrades to both operating systems and applications software. Given the fact that even Windows NT users had local administrator privileges, there was little hope for truly consistent configurations across the board. By creating a matrix of all possibilities, MCS decided that at least 25 variations *could* exist and that the actual number was probably higher. In the end, since even a relatively targeted scan of over 50 applications was known to occasionally slow down logons, administrators were reluctant to use it.

Because most companies update and patch software on a regular basis, conducting centralized software inventories is a major challenge. You need to create software inventory requests that are neither too complicated (which can slow down workstation performance) nor too narrow (which can miss slight variations to the original software you are trying to document). MCS encountered this problem at Trey Research, and it was complicated by the existence of low-grade hardware (left over 486 systems) and many different types of software.

So MCS experimented with other ways to capture critical-software information, using methods developed in previous projects and developing some on the spot. The key to this process was prioritization: identifying what was most important then narrowing down the requirements. The sections below explain how they determined which information was important and why. Any methods applicable in general situations are described. Here are their two early attempts:

- First, MCS built a custom package to obtain software inventory via relatively lightweight queries to the users' registries—a method that also could be counted on to capture more information than the usual IDX file. The package could be sent as part of the logon script if SMS was not available for some reason—a handy capability when systems lack SMS infrastructure.

- Second, they focused on extracting the versions of the logged on e-mail clients from the Exchange server logon window. This is described more fully later in this chapter.

As this chapter was being written, the first SMS software inventory with the package that checks registry entries was underway. MCS expected this package to greatly enhance the overall picture of the environment and to extract the lists of Office 95 users.

Soft Data

In addition to hardware and software information, you need to survey the enterprise for *soft data*, which includes users' reports on their experiences (past and present) with software and deployments. This is explained in detail in the section "Collecting Soft Data" on page 180.

Deciding Which Data to Capture

To inventory hardware and software (the components of the in-place system environment) and soft data (usage patterns and other factors that can affect deployment) you first have to figure out which information to capture. This section walks you through the decision processes with which you can shape an inventory plan.

Hardware

Hardware inventory data falls into two categories: workstation and server.

Workstation Hardware

Ask these questions about the workstation hardware targeted for deployment:

- **New or existing?** In most situations where a major deployment is planned, new workstations are purchased to provide two benefits:
  - Systems targeted for replacement don't need to be inventoried.
  - Images for the new systems can be predefined and tested in the laboratory. If deployment schedules allow, you can usually provide the manufacturers with custom images suitable for your environment, eliminating the need to rebuild the workstations upon delivery.

Note   If new systems are the primary platform for your deployment, they need to be taken into account as early as possible in the testing cycle. Being able to deploy *out of the box* saves the support staff significant time and effort. If you plan to buy new systems, purchase the same model in one block from the same manufacturer and take the first system delivered to the computer lab for testing.

- **Hardware configuration?** The minimum requirements for each system are:
  - **Size and number of hard disks.** In most cases, you are concerned with the first hard disk in a chain because the operating system and applications will be loaded there. If you plan on another arrangement (such as the OS on the first hard drive, and applications on a second), you will need to know the volumes on each hard disk.

- **Remaining space on hard disks.** You need to know this if you plan on upgrading instead of performing an installation from scratch.

- **Memory.** Make sure you have enough to meet the minimum recommendation for the operating system and Office 2000. 64 MB is usually adequate, but more is better for Windows NT because it takes unusual advantage of additional memory.

- **Processor type.** MCS considers a Pentium 150 MHz to be the minimum. The main goal in gathering processor data is to isolate 486 systems and target them for early replacement. You could keep them and run them as Terminal Server clients. Either way, you incur additional preparation for these systems.

- **Network Interface Card (NIC) manufacturer and model.** This is useful for situations where Windows NT 4.0 is planned for deployment on systems built from scratch. Windows NT 4.0 is not plug and play, so you must plan to add the necessary drivers or provide an unattended installation that will preload NIC drivers. Specific Windows NT strategies to simplify this situation are addressed later in this chapter.

Note   Most of the above hardware information was obtained from a standard SMS hardware inventory, which was reworked through an Excel spreadsheet and PivotTable to produce one stock report of the existing environment. "Using Excel 2000 and PivotTables to Categorize Inventory Data" on page 182 in this chapter describes this reworking process.

MCS found that the Excel 2000 PivotTable Wizard helped isolate important information in the rather long and repetitive inventory entries. Extracting the information into a PivotTable made inventory data easier to study and made it possible to obtain roll-up numbers flexibly. For more information, see "Using Excel 2000 and PivotTables to Categorize Inventory Data" on page 182 in this chapter.

Server Hardware

The main goal in this inventory is to identify potential distribution or source servers. In most cases, source servers will require only enough space to store Office 2000 files, and, if users are running the application from the network, enough processor speed and RAM to handle the higher traffic volume.

When deploying Office 2000, you must keep a source server or servers available because Office 2000 offers self-repair and Install on First Use functions via the Windows Installer service. Whenever a client chooses a module that is not preinstalled but is marked for Install on First Use, the first server in the list is accessed. This list of servers is defined in the Transform (.MST) file created by the Custom Installation Wizard. For more information, see Chapter 4, "Customizing an Office 2000 Installation."

If you are planning a Terminal Server and Office 2000 system, follow the guidelines established in the *Microsoft Office 2000 Resource Kit* and in Chapter 12 of this book, "Deploying Office 2000 on Windows Terminal Server," for minimum hardware configurations (particularly with respect to RAM). Use a dedicated server to support Terminal Server clients; it severely degrades performance to run other server applications, such as logon validation stand-alone server applications like SQL Server.

Obtain this information on the servers:

- **New or existing.** As with workstations, you have to plan around deployment of new servers if hardware is being delivered in the same timeframe. If at all possible, bring the new servers up before the workstation deployment launches instead of trying to coordinate server installation simultaneously. This primarily affects schedules, so it is more of a planning issue than a technical one.

- **Size of hard disks, partition/volume sizes, and remaining space on partitions/volumes.** Importance depends on whether you deploy Office 2000 from custom CDs or over the network.

  - If you use the server strictly as a source server for self-repair and the occasional *Installed on First Use*, you should need less than 1 GB on one volume of an array with average access times under 10 ms. MCS sometimes sets up one server as a source and, when deployment starts, a second as a backup.

  - If you plan to use the server as the primary source for brand-new installations of Office 2000 through the network, you have to consider hard disk speed and performance. RAID setups provide for speed and fault tolerance, but you also have to examine the health of the network backbone, and whether hubs and media can handle downloading 100 MB or more (depending on installation choices) to each workstation.

- **Memory.** More RAM boosts Windows NT-based servers response to user requests. You may have to upgrade memory on the deployment and/or source servers. Based on projected server usage, Trey Research required each server to have at least 128 MB of RAM.

- **Processor type.** Alpha versus I386 distinctions are important when you set up new servers and apply service packs.

- **Number of processors.** Evaluate servers' power and robustness. The most powerful server should function as the Office 2000 network application server, the next in line should be used as the first source server, and the least powerful as backup source server.

When reviewing server hardware results, remember that Office 2000 allows you to define multiple source servers. The original customized transformation (.MST) file defines which server is queried first, which second, and so on. Out of the box, Office 2000 does not distribute user requests across source servers (although it does offer what amounts to a fail-over solution). The first server on the list is hit hardest. You can deal with this by placing the strongest server first in line and upgrading it as necessary to handle increased loads. You can add on other load balancing solutions such as DNS round robin.

At Trey Research, MCS ran the first network deployment (to 24 alpha users) on a single-processor Pentium II box with 128 MB RAM. No performance issues were reported during the maintenance phase, when occasional downloads of uninstalled modules were occurring. The same server was already the primary central storage for software, which was one reason for choosing it.

Software inventory data also falls into workstation and server categories.

Workstation Software

Workstation software data is important, but don't waste energy gathering data of questionable importance. For instance, if you plan on a complete re-installation, all existing software will be overwritten and software information won't be worth capturing. Rule of thumb: when you upgrade existing systems you need to gather information on workstation software.

If you are upgrading from Office 95 to Office 2000, a software inventory should:

- Identify the operating system, especially service pack levels. Office 2000 requires certain service pack levels.

- Isolate all non-Outlook mail clients (typically these are Exchange clients). Because of incompatibilities between Outlook and Exchange schedulers and forms designers, you need to upgrade non-Outlook clients as early as possible in the deployment. For more information, see Chapter 8, "Deploying Outlook 2000."

Office 2000 upgrades over existing software relatively cleanly if the latest operating system service packs have been applied and users' configurations are not cluttered with multiple loads and flawed uninstalls of older software. At Trey Research, MCS laboratory tested upgrading clean installations of Office 95 and Office 97 and found few or no significant problems or halts during installation. In the field, however, you can save time and avoid problems by researching these items before upgrading:

- **Operating system type.** Determine which service releases or service packs must be present for a smooth Office 2000 installation. Rule of thumb: apply the latest service packs and recommended security patches before installation. You can do this with silent, non-interactive scripts (if users have administrative rights to their workstations) so installers don't have to go to workstations. Minimum SP requirements:
  - Windows 95: Service Pack 1.
  - Windows 98: no additional service packs or patches required.
  - Windows NT: SP 3 or 4. For security reasons, you should have SP 4.

- **Office versions.** Isolating Office 95 users is the main issue. Office 97 (Service Release 1 or 2) is more compatible with Office 2000 because it handles the same binaries. Access is not completely compatible, but there usually are fewer Access users and you can identify them easily.

- **Office and/or e-mail software installation source: network or local.** If you plan a local Office 2000 installation, MCS recommends uninstalling Office 95 and Office 97 before the install. This applies to classic network application configurations, not to Terminal Server, which you can upgrade centrally.

- **Type of e-mail client.** This can be important information. Trey Research was running Scheduler on an Exchange client, which is not fully compatible with the more advanced Outlook Calendars.

At Trey Research, the functions lost between Outlook and Exchange schedulers were not terribly significant to the department being upgraded; they had to do with delegate access to manage someone else's calendar (the administrative assistant and manager scenario) or with the ability to exchange e-mail forms. But in other departments this might have been significant. Trey Research also had a lot of Macintosh Outlook 98 clients, creating more compatibility concerns.

At Trey Research, MCS issued an SMS query and found that only one of the two locations had a significant number of Office 95 clients (about 80). It was unrealistic to expect *all* of these users to move to Windows NT 4.0, so MCS had to test the upgrade.

MCS found few network application-based systems, so they handled them case-by-case. If there had been more, MCS would have had to sense the network installation and handle automatic uninstalls. This can be done by adding the **/u** flag to the setup.exe command (**setup.exe /u**).

Server Software

You need to identify only the network operating system software and any client/server applications or e-mail functions.

- **Network Operating System (NOS) software.** This determines to client network protocol if you are going to use a customized bit-copy image installation for some or all workstations. It is not essential, but you should install Service Pack 4 for Windows NT Server, and at least Service Pack 3 for Windows NT.

- Terminal Server, version and service pack number

- Operating system: Novell, Windows NT, version and service pack numbers

At Trey Research, the servers were running Windows NT 4.0 with the latest service packs and the IT group planned to implement a Windows 2000 and/or Windows NT 4.0 Terminal Server configuration with Office 2000 for the UNIX and Macintosh clients in their areas.

- **Server software.** Software on the target servers that could affect performance (Exchange, SQL Server, anti-virus software distributed from the server, and so on). In Novell environments, you might find ManageWise, GroupWise, or ZenWorks.
- **Network traffic analyses/profiles for key sites.** Get an idea of the typical server-server and server-client communications speeds. Look at:
  - **Server backbone.** Determine the hub, distribution, and NIC types.
  - **WAN link types and costs.** Scattered sites and distributed traffic create special requirements for Office 2000 source servers and deployment methods.
  - **Typical load.** Investigate loads during hours or hours during which upgrades will most likely be scheduled. If you have tools to analyze network traffic throughout the day, look for the best times for an Office 2000 network installation. Use Network Monitor (in SMS 1.2) to get snapshots of servers' network traffic.

Soft Data

Soft data is unquantifiable but it can profoundly affect deployment planning and execution. Don't underestimate its importance—there are cases where users resistant to change or totally unfamiliar with the new interface have stopped deployments by revolting against sudden and unwanted changes in the way they do business.

Soft data often helps you determine how much training you should plan for. It can also indicate if you should introduce users to new software in nonthreatening, informal situations such as brown bag lunches. Provide some food and some computers and let users test drive hands-on the new software in a relaxed environment.

Collecting Inventory Data with Systems Management Server

Rule of thumb: inventory results are never perfect or even complete. At best, they are a snapshot of the existing environment at some recent time. Things large and small are missed—some users may be on vacation so that their systems are not found during the hardware and software scans.

Rather than trying to capture *all* information, concentrate on information on the majority of systems so that you can accurately estimate how many Office 95, Exchange, and Office 97 systems installers and scripts can expect.

Systems Management Server 2.0 extracts much more granular inventory data than SMS 1.2. If you plan to deploy to a site that can access SMS on the network, you will find it worthwhile to upgrade to SMS 2.0 before inventorying equipment.

SMS 1.2: The Audit.rul Method

Classic SMS 1.2 software surveys make use of an audit.rul file. If you plan to use this method, get the latest audit.rul file from ftp://ftp.microsoft.com/bussys /winnt/sms-public/. Rather than trying to inventory all 5,300 products listed in this master file, narrow it down to products likely to be on your systems so that users don't encounter long, irksome logons.

In its original form, audit.rul looks for executables or .DLLs needed to run the program, checks the sizes of the files it finds against a list of executables and .DLLs, and, if there is a match, adds the file to the workstation's software inventory.

Below are some audit.rul extracts for Trey Research. Note that it is limited to look only for Office versions and Exchange clients, so that it can complete faster.

```
package 7496 "MICROSOFT OFFICE, MICROSOFT CORPORATION"
  file "MSOFFICE.EXE" size 183168

package 7499 "MICROSOFT OFFICE FOR WINDOWS 95, MICROSOFT CORPORATION"
  file "MSOFFICE.EXE" size 356056

package 7501 "MICROSOFT OFFICE Version?b, MICROSOFT CORPORATION"
  file "MSOFFICE.EXE" size 193600

package 14370 "MICROSOFT OFFICE 97 PROFESSIONAL EDITION FOR WINDOWS 95,
MICROSOFT CORPORATION"
  file "MSOFFICE.EXE" size 333824

package 14394 "MICROSOFT EXCHANGE 4.00.993.4, MICROSOFT CORPORATION"
  file "EXCHNG32.EXE" size 83776

package 14395 "MICROSOFT EXCHANGE 5.0.1457.3, MICROSOFT CORPORATION"
  file "EXCHNG32.EXE" size 175376

package 14389 "MICROSOFT SCHEDULE+ 7.0 FOR WINDOWS 95, MICROSOFT
CORPORATION"
  file "SCHDPL32.EXE" size 93040

package 14390 "MICROSOFT SCHEDULE+ 7.5 FOR WINDOWS 95, MICROSOFT
CORPORATION"
  file "SCHDPL32.EXE" size 184080
```

Using CRC Checks

If there are a lot of packages and you want a good snapshot, you can survey the system faster and affect users less by checking the CRC instead of the size of the file. This method (detailed in "Package and Audit Rule File Formats" on TechNet) involves more work because you have to extract the proper CRC numbers from the original executables (detailed in "Inconsistent CRC or Checksum Values on Large Applications" on TechNet). This is an effective method *if* the configurations are relatively stable and you know the target applications.

Using Registry Scans: App-Reg

At Trey Research, MCS experimented with a freeware utility called *app-reg*, which essentially scans the registry for program listings, then produces the list of programs found under the **Control Panel, Add/Remove Programs** applet. You can also use it with the **/E** flag to convert the list to a suitable .MIF format so that the information is deposited automatically into the SMS database and examined with normal SMS queries.

MCS used app-reg at Trey Research because:

- It queried the registry at high speed
- It could be dropped into logon scripts (speeding information delivery)
- It could gather information on applications that administrators might not be aware of and thus could not include in the audit.rul file
- All the applications MCS wanted to capture appear in the **Add/Remove Programs** section

Automatic insertion of the information into SMS makes it possible to use SMS as the central inventory tool for future maintenance. Data doesn't have to be concatenated, it is already available in the SMS SQL Server database.

App-reg works only for Windows 9*x* and Windows NT systems. Numerous other freeware utilities are available for inventory.

Pulling Data Together with SMS

MCS used Systems Management Server 1.2 to inventory hardware and software, and used queries to identify substandard computers needing immediate hard disk, memory, or processor upgrades (486 processors were marked for replacement). Here is an example of this type of query:

```
(
MICROSOFT|DISK|1.0:Free Storage (MByte) is less than or equal to '400'
AND
MICROSOFT|DISK|1.0:Disk Index is 'C'
)
```

```
OR
MICROSOFT|X86_PC_MEMORY|1.0:Total Physical Memory (KByte) is less than
or equal to '32000'
OR
MICROSOFT|PROCESSOR|1.0:Processor Name is like '486'
```

MCS also examined raw SMS data dumps to get an overall view of data quality, although they had to use additional steps to format key fields in the previous section.

First, MCS ran a standard SMS inventory that included these important fields: Site (the Site Server), SMSID, LogOn Name, Name, UserID, Room, Last Hardware Scan, System Type, Processor Name, Total Physical Memory, Operating System, Version, Service Pack, Free Disk, and Total Disk. They exported the results into a CSV file that could be imported into Excel.

Trey Research's inventory showed two sites (as expected): one for the main offices and one for a second division. Some information was missing because the SMS gathers statistics on the first drive found, which is A, the floppy. So *free disk* and *total disk* were often blank (meaning users did not have a floppy in Drive A) or contained data that was old or based on the floppy drive.

MCS used another routine to derive *free disk* and *total disk* statistics for the hard disk. TechNet article Q134717, *SMS: Query Results Display Only First Data Record*, details a way to extract information directly from the SMS database on the SQL Server (by using an ODBC connection through Access). You can use Office 2000 to pull this information into Excel 2000 or Access 2000. TechNet article Q153534, *Retrieving SMSVIEW Data Using Microsoft Access*, explains.

Other Methods of Gathering Data

If you can't use SMS or a similar distribution mechanism, here are some other ways to gather data.

Manual Checks

If you are dealing with a small site, automating inventory may take more effort than simply visiting each computer. If you do this, create an inventory form with check boxes and options to take along and simplify information gathering.

User Interviews

You can interview users through e-mail or ask them to complete forms on an intranet site. This is not the best way to gather information. Many users don't know what hardware or software they have and therefore provide incorrect responses—especially when it comes to memory or hard disk space.

Remote Scans of the Registry and Disks

The Windows NT and Windows 9x resource kits contain utilities for remotely monitoring registry entries—a useful capability if users routinely leave their machines on. You can store the data in individual files (one per machine) on a single server share and then use a text utility to combine it. Or you can redirect the results to a concatenating file on a network share. This method saves a step and, by limiting the number of servers you have to consult, makes it much easier to gather inventory results and monitor progress.

Logon Scripts

You can insert commands into logon scripts to capture information about the size of hard disks, registry entries, and the existence of certain executables. Redirect results to a central server and share if possible, so that you reduce the number of servers you have to consult. Use this method sparingly because it can delay logon execution for users.

Collecting Soft Data

Generally speaking, you can't extract soft data from reports. MCS often has to capture it by distributing (in e-mail or on paper) a questionnaire, or by talking to as many users, administrators, and technicians as possible. Take advantage of all contact with users: swap tips and ideas with Alpha clients while you troubleshoot problems, stay open to user comments and feedback. This effort creates good will and a sense of security in the user community, and helps you assess users' technical sophistication and their attitude toward the new software.

Past History of Upgrades

However you approach information gathering, try to:

- **Determine if people see previous upgrades as successful or unsuccessful.** You'll have to take negative feelings into account and work to allay misgivings. Use training and early adoption to overcome these obstacles.

- **Identify/assess methods used in previous upgrades.** Which distribution vehicles were used (SMS, Tivoli, unattended scripts, logon scripts) and how well did they work? How much user interaction was there (did users have to start the script or was it started for them on logon)? Was upgrading optional?

- **What are users accustomed to seeing and doing during an upgrade?** Have previous upgrades been noninteractive, or have users been offered several options? If users are experienced with one method (for example, SMS Package Command Manager or standard prompts in a logon script) use it if you can. For example, if users have always seen progress bars during installation, include them.

- **Find out what didn't work.** Then figure out how to use Office 2000 upgrade tools to avoid those problems. For instance, if silent installations confused users and made them reboot before the package was complete, you can use an unattended Office 2000 installation but add foreground notices to keep users informed.

Some Trey Research users had strong opinions as to what was appropriate on their desktops and were traditionally allowed to be extremely independent in their choices. MCS realized it would have to proceed carefully when the Windows NT 4.0 and Windows 2000 portions of the rollouts required locking down desktops by implementing policies and restricting users to Domain User status.

Users' Experience with Microsoft Office

1. **Find out if requests for Office 2000 already exist.** Do users need to be educated on Office 2000 benefits, or do they just want it on their desktops ASAP?

2. **Determine previous issues/complaints with previous software.** Users will more readily adopt Office 2000 if it will solve or mitigate existing problems.

Trey Research users complained of incompatibilities (systems and software) and of difficulties importing and exporting data. Problems recurred when users tried to color-print EPS files embedded in Office 97 PowerPoint documents. This is not something you would predict, but it was a source of serious contention at Trey Research.

Current Methods of Communicating with Users

- **How are users currently alerted of IT changes?** Use the most familiar method—e-mail, voice mail, bulletin boards, and so on.

- **Are current methods effective?** Do they provide users with timely upgrade information—what it involves, what to expect, and when it will occur. If users received alerts but were still surprised, find a better way to notify them.

At Trey Research, MCS IT technicians had good relationships with users and tended to distribute information one-on-one. They created intranet pages (including a FAQ), and used e-mail as a primary information delivery tool because they knew that users checked their e-mail daily. About six weeks before deployment was scheduled to start they held an open house where users got hands-on experience with machines running Office 2000 and could watch demonstrations.

Using Excel 2000 and PivotTables to Categorize Inventory Data

MCS used Excel 2000 PivotTables to analyze raw data and parse it into a usable format. SMS has query tools and report-generating capabilities (including customizable Crystal Reports) but MCS found good reasons to work in Excel:

- With Excel 2000 you can review all data in one place at one time, making it easier to find anomalies and assess validity.

- You can use Excel 2000 to extract information from the overwhelming amounts of data that some sites produce. Quick replies to *Where Are, Who Has*, and *How Many* questions are now enhanced. Excel 2000 PivotTable drill-down capabilities make it allow you to get a second tier of information by double-clicking and choosing which field would show up as subdata. Excel 2000's new wizard and its extended drag-and-drop features are easier to use than Excel 97.

- Excel tools make report creation easier than SMS Administration tools. At Trey Research, three technicians handled most of the administrative duties at both main locations. They could drop information into an Excel workbook, then examine it on their own desktops, and could use PivotTables too manipulate their view of the information.

You can apply advanced filters to eliminate data more than a month old. A range of criteria was named *Criteria* to make it the default for all filter criteria. Figure 6.3 shows the criteria that limit the advanced filter to data gathered in the previous month, run on a 2/19/1999 inventory list:

Last Hardware Scan
>1/19/1999 12:01:00 PM

Figure 6.3   An example of criteria that determines the data gathered.

This reduced entries by about half (480 to 250). SMS can also eliminate earlier hardware scans before performing the export.

To improve readability, filtered data was copied into a fresh worksheet and then run through a PivotTable. Table 6.1 shows how you can filter a raw data sample to produce a quick view of critical information.

Table 6.1   Filtered Data That Was Run through a PivotTable.

LogOn Name	Building	Room	Last Hardware Scan	System Type	Processor Name	Operating System	Version	Service Pack
USER1	BLDG1	B207	1/19/99 12:04	X86-based PC	INTEL PENTIUM-120	MS DOS	7.1	
USER2	BLDG1	D115	1/19/99 15:00	X86-based PC	486DX-33	MS DOS	7.1	
USER3	BLDG1	A112	1/20/99 16:22	X86-based PC	INTEL PENTIUM-100	MS DOS	7.1	
USER4	BLDG1	B104	1/21/99 10:45	X86-based PC	INTEL PENTIUM-100	MS DOS	7.1	
USER5			1/21/99 13:24	X86-based PC	INTEL PENTIUM-166	MS DOS	7.1	
USER6	BLDG1	B124	1/21/99 16:17	X86-based PC	INTEL PENTIUM-166	MS DOS	7	
USER7			1/22/99 8:20	X86-based PC	INTEL PENTIUM II-398	Microsoft Windows NT	4	Service Pack 4
USER8	BLDG1	B211	1/22/99 9:16	X86-based PC	INTEL PENTIUM-200	MS DOS	7.1	
USER9	BLDG1	D205	1/22/99 15:43	X86-based PC	486DX-75	MS DOS	7	
USER10	BLDG1	C206	1/23/99 7:57	X86-based PC	INTEL PENTIUM-90	MS DOS	7	
USER11	BLDG1	B102	1/26/99 12:33	X86-based PC	486DX-66	MS DOS	7	
USER12			1/26/99 12:39	X86-based PC	INTEL PENTIUM-90	MS DOS	7.1	
USER13	BLDG1	C217	1/27/99 8:20	X86-based PC	INTEL PENTIUM-166	MS DOS	7	

(continued)

LogOn Name	Building	Room	Last Hardware Scan	System Type	Processor Name	Operating System	Version	Service Pack
USER14	BLDG1	B222 M	1/27/99 9:13	X86-based PC	INTEL PENTIUM-166	Microsoft Windows NT	4	Service Pack 3
USER15	BLDG1		1/27/99 17:51	X86-based PC	INTEL PENTIUM II-451	Microsoft Windows NT	4	Service Pack 4
USER16			1/28/99 8:55	X86-based PC	INTEL PENTIUM II-266	MS DOS	7.1	
USER17	BLDG2		1/29/99 10:07	X86-based PC	INTEL PENTIUM PRO-200	Microsoft Windows NT	4	Service Pack 4, RC 1.43
USER18	BLDG2	D2	1/29/99 12:09	X86-based PC	INTEL PENTIUM-90	MS DOS	7.1	
USER19	BLDG2	D208	1/29/99 14:56	X86-based PC	INTEL PENTIUM PRO-200	Microsoft Windows NT	4	Service Pack 1
USER20	BLDG2	C235 M	1/29/99 15:23	X86-based PC	486DX-66	MS DOS	7	
USER21	BLDG2	C222 M	1/30/99 12:13	X86-based PC	486DX-66	MS DOS	7	
USER22	BLDG2	C103	1/31/99 10:17	X86-based PC	INTEL PENTIUM-166	Microsoft Windows NT	4	Service Pack 3
USER23	BLDG2		1/31/99 17:31	X86-based PC	486DX-66	MS DOS	7	
USER24	BLDG2	A120 M	2/1/99 7:09	X86-based PC	INTEL PENTIUM II-233	MS DOS	7.1	
USER25	BLDG2	C230 M	2/1/99 7:38	X86-based PC	486DX-66	MS DOS	7	
USER26	BLDG2	B111	2/1/99 7:42	X86-based PC	Internal	MS DOS	7	
USER27	BLDG2	C221 M	2/1/99 7:48	X86-based PC	INTEL PENTIUM II-300	MS DOS	7.1	

LogOn Name	Building	Room	Last Hardware Scan	System Type	Processor Name	Operating System	Version	Service Pack
USER28	BLDG2	D219 M	2/1/99 7:51	X86-based PC	486DX-66	MS DOS	7	
USER29	BLDG2	A101	2/1/99 8:14	X86-based PC	INTEL PENTIUM-166	MS DOS	7.1	

Here is how to build a PivotTable on top of this data.

1. Select all the data (use CTRL+A on the keyboard, or click on the upper left corner of the worksheet).

2. Click on **Data**, then click **PivotTable and PivotChart Report**.

3. Make sure the **Microsoft Excel list or database** and **PivotTable** option buttons are selected (Figure 6.4).

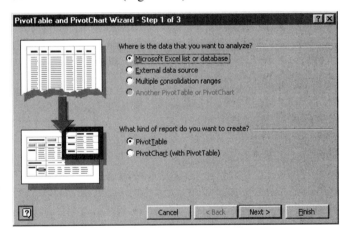

Figure 6.4   PivotTable and PivotChart Wizard.

4. Click **Next** and leave the current default entry since the selection has already been made (Figure 6.5):

Figure 6.5   Selecting data.

5. In the next Wizard screen, leave the setting for the default PivotTable location (in a new worksheet) as is, and click the **Layout** button.

6. In the **Layout** dialog box, drag **Processor Name** from the right listing of buttons to the area of the dummy PivotTable labeled ROW, and then drag **Count of Processor Name** from the right again, this time to the area labeled DATA. Leave COLUMN blank. The layout should resemble Figure 6.6.

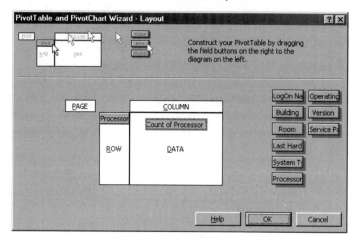

Figure 6.6   The PivotTable layout.

7. Click **OK**, and then click **Finish** to generate the PivotTable.

The PivotTable is dynamic, not static, as are most database reports. The first PivotTable created after completing the above steps would resemble that in Figure 6.7.

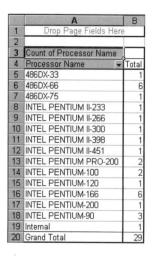

	A	B
1	Drop Page Fields Here	
2		
3	Count of Processor Name	
4	Processor Name	Total
5	486DX-33	1
6	486DX-66	6
7	486DX-75	1
8	INTEL PENTIUM II-233	1
9	INTEL PENTIUM II-266	1
10	INTEL PENTIUM II-300	1
11	INTEL PENTIUM II-398	1
12	INTEL PENTIUM II-451	1
13	INTEL PENTIUM PRO-200	2
14	INTEL PENTIUM-100	2
15	INTEL PENTIUM-120	1
16	INTEL PENTIUM-166	6
17	INTEL PENTIUM-200	1
18	INTEL PENTIUM-90	3
19	Internal	1
20	Grand Total	29

Figure 6.7   Sample PivotTable.

PivotTables help you research a particular detail, something *behind* the listed count. For example, if you did not expect to see the six 486DX-66 machines listed in Figure 6.7 and you want to see who logs onto those machines, you can double-click on that row to list fields you can drill down into. Clicking **LogOn Name** to produces this change:

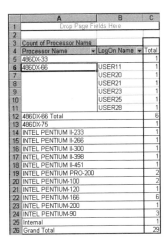

Figure 6.8   Drilling down with a PivotTable.

To the right of the PivotTable itself is a floating toolbox for the PivotTable controls. Click inside the PivotTable to expand the toolbox (Figure 6.9).

Figure 6.9   The PivotTable toolbox.

Drag the **Building** button to the top cell on the PivotTable where the gray text *Drop Page Fields Here* appears. Page fields allow dynamic changes to filter the entire table—for instance, to see where the 486DX-66 users are located. Note that the resulting **Building** field becomes a drop-down box, where **All, Bldg1,** or **Bldg2** are available. You can choose **Bldg2** to collapse the table to show only machines in **Bldg2,** which shows five users (Figure 6.10).

	A	B	C
1	Building	BLDG2	
2			
3	Count of Processor Name		
4	Processor Name	LogOn Name	Total
5	486DX-66	USER20	1
6		USER21	1
7		USER23	1
8		USER25	1
9		USER28	1
10	486DX-66 Total		5
11	INTEL PENTIUM II-233		1
12	INTEL PENTIUM II-300		1
13	INTEL PENTIUM PRO-200		2
14	INTEL PENTIUM-166		2
15	INTEL PENTIUM-90		1
16	Internal		1
17	Grand Total		13

Figure 6.10   A new drop-down box.

You can also drag and drop fields such as **Machine's Name** to put them next to the **LogOn Name**. Excel 2000 PivotTables manipulate data more flexibly than standard database reports. Trey Research used these capabilities to distribute results to administrators without sacrificing the flexibility of roll-up reports.

After-Inventory Tasks

Once you have substantial data you have to make decisions. To solidify plans you have to define this information:

- Hardware that needs complete replacement
- Hardware that requires upgrades
- Whether rollback is an option
- Which applications are mission-critical

List Hardware That Needs Complete Replacement

To some degree, hardware requirements depend on budget and on what level of performance users require. Office 2000 publishes recommended configurations, but MCS often sees lower standards applied onsite.

After lab testing, Trey Research decided they would permit users with 120 MHz or higher Pentiums and at least 64 MB RAM to upgrade to Office 2000 (installed locally).

These criteria indicated that about 25 percent of Trey Research's computers had low-end processors (386 and 486 chips) and had to be replaced. Roughly 10 percent of these were already slated for replacement within the month, but this information helped the team decide to build a Terminal Server (for which hardware and software had already been purchased) to serve slower clients until replacement funds became available.

List Hardware That Requires Upgrades

Hardware that requires upgrades falls into two basic categories: memory and hard disks. Although 32 MB of RAM is technically sufficient, reasonable performance requires at least 64 MB. Early surveys indicated that no systems had less than 32 MB RAM but some had less than 64 MB. RAM upgrades require sending a technician to the machine, so Trey Research decided to install Office 2000 to these systems via CD-ROM so that the technician could upgrade the hardware and then install Office 2000, saving time and reducing network traffic.

Calculating necessary local client disk space is harder: it depends on decisions made in the Custom Installation Wizard and varies widely. To determine real hard-disk space requirements, run the standard installation with the custom transformation files and add up the size of the installation. Don't forget to include all Install on Demand options to obtain the worst-case scenario for what the client *could* have on the local drive. If the base RAM is 64 MB and Windows NT workstations are the target, add 100 MB for paging files and storage. For systems with more RAM, add 1.5 of the RAM capacity. These operations yield a final requirement: systems without this much space will need hard disk upgrades to avoid undue fragmentation of files.

You can sometimes avoid upgrading disk space by asking users to delete older files, or offering them good removable disk alternatives or larger network shares. In most cases, though, you'll have to upgrade.

To determine memory requirements in your environment, assess current performance metrics, then do some testing. MCS knew that some Trey Research users were happily running Windows NT 4.0 with Office 97 on 32-MB systems. Lab tests and a short alpha stage proved that Office 2000 was never slower than Office 97 and was occasionally much faster. On the basis of these tests, Trey Research kept the RAM upgrades scheduled but allowed users with 32 MB to upgrade to Office 2000 and add RAM later.

Determine If the Rollback Feature Is an Option

Office 2000 has a rollback feature that automatically restores computers to their original configuration if the installation fails. This requires enough hard-disk space to store the old configuration files and settings, which can be a challenge at sites with hard disks of 2 GB or less. If you select the rollback feature, installation will not start unless the hard disk has enough room to store the old configuration *and* complete the Office 2000 installation (you define this amount).

This leaves you with two alternatives: either use the rollback feature only for computers with adequate storage space, or disable it completely. If you decide not to use rollback, tell users well in advance to back up their data thoroughly, and make sure they understand that there will be no auto-recovery to a previous state should the upgrade fail. If you must be able to return to a previous configuration rapidly, make a bit copy of the hard disk before beginning the installation.

Identify Mission-Critical Applications

It is not always obvious which applications are mission critical, though it is significant when you are deciding whether to use rollback. To decide if an application is mission-critical, ask the following questions.

How much downtime for a failed installation is acceptable? Estimate the maximum allowable recovery time upon report of a problem with the installation. Users will have various tolerances for downtime on which you will need to base your approach. Here are some examples.

Example: In a 24-hour working environment, operations cannot tolerate *any* downtime. In this case, one solution would be to buy a small block of new machines and preconfigure them with Office 2000. Then, you would provide a new parallel system for a specific period. Once users were working purely on the new systems, claim the older machines for the upgrade and repeat the cycle.

Example: Users can tolerate only the 30 to 60 minutes of downtime estimated for installation. In this case, you must provide for rollback. This process may include upgrading hard-disk space on each machine to make sure enough is available.

Example: Users can afford to lose access to their Office applications for as long as half a day. In this case, you should set expectations by explaining that a failed installation may extend downtime beyond a half day. The additional time may be necessary because your recovery plans will center on a completely new build from scratch—as compared to trying to back out of a failed installation that is proving difficult to recover.

Example: Users can afford to lose access to their Office applications for an extended period of time if troubleshooting is necessary. For example, they are away at training for a week. Administrators should turn off the rollback option completely to save time and space.

How do users assess priority? Ask users which is more important to them—faster upgrades or better insurance against downtime. If users are willing to accept the risk of an unprotected upgrade to be able to run the new software sooner, you have an answer. Always remember that users' answers will reflect their own points of view, and this is *not necessarily* the same as an application's actual value to the organization.

CHAPTER 7

Distributing Microsoft Office 2000

When you upgrade existing systems, you face certain basic challenges. If your enterprise is large or small, if you use third-party software distribution tools or the ones that come with Windows NT or Windows 9*x*, you *still* have to make basic decisions and perform specific activities in *all* distributions.

Note   Windows NT clients are a special case. If users of these clients do not have local administrator permissions, you have to visit each computer or take other steps to allow these users to perform the installation.

This chapter discusses three basic Office 2000 distribution methods: Systems Management Server (SMS), network administrative share, and CD. The methods are suited to different circumstances, and have different advantages and drawbacks. The sections that follow examine your options from various points of view to help you choose which method or combination of methods will serve you best. Along the way, the discussion taps into MCS experience for explanations and examples of important points.

What You'll Find in This Chapter

- A flowchart of the distribution decision-making process for large- and small-scale organizations. (See Figure 7.1.)

- An in-depth analysis of how to use Microsoft Systems Management Server to distribute Office 2000 to minimize the impact on users and lower total cost of ownership (TCO).

- Detailed instructions for many distribution processes.

- How to choose and execute alternate distribution methods (large- and small-scale) when you cannot use SMS.

- How to choose the best distribution medium for deployment in your environment.

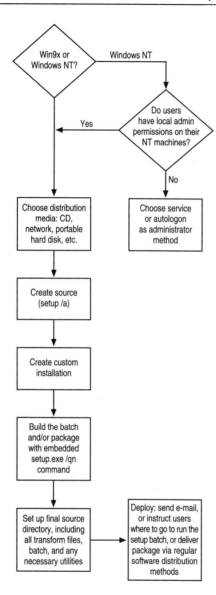

Figure 7.1   Decision flow for distributing Office 2000.

Distributing Office 2000 with SMS 1.2

To help reduce total cost of ownership (TCO), software distribution must be efficient, timely, and cost-effective. You have to implement inventory and support strategies that provide a stable and effective operating environment.

A software distribution strategy must deliver a clearly defined data set to users with varying computer types and link speeds. It must use a minimum of scripting, provide installation options, and have minimal impact on day-to-day operations.

Microsoft Systems Management Server (SMS) can help address these needs. The following sections explain how Microsoft Consulting Services (MCS) used SMS 1.2 to distribute Office 2000 in a complex environment. The discussion is detailed, but it is not a step-by-step manual. For more details see the *Guide to Deploying Office 2000 with Systems Management Server 1.2* and the *Guide to Deploying Office 2000 with Systems Management Server 2.0* in the Deployment section of the Microsoft Systems Management Server Web site at http://www.microsoft.com /smsmgmt/deployment/default.asp.

Previous Microsoft Office Rollouts

To plan a deployment, you should start by examining how previous versions of Office were rolled out. Examining the successes and failures of previous rollouts can help make your Office 2000 rollout smoother.

SMS Installer

One company used SMS Installer to distribute Office 95, then later used it to distribute Office 97. To minimize installation time on shared machines where multiple users logged on, scripts were modified to allow for a machine portion and a user portion. The machine portion installed all files and made registry changes to the HKEY_LOCAL_MACHINE hive; the user portion created desktop icons and made changes to the HKEY_CURRENT_USER hive.

Network Bandwidth

When distributing the Office 97 package, MCS found that the links to some of the 56-KB sites became saturated. MCS had scheduled the SMS distribution to servers to begin after the work day ended and finish before employees arrived the next day, but saturated lines slowed things down and the distribution ran into the next business day. Rather than back out and refigure, MCS completed the distribution, which went quickly once the package hit local distribution servers and became available to clients. Rule of thumb: determine bandwidth issues and study them before deploying Office 2000.

Assessing End-User Requirements and Constraints

This company's objectives for the Office 2000 deployment project were:

- Deploy Office 2000 to 2100 desktop computers within four weeks.
- Add regional support staff to manage the deployment schedule.
- Deploy Outlook 2000 later, in a separate package developed by the messaging team.
- Configure Internet Explorer to use proxy server with AutoConfiguration URL set to the http location of your autoconfig.ins file.
- Install Word and Excel to clients; configure other applications to Install on First Use to reduce disk space requirements and bandwidth requirements by installing only Word and Excel at deployment—other components will be installed at random times as users select them.
- Design the Office 2000 package so that SMS is not required in all cases.
- Provide enough documentation and training that support staff can further customize the Office 2000 deployment package at the end of this project.

These were required; in addition, the company wanted, if possible, to:

- Save documents by default to user shares on local servers
- Set the default Internet Explorer Home page to a specific intranet page
- Set Internet site restrictions

Tools and Utilities Required

To use SMS to distribute Office 2000 you need:

- Office 2000 Source Files
- Office 2000 Resource Kit (ORK)
- Custom Installation Wizard (CIW) from the Office 2000 Resource Kit
- OFF9SMS.BAT from the ORK
- SHUTDOWN.EXE from the ORK
- REBOOT.EXE from the ORK
- O2KSETUP.EXE from the ORK; you need to modify this compiled SMS installer script for Windows NT Workstation deployment
- OFFSPEC.INI—an empty, uniquely named file in which SMS can place Office 2000 Professional inventory information
- SMS Hotfix for SMS 1.2 SP4 (SMS12O2K.EXE)
- Service Pack (SP) 4 or above for Windows NT workstations

- Administrator password for Windows NT Workstation deployment
- SMS Installer to modify O2KSETUP.IPF script
- 1.7 GB of free disk space on distribution server: 550 MB for source files on any network share, 600 MB for compression files on the site server, 550 MB for decompressed distributed source files on distribution point servers

Administrative Install

Office 2000 requires that you enter a license during setup. If you don't enter it, users are asked to enter key the first time they attempt to use an Office 2000 component. To avoid this issue, run the Office 2000 Setup in *Administrative* mode (**setup.exe /a**) to a network share. To create an administrative install point:

1. Create a directory on a network server with more than 550 MB of disk available.
2. Make sure the SMS Service Account has *read* permissions to this share.
3. Map a drive letter to this share. You must be logged on with *write* permission to this share.
4. From the Office 2000 CD, run Setup in Administrative mode (**setup.exe /a**).
5. When prompted for destination, enter the path to the network share.
6. Enter the license key when prompted.

The Windows Installer places an administrative copy of the Office 2000 source files in the specified directory.

Office 2000 Resource Kit

To customize Office 2000 installation features and options you must have the *Microsoft Office 2000 Resource Kit* (ORK).

Custom Installation Wizard

The Custom Installation Wizard (CIW, included in the ORK) lets you install a subset of Office 2000 components, choose their installation states (local computer, source, on first use, not available), and set most customization options.

The Windows Installer uses an .MSI file that contains default setup information about the software being installed. The CIW reads the .MSI file and presents you with setup options and defaults which you can change. You save the changes in a custom transform (.MST) file that customizes Windows Installer execution when you supply it on the Office Setup command line.

SMS 1.2 Hot Fix

SMS 1.2 Package Command Manager (PCM) maps a drive letter when executing a command. This drive letter is arbitrary, and it exists only during the execution of the command from PCM. Office 2000 cannot use this drive letter to perform *Detect and Repair* or *Installed on First Use*, which require accessing the original installation location. You can correct this with an SMS 1.2 hot fix (SMS12O2K.EXE), which causes PCM to create an environment variable *PCMUNC* containing the UNC path to the setup files.

Important   Service Pack 4 must be installed before you install the hot fix. If Service Pack 5 is installed, you don't need the hot fix.

OFF9SMS.BAT

This ORK file, used on the command line of the SMS 1.2 package, uses the PCMUNC environment variable to launch Office 2000 Setup with the UNC. Setup stores the UNC so the SMS package can be used later for *Detect and Repair* and *Install on First Use*. You can add other source file locations through .MST files or by adding command line parameters to the Office Setup command line.

SMS Installer Script—O2KSETUP.IPF

When the SMS 1.2 package arrives, Windows NT 4.0 requires administrator rights to install software, and not all users have this level of permission.

You can solve this problem with the SMS Installer Script O2KSETUP.IPF (from the ORK). An SMS administrator has to edit the file to insert the username, password, and domain of an account with administrator privileges (it must have this level of permission or the script can lock the client) and any custom .MST filenames. Then, when it is compiled, O2KSETUP.EXE performs these tasks on a Windows NT 4.0 computer:

1. Enables autologon and sets the default username, password, and domain so that upon reboot, the machine starts up with an administrator account.

2. Locks out the keyboard and mouse to prevent any misuse of this heightened capability.

3. Restarts the computer to begin Office 2000 Setup (Stage 1).

4. Restarts the computer (Stage 2) to finish Setup.

5. Disables Autologon and resets username, password, and domain to the original settings.

6. Reboots.

OFFSPEC.INI

Office 2000 comes in Professional, Premium, and Developer editions. SMS cannot distinguish between Office 2000 editions during inventory, so you have to create an .INI file and install it during Office 2000 Setup, which adds it to the SMS package's inventory rules so that SMS can use it to differentiate Office 2000 editions. SMS inventory requires that Offspec.ini file be installed to the same directory as the other file specified in the SMS package inventory rules. Use the CIW to include this file in the Office 2000 installation in the directory **<Program Files\Microsoft Office>\Office**.

Rebooting Utility Programs

REBOOT.EXE and SHUTDOWN.EXE (from the ORK) are required for the SMS 1.2 installation of Office 2000. OFF9SMS.BAT and O2KSETUP.IPF supply a switch to the Office 2000 Setup program that disables automatic shutdown and restart of Windows. REBOOT.EXE and SHUTDOWN.EXE control rebooting, and they must exist in the root of the directory containing the source of the SMS Package.

When Windows Installer finishes Office 2000 Setup, it executes Reboot.exe on Windows 9*x* computers and SHUTDOWN.EXE on Windows NT computers.

SMS 1.2 vs. SMS 2.0

Systems Management Server 2.0 provides features that allow you to install packages using a UNC name and to set packages to install under the context of an account with administrative privileges. Both of these can simplify Office 2000 distribution.

UNC Names

Office 2000 Setup records the location from which Office is installed so that *Self-Repairing Applications, Detect and Repair,* and *Installed on First Use* features can use the required source files. SMS 2.0 can launch applications using UNC paths, but SMS 1.2 requires the SMS 1.2 hot fix and the OFF9SMS.BAT file for Office 2000 Setup to detect a UNC name instead of a drive letter when launched by Package Command Manager.

Windows NT Permissions

On Windows NT clients, SMS 1.2 SP 4 can run the Package Command Manager as a service, and you can run the *Rservice* utility to set it up with administrative rights on the clients.

With SMS 2.0 you can specify that Office 2000 Setup runs with administrative permissions on Windows NT computers. The permissions are restricted to Setup—the logged on user retains existing permissions.

Creating the Office 2000 Installation Location

To create the administrative installation location for Office 2000:

1. Apply the SMS hot fix to the primary site servers.
2. Create the administrative share point, making sure the SMS Service Account has access.
3. Run Office 2000 Setup in Administrative Mode (**setup /a**).
4. Use ORK tools to customize Office 2000 Setup.
5. Copy these files from the ORK to the Office 2000 administrative share:
   - OFF9SMS.BAT
   - SHUTDOWN.EXE
   - REBOOT.EXE
   - OFF9SPEC.INI
   - O2KSETUP.IPF
   - SETUP.EXE (see note below)

Note   The updated SETUP.EXE (on the ORK at <CD Root>:\PFiles\ORKTools \ToolBox\Tools\SETUP\SETUP.EXE or search http://www.microsoft.com /office/ork) provides better network resiliency for use with SMS, allows SMS to roll back a failed installation, and lets you use the /chained command to include multiple installs in one process. Use of the updated SETUP.EXE is strongly recommended.

6. Install the SMS Installer, available at http://www.microsoft.com/smsmgmt (select the Downloads link).
7. Open O2KSETUP.IPF and enter the account information for the administrative account that will run the Office Setup program on Windows NT computers.
8. Compile and save O2KSETUP.EXE into the root of the Office 2000 administrative share using SMS Installer.
9. Remove the copy of the O2KSETUP.IPF with the administrator's password from public shares. Anyone can use this file's information to access secure data.

SMS 1.2 Package Creation

The figures below demonstrate the SMS 1.2 Package definition for Office 2000. Before creating the package, save all utilities and files in the location where the administrative copy of Office 2000 is installed. This will be the source for the SMS Package (see Figure 7.2).

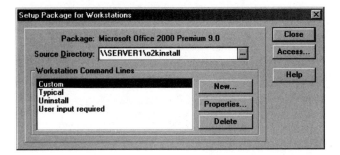

Figure 7.2   UNC name where administrative copy of Office 2000, the customized Transform file (*.MST), the OFF9SMS.BAT file, and O2KSETUP.EXE have been placed. Note that the SMS Service Account must have read access to this directory.

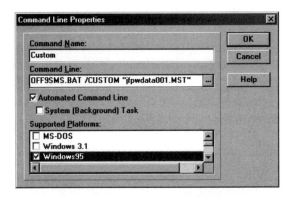

Figure 7.3   The command line definition for the Office 2000 SMS 1.2 package. Note that the name of the .MST File created by running the Custom Installation Wizard is specified.

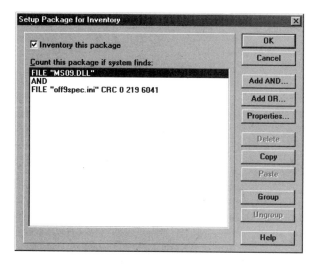

Figure 7.4   Software Inventory Definition for Office 2000. Note for SMS Inventory rules to evaluate to TRUE, both files must exist in the same directory. OFF9SPEC.INI is a custom file defined in the Transform file (*.MST) and is used only to allow various versions of Office 2000 to be inventoried.

SMS 1.2 Job Creation

Figure 7.5 demonstrates the creation of the SMS 1.2 distribution job for Office 2000.

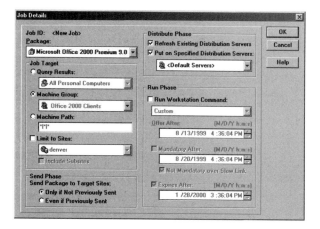

Figure 7.5   To distribute an SMS package to distribution servers but not clients, clear the *Run Workstation Command* option button in the *Run Phase*. Office 2000 will be placed on Distribution servers but not distributed to clients.

LAN/WAN Considerations

The company was concerned about the 56-KB frame relay links from one of the regional offices to other operating divisions. They are usually heavily loaded—with business traffic during office hours and with automated processes during the evening—so SMS could not be used to distribute the 570-MB Office 2000 installation package to the operating division distribution servers.

Skeleton SMS Package Created

The team created a second small package (OFF9SMS.BAT), placed it by itself on a new share point, and used it to distribute a skeleton package to the operating division distribution servers over the frame links.

Office 2000 and Skeleton Package Distributed

The team created two SMS machine groups for the distribution servers: *HighBandwidth* (servers with T1 links) and *LowBandwidth* (servers with 56-KB links).

The team created two SMS distribution jobs, leaving the *Run Phase* of each job definition unchecked so that the package would be distributed to SMS Servers but not made available to clients. The first job sent the full Office 2000 package to the *HighBandwidth* servers; the second sent the *Skeleton* package to the *LowBandwidth* servers.

They then burned CD images of the Office 2000 administrative share and sent them by courier to the operating divisions—a low-tech but effective tactic—where the image was copied into the SMS package installation point that had been created on the *LowBandwidth* servers by the Skeleton package.

SMS Run Jobs Sent to Clients

The second phase executed the SMS Office 2000 package on the client computers, created new SMS jobs, and set these options:

Option	Setting
Send Phase...	CHECK Only if Not Previously Sent
Distribute Phase...	UNCHECK Refresh Existing Distribution Servers
Run Phase...	CHECK Run Workstation Command

To reduce impact on the network, the team created machine groups and SMS jobs so that groups of 100 users would receive the package, and set the Run phase so that each day for five days, two sets of 100 users would get the package at each of the four regional offices.

They created operating divisions jobs, but did not stagger them because the divisions averaged only 50 users and tests showed that shipping to them would not place an unacceptable load on the LANs.

Non-SMS Installation Techniques for Office 2000 Deployment

When you cannot use SMS, you have other distribution options, which are discussed in this section. The treatment divides companies into two categories. *Large* ones tend to have at least one type of distribution mechanism—such as WinInstall, ZenWorks, Tivoli, or a proprietary internal system—and locked-down desktops that do not enable users to load software. *Mid-size and smaller* lack large-scale distribution mechanisms, so their administrators often set permission levels so that users can load and maintain software on their own computers. This saves effort but leaves administrators unaware of precisely what is installed, making it more difficult to plan deployment. This section offers some help for these situations.

Even though this discussion has concentrated on using SMS, most recommendations in this and other chapters hold true when you use other distribution means. You can choose the distribution scripting method or packaging software you are most familiar with, and apply the same methods you apply when using SMS *if* you understand how the SMS scripts work. This section explains them, but it cannot address every possible variant in scripting languages. It gives some basic routines in what you cold call the lowest common denominator for scripting (MS-DOS batch files) and it outlines some basic rules that can help you distribute Office 2000.

Large-Enterprise Scenario: Packaging and Distribution Software

This section explains how to incorporate the Office 2000 Setup into existing distribution structures that are not run on SMS: ZenWorks, WinInstall, Tivoli, and so on. Rather than offer specific scripts or packages for each product, it suggests how to approach deployment.

If you are an administrator for a large enterprise, you should review the sections for the mid-size and small companies. These outline basic MS-DOS batch scripts that you can easily turn into more sophisticated packages and scripts.

Packaging

You should run the Custom Installation Wizard to build suitable transform files for each custom installation, then use a simple call inside the packaging software to run Setup with the *TRANSFORMS=* command and the appropriate .MST file.

This approach does not attempt to *capture* the Office 2000 installation with SMS Installer; it doesn't have to because .MSI technology makes customization more complete and flexible. Most current distribution software, such as WinInstall and ZenWorks, allow you to capture (take a snapshot of) the system before installing software, then, after installation, capture the differences (files added, registries edited) discovered by comparing the system's present and pre-installation states.

Rule of thumb: Transform file installations are much cleaner and more adaptable (for example, one per department with multiple transformation files stored in the same source directory) if you use methods *other* than running a before and after snapshot, or capture, with software such as WinInstall or ZenWorks. Some common issues:

- Capturing can grab elements that are not part of the Office installation. For instance, background operations running in Windows NT workstations can change a log or update a registry key, and you can't be sure this isn't captured in the difference file. Stray entries buried deep in the difference file can cause havoc for users.

- Capturing requires the same testing you should apply to any custom program to be distributed to users. It is, after all, a new package that is not guaranteed to be identical to what the manufacturer planned for installation. When you repackage a product, you have to test it.

- Capturing breaks Office 2000's *Automatic Repair* and *Install on First Use* features, rendering .MSI technology almost useless.

- Capturing each program out of a suite of software and applying them in a new combination is almost impossible to do well. To operate as intended, Office suites usually have to be captured in one massive package and you may have to complete captures for each configuration or department or need.

- Capturing does not deal with variations among computers. Many administrators have been surprised to find users who still have Office 4.*x* or other software (once approved, but no longer standard) that affects how Office 2000 installs.

- Capturing leaves you between the manufacturer's approved installation and the user. Troubleshooting is more complicated because you have to check an extra level (the package itself) to make sure it is not causing the problem.

Note   ZenWorks has its an auto-repair feature that restores deleted or corrupted files, but it requires capturing the software. .MSI technology offers *Self-Repair* and *Install on Demand/First Use Install* capabilities out of the box.

All packaging software offers a way to embed a simple batch file inside the package, which should be the starting point for building the custom installation package. You should use a manufacturer's silent installations when available.

Warning Do *not* re-capture Office 2000; use the CIW and silent or non-interactive installation flags, and embed the resulting command inside the packaging software. An example of such a command is:

```
setup.exe TRANSFORMS="filename.mst" /qb-
```

Distributing to Users Who Do Not Have Local Administrator Permissions

You can implement Windows NT Workstation 4.0 with a locked-down environment, in which users' *Domain User* or *Power User* permissions do not enable them to install software.

Most enterprise-level software that provides distribution also provides a service that can install a package on behalf of the user. The service is installed in one of three ways, typically:

1. During rollout of the distribution software.

2. Through an administrative console that accesses machines remotely.

3. With a utility that remotely installs services, such as RSERVICE.EXE, provided in Supplement 3 of the *Microsoft Windows NT Resource Kit*.

The service typically uses one of two accounts: a *local administrator* account created and defined by the administrator or the package installation, or the machine's *system* account. The *system* account offers better security, because if the *local administrator* password account is breached you have to update passwords across multiple workstations.

Rules for using this feature vary with the software, but the concepts are the same: make a package that includes a setting that forces the service to install it once it reaches the workstation. For instance, the WinInstall scheduler service has a special executable to which the administrator passes the package name. This call tells the service to go into action, installing the identified package using administrative rights.

Experience shows that using the background services to take over for a user who does not have adequate rights has drawbacks that are particularly apparent when it comes to large package installations (such as Office 2000 Setup):

1. The services run a background operation, so the entire installation is silent. If users don't understand that the installation is continuing they often shut down prematurely or try to run the application—halting or seriously damaging the installation. The Office 2000 Setup switches allow you to use an Office command line that installs the software without user interaction but with a progress bar that informs users of the installation.

2. A service announces the beginning of the installation and keeps the user informed for a period that the installation is still executing, but the service usually drops out once the package command has been called, leaving the threads to execute in the background. Most software distribution services working with a batch file regard their job as complete once they call the batch: they do not track all the threads spawned by the initial command, which can be numerous for some packages. This creates a false impression that the package is complete, and users often try to reboot at this point.

3. Without progress bars, users grow uneasy.

4. You can build feedback around the beginning and end of the background installation, but it is often difficult to create a foreground message that remains throughout Setup. Services tend to operate in one mode—foreground or background—at a time, and it is not always easy or possible to pass useful information back to the foreground, where the user can see it.

If you get lucky and end up with a package that solves the first two problems by locking the keyboard and mouse, see the section on page 210 that describes how to edit the registry and autologon to complete the installation with the user locked out.

Unfortunately, none of these methods prevents users from simply hitting the power button once they discover the keyboard and mouse are frozen. This is easy to understand: it is unnerving to feel lost or locked out, and most users react to this frustration by cycling power. Educating users and telling them what to expect can help ensure the success of such operations. Rollback can usually rescue power cycling users, but there are places in the process where a power loss prevents rollback from returning the system to its original state.

To solve problems three and four, you can wrap the command inside a shell batch file, which, roughly, does this:

1. At the beginning of the file, issues the usual warnings and explanations of what is to come.

2. Starts a timer (the WAIT.EXE command or another utility).

3. Executes the background command that takes advantage of the service's permissions (depending on which distribution software is being used).

4. Issues a final message once the timer runs out, or generates a restart within the package.

This covers most situations, but it doesn't always do the trick because you have to guess what the worst-case installation time will be, and this can be hard to predict. Also, you have to instruct users to wait for a restart before assuming the installation is complete.

As packaging software grows more sophisticated, it offers more ways to send messages back to the foreground, where users can see them. Research products carefully and use this functionality if you can.

Mid-Size to Small Distribution Scenario: Basic Distribution and Scripting Methods

Smaller companies often can't afford to use services that take over the installation for the user, under an administrative context. This section describes distribution and scripting options for these groups.

Distributing to Users Who Do Not Have Local Administrator Permissions

If you want to keep users locked down on Windows NT workstations, giving them only *User Domain* rights, then you face this problem each time you roll out software. You have two alternatives that are basically free.

You can use SU.EXE, which you can get in the *Windows NT Resource Kit*, Supplement 3, or from the Microsoft Web site. Similar to the UNIX SuperUser concept, SU.EXE runs as a service under Windows NT 4.0 and enables certain commands under the *SU* account privileges. There are other freeware and shareware products that perform this and similar tasks, and you can use them just as easily, distributing them remotely with the RSERVICE.EXE utility (described on page 218). The biggest challenge usually is getting the service installed before deploying Office. You can install RSERVICE.EXE remotely using a script, but severe security problems can result if anyone finds and misuses the account password used by these services.

The second method is actually the same one used in the SMS Installer script: Setup disables the client computer's keyboard and mouse, then automatically logs on as administrator and proceeds without interruption. The disabled input devices prevent users from taking over the system while the client is logged in with administrative rights. Because user accounts cannot disable the keyboard and mouse, you have to arrange a task and schedule it so that it does not kick off at an awkward or inconvenient time. Generally, you run it at night and tell users to leave their computers on when they go home.

Using a Service to Install for the User: Three Examples

If a service to handle software installations under another set of permissions is not already available, you have to get one on the Windows NT workstations. Often, you have to go to each computer, log in with a user account with local administrator rights (at least), and install the service. Three services (described below) can help you deploy Office 2000 without giving a local administrator password to users who do not have permission to install software. Each offers a slightly different approach, and each can be used alone or in combination with others.

When users cannot install software or services, you have to install the service on each user's machine. Once the service is in place, you can send a script that uses the service's account permissions to install Office 2000, and can continue to use the service for any updates that require administrator privileges.

Schedule Service

You can enable the Schedule service on all computers. You can do it one computer at a time remotely: run REGEDT32.EXE, open the remote machine's registry keys, and navigate to this key on the remote machine:

HKLM\System\CurrentControlSet\Services\Schedule\Start

Set it to **2** to start the service automatically. The next time the user reboots and logs on, the Schedule service runs and continues to start up automatically through multiple reboots. You can also run the NETSVC.EXE utility (from the *Windows NT Resource Kit*) and start the service immediately and remotely with the command:

```
Netsvc Schedule \\remote_machine_name / start
```

If you have too many machines to enable the Schedule service manually, run the batch file (SCHDRUN.BAT) that uses REG.EXE (also from the Resource Kit) to change service's state from *manual* to *automatic*, then uses netsvc to start it immediately. You have to enter a computer name, (for example, *schdrun.bat computername*) that is substituted in the batch for the %1 variable:

```
echo y | reg delete
HKLM\System\CurrentControlSet\Services\Schedule\Start \\%1
reg add HKLM\System\CurrentControlSet\Services\Schedule\Start=2
REG_DWORD \\%1
netsvc schedule \\%1 /start
```

You can call the batch file from a FOR statement if you are running the remote installations on Windows NT. FOR is a powerful utility, worth investigating for use in Windows NT scripting (type **for /?** at the command line to get a good explanation of the options with this command). FOR can in turn take a list of machine names from a text file. In the example below the text file is called WKSLIST.TXT:

```
FOR /F %%i IN (wkslist.txt) DO schdrun.bat %%i
```

Note that within a batch file, the %i variable has to have a second percentage mark (*%%i*); in a straight command line, outside of a batch, it would be simply *%i*.

WKSLIST.TXT would look something like this, with computer names separated by carriage returns:

```
COMPUTER1
COMPUTER2
COMPUTER3
```

SU (SuperUser) Service

You can use the AT command to extend the schdrun.bat script so that it installs other services. Here is an example that works for SU.EXE.

```
copy suss.* \\%1\c$\winnt\system32
FOR /F "eol=E tokens=5 delims= " %%i in ('time') do at \\%1 %%i
"c:\winnt\regedit.exe /s c:\winnt\system32\suss.reg"
wait 120
shutdown \\%1 /R /T:120 "Please Close All Applications Immediately,
System Must Shut Down Now"
```

SUSS.REG is a straight export of the service key HKLM\System\CurrentControlSet \Services\SU from a working system. You could also accomplish this by running the **suss –install** command.

Shutdown (another resource kit utility) allows you to shut down other computers remotely, if you have domain administrator status.

Once the services are in place, you can schedule a command similar to the one below, which applies Office Setup to the *Administrator* account—just as it would if installers had to come by and apply the software:

```
Su username "setup.exe /qn /wait TRANSFORMS=filename.mst
REBOOT=ReallySuppress /x"
```

The password for the *username* account could either be piped in (via a < USERNAME.TXT) at the end of the command, or you can give users a temporary password to an account. When the installation is complete, the account can remove itself from the Local Administrators group to prevent security problems, but it retains its Administrative status until auto log off is complete.

Remote Command Service

With RCMDSVC and RCMD.EXE you can log in remotely and execute a package on behalf of the user. This service can substitute for more sophisticated commercial software distribution packages when you are installing Office in smaller environments. It uses installation routines similar to SU.EXE. You can touch machines to install this service or use the Schedule service to install remotely.

Locking the Keyboard and Automatically Logging In as Administrator

Because users cannot disable their keyboard and mouse, you must use the Schedule Service to arrange for this service. This section discusses how to run this type of installation with a batch file.

The batch file uses the same basic methods as O2KSETUP.IPF (the SMS Installer script from the ORK) and it uses utilities from the *Windows NT Resource Kit,* such as REG.EXE.

First, to disable the keyboard and mouse, you have to be in a valid service account with administrative rights, or you have to run the batch through the Schedule service. The commands passed to the service you decide on should look like the batch listed below. Second, the system reboots and automatically logs in with an Administrator account. You can accomplish this with a registry edit that allows auto logon with specific parameters (account, password, and so on). Third, the system starts the Office 2000 installation (here called O2KINST.BAT). When that is complete, O2KINST.BAT re-enables the keyboard and mouse and reboots one last time, using the shutdown command. As shutdown is counting down, O2KINST.BAT removes itself from the Startup group.

 Here is an example of core commands that would need to be in the first batch, preparing for O2KINST.BAT.

```
:: Disable Keyboard and Mouse
Reg update HKLM\System\CurrentControlSet\Services\Mouclass\Start=4
Reg update HKLM\System\CurrentControlSet\Services\Kbdclass\Start=4
:: Enable Auto Logon the next time we boot
Reg update
"HKLM\Software\Microsoft\Windows NT\CurrentVersion\Winlogon
\AutoAdminLogon=1
Reg update
"HKLM\Software\Microsoft\Windows NT\CurrentVersion\Winlogon
\DefaultDomainName=domainname
Reg update
"HKLM\Software\Microsoft\Windows NT\CurrentVersion\Winlogon
\DefaultPassword=password
Reg update "HKLM\Software\Microsoft\Windows NT\CurrentVersion\Winlogon
\DefaultUsername=username
:: Disable the welcome screen (which can halt the script)
move %windir%\welcome.exe %windir%\welcome.old
:: Copy the o2kinst.bat file (in which the call to setup.exe for Office
    2000 exists) to the Startup directory
copy o2kinst.bat "c:\winnt\profiles\all users\start
menu\programs\startup"
```

Common problem: auto logon doesn't work very well if this key is set to 1:

```
HKLM\Software\Microsoft\Windows NT\CurrentVersion\WinLogon
\DontDisplayLastUserName.
```

You an eliminate this problem by adding a **reg del** command to the batch, and restoring it at the end of the Office 2000 installation script.

O2KINST.BAT might look like this:

```
Start /wait \\server\share\setup.exe /qn /wait TRANSFORMS=filename.mst
REBOOT=ReallySuppress /x
:: Enable Keyboard and Mouse
Reg update HKLM\System\CurrentControlSet\Services\Mouclass\Start=4
Reg update HKLM\System\CurrentControlSet\Services\Kbdclass\Start=4

:: Enable Auto Logon the next time we boot
Reg update
"HKLM\Software\Microsoft\Windows NT\CurrentVersion\Winlogon
\AutoAdminLogon=0
Echo y | Reg del
"HKLM\Software\Microsoft\Windows NT\CurrentVersion\Winlogon
\DefaultDomainName=domainname
Echo y | Reg del
"HKLM\Software\Microsoft\Windows NT\CurrentVersion\Winlogon
\DefaultPassword=password
Echo y | Reg del
"HKLM\Software\Microsoft\Windows NT\CurrentVersion\Winlogon
\DefaultUsername=username

:: Enable the welcome screen (which can halt the script)
move %windir%\welcome.old %windir%\welcome.exe

::
shutdown /l /r /t:120 "Shutting down now, Installation is Complete"

:: Delete the o2kinst.bat file (in which the call to setup.exe for
     Office 2000 exists) to the Startup directory
del "c:\winnt\profiles\all users\start
menu\programs\startup\o2kinst.bat"
```

Advertising the Windows Installer Package

Another way to elevate privileges on a Windows NT 4.0 computer is to advertise the package to the workstation (by running Setup with the **/jm** switch) and let the Windows Installer perform the installation the first time the client attempts to use an Office 2000 component.

You can specify transform files in the command line, which speeds up installations when you have to go to each computer. For example: *setup.exe /jm data1.msi /t officestation.mst* installs Office using the **Office station** transform file.

Issues: the advertisement requires *administrative* privileges, and Internet Explorer (not a Windows Installer package) requires *user* privileges for installation.

Using Windows System Policies

You can use local system polices to elevate the privileges of the Windows Installer permanently.

Under the local Windows NT registry: HKEY_LOCAL_MACHINE\Software \Microsoft\Windows\Installer, setting the value of **AlwaysInstallElevated = 1** enables the Windows Installer to install applications using elevated privileges. You can also set this value with the Windows Installer *.ADM file. When the value is set, you install to computers running Windows NT 4.0 the same as to those running Windows 9*x*.

Steps to Creating Custom Scripts

Basic steps:

1. Decide what type of feedback users will require and whether they will have choices during installation or the installation will be completely non-interactive (necessary if using one of the services, or if the keyboard and mouse are disabled).

2. Create the final script file. Keep in mind the following:

   a. Windows 9*x* and Windows NT syntax differences. For instance, the FOR statement does more in Windows NT than it does in Windows 9*x*. If you are developing the batch for multiple operating systems, use the lowest common denominator.

   b. You can use *Windows NT Resource Kit* utilities such as IFMEMBER.EXE to branch out in one batch and apply different configurations to different departments (the user's group becomes the deciding factor).

   c. If you want to target only Windows NT workstations, consider using the IF statement, which can take input from a file in Windows NT (for instance, a list of workstations or usernames) and thus can sort which users get which configuration.

The basic batch file below provides one possible approach to such a script. You have to set the source (in *italics*) to the proper server, insert the share names for your environment at the top of the batch, and substitute suitable .MST filenames at each SETUP.EXE command line.

```
@echo off

set source=enter your source UNC here (ex: \\server\sharename\)

rem ensure batch file not triggered by double-click
  if "%1"=="" goto end_args

rem detect OS
  if "%OS%"=="Windows_NT" set start=
  if "%OS%"=="" set start=start /wait

rem set message to be displayed when product gets installed
  set product=Microsoft Office 2000 Premier
  set message=installation in progress.

rem setup detection
  if "%1"=="/TYPICAL" goto typical
  if "%1"=="/CUSTOM" goto custom
  if "%1"=="/MANUAL" goto manual
  if "%1"=="/UNINSTALL" goto uninstall
  goto end_args

:typical
  echo    -======- %product% %message% -======-
  %start% %source%setup.exe /qn /wait TRANSFORMS="AddFile.mst"
REBOOT=ReallySuppress /m off2000
  goto install_complete

:custom
  if .%2 == . goto end_notransform
  echo    -======- %product% %message% -======-
  %start% %source%setup.exe /qn /wait TRANSFORMS=%2
REBOOT=ReallySuppress /m off2000
  goto install_complete

:manual
  echo    -======- %product% %message% -======-
  %start% %source%setup.exe /wait TRANSFORMS="AddFile.mst"
REBOOT=ReallySuppress /m off2000
  goto install_complete

:uninstall
  echo    -======- %product% %message% -======-
  %start% %source%setup.exe /qn /wait REBOOT=ReallySuppress /x
  goto install_complete
```

(continued)

```
:install_complete
  if Errorlevel 3011 GOTO end_install_fail
  if Errorlevel 3010 GOTO reboot
  if Errorlevel 1605 GOTO end_install_fail
  if Errorlevel 1604 GOTO reboot
  if Errorlevel 1 GOTO end_install_fail
  if Errorlevel 0 GOTO reboot
  if Errorlevel -2147024891 GOTO end_install_fail

:reboot
  if "%1"=="/UNINSTALL" goto end
  reboot.exe
  goto end

:end_notransform
  echo ERROR: An .MST file must be specified with a custom setup.
  pause
  goto end
:end_args
  echo ERROR: Command line parameters are not set correctly.
  pause
  goto end
:end_install_fail
  echo ERROR: Installation failed.  Check the installation logs for
    more details.
  pause
  goto end
:end
```

Tip Provide users with as much feedback as possible; use the progress indicator, alerts, and echoed text in the batch files.

Distribution Media

If you don't have access to a software distribution vehicle, you have other options: the network, CD, portable hard disks, and removable hard disks. Network installation is common, but large suites generate considerable network load and can take a long time, especially over WAN links, impelling many administrators to choose one or more of the other methods. Benefits and disadvantages of the methods are summarized below.

Network Share

The most common choice is a simple batch file that installs Office 2000 from the network, delivering it to users through e-mail or a Web site. Installation instructions can be passed over the phone, on paper, in e-mail, and so on. You generally will want the batch file to run a completely self-contained set of operations—not stopping to ask the user questions or offer options.

One company MCS worked with used profiles. When users logged on to the Windows NT domain, some were automatically directed to an installation Web server which prompted them for username to verify installation, checked system requirements, and began installation. When the installation was complete, the program removed the user from the installation group and informed the manager that installation was complete.

A more detailed installation process flow is illustrated in Figure 7.6.

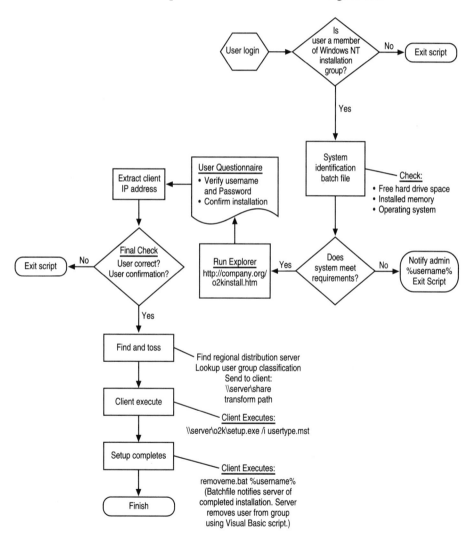

Figure 7.6   Office 2000 installation flow process.

Distribution Server

Administrative installation requires about 500 MB. You can distribute to multiple network locations by making a single installation and copying the files, or by performing an administrative installation on each network share point.

Distribution server performance is sometimes a concern. At one installation, testing showed that each server could service 50 clients simultaneously at LAN speed. The team created a plan and a schedule to ensure that no more than 75 users received Office 2000 on the same day.

CD-ROM Media

CD-ROM is usually the most cost-effective, familiar, and portable delivery mechanism. You can set up CDs so the autorun features of the latest CD drives automatically open up the Setup screen when the user loads the CD. CD-ROM recorders are becoming cheaper every day, and CDs run less than U.S.$1 apiece. The basic Office installation fits on a single disc.

CDs for Remote Users

At one company, many remote users use the corporate network, so it was expected that some of them would install Office 2000 from shared network distribution points. The team established a corporate Office intranet site, which provided information and downloads, and made it possible to schedule installation, verify versions, and so on. The team made sure that:

■ The administrative share points where Office 2000 was installed were *hidden* using the *$* after the share name. This made them invisible to normal browsing.

■ The intranet site was kept very simple. Its purpose was to guide users to the correct version of Office 2000 with a two-question wizard that verified the user name and confirmed installation. When the user was verified, the site detected the client IP address and had it launch Office 2000 Setup from the proper location with the correct transform. This method provided remote users with the same installation they would receive from the CD, as long as they indicated that the machine they were using was also used to access the network via dial-in, or used offline.

Scheduling was simple and automated. Department managers coordinated the period for Office 2000 upgrades and created and published a schedule that showed which users were to be upgraded. On the scheduled date, a simple logon script launched the client's Web browser and loaded the corporate Office 2000 Web site. Users followed a brief questionnaire and Office 2000 was installed.

Portable Hard Disks

Typically, these are connected to the back of the machine via a SCSI or a slower but more common parallel cable. If SCSI connections are available, a hard disk-to-hard disk installation is fastest by far. If installers have to carry the hard-disk pack to each station and plug a new parallel cable into the back of each machine, the process is slow and labor-intensive.

Removable Disks

These are as time consuming to connect as hard disks, but are generally more portable and less fragile. Iomega's Zip drives are too small for a typical Office installation, but Jazz and SyQuest drives (at 1 GB and larger) are more than adequate. Speed can be similar to CDs but it depends on whether you have SCSI or parallel connection.

Other Useful Utilities and Commands

In constructing a customized script for a non-SMS environment, check out the utilities available in the *Microsoft Windows NT 4.0 Resource Kit* and the Microsoft Web site. These (and other free ones on the Internet) provide options for performing branching based on information gathered by the utility. They are especially useful when you have mixed Windows 9*x* and Windows NT environments, and the lowest common denominator (Windows 95 command line options) can't do what the script needs to do.

IFMEMBER.EXE

This determines if the current user is a member of a specified group or groups in a Windows NT domain. In a typical Office 2000 installation this command can help you match Office 2000 configurations to groups. For instance, you can install one for the Accounting department (including Access) and another for the salespeople (adding all clip art). You would do this by creating two .MST files (ACCTG.MST and SALES.MST), and then using IFMEMBER.EXE in the batch file to kick off the appropriate Office 2000 installation, depending on which group a user belongs to.

For instance, the simple batch below would handle both groups of users and would exit if a user did not belong to either.

```
Ifmember Sales
If not errorlevel 1 goto ACCTG
setup.exe /qn /wait TRANSFORMS=sales.mst REBOOT=ReallySuppress /x

:ACCTG
Ifmember Accounting
If not errorlevel 1 goto FINISH
setup.exe /qn /wait TRANSFORMS=sales.mst REBOOT=ReallySuppress /x

:FINISH
exit
```

AT, WinAT

The AT (Schedule) service runs under system account privileges and is built into Windows NT and Windows 9*x*. WINAT.EXE is a simpler GUI utility that does everything AT.EXE does when you enter it at the MS-DOS command line. With the service and the tools you can schedule any task under the System Account privilege.

To use the AT service, you have to enable the Schedule service so that it loads automatically each time a computer is restarted—which is not always the case, especially with Windows NT. Use Server manager to check workstations, determine that the Schedule service is set to *Automatic* load, and verify it is started. Or you could use rservice to gather information on the status of services running on remote machines, then drop the results into a log you can check later.

XSET.EXE

XSET.EXE is a shareware utility that offers a lot more functionality at the MS-DOS command line for setting environmental variables, calculating and manipulating results, then branching to subroutines. Two of Xset's tools are particularly useful: it can calculate (it has a full set of mathematical functions) and it can capture and manipulate strings into environmental variables that can be called out later in a batch.

Use of Environmental Variables

Windows NT and Windows 9*x* have numerous environmental variables you can use, but be aware of these two limitations:

- A lot of Windows 9*x* workstations have limited memory set aside for this kind of effort. It you use variables too heavily, an error is returned, advising that you open up more memory for storage. This requires a reboot, but once you do it the batch usually continues. You are more likely to hit this limit in Windows 9*x* computers than in Windows NT computers.

- Windows NT and Windows 9*x* share many *but not all* variables. Windows NT, for example, has an %OS% variable that Windows 9*x* does not. Rule of thumb: to determine OS, check for a Windows NT variable—if it isn't found, the script can proceed on the assumption that the OS is Windows 9*x*.

RSERVICE.EXE

RSERVICE.EXE was built to install services remotely, and it works better than command-line utilities such as INSTSRV.EXE. For one thing, it includes definition of accounts the service must run under. It was originally part of the *Microsoft SMS Resource Kit*, but you can now download it free from the Microsoft Web site.

Complete Replacement of Existing Software and/or Hardware

This section discusses complete-system deployment, focusing on Windows NT 4.0 and Office 2000 rollout. Usually these are delivered new by a manufacturer, and users are scheduled for complete hardware replacement. Sometimes, existing software is slated for replacement with a new installation of operating system and Office 2000.

This is always the cleanest and least expensive way to install Office 2000— sometimes it is the *only* way to ensure a fool-proof installation.

Even if you plan to install over the existing operating system and software, you should read this section to find out how to rebuild a system from scratch rapidly and reliably. Older systems can have numerous problems that complicate an upgrade. MCS experience shows the most common are undetected viruses, deeply fragmented disks, and registries full of unused and misleading entries left over from botched installations or uninstallations. You can address these problems by carefully preparing the systems, running anti-virus with the latest signatures, making sure files are clean and contiguous with de-fragmentation software, and running registry cleaning utilities.

 Rule of thumb: Regardless of how you plan the upgrade, it is always a good idea to have a fall-back position from which you can build the system up again from scratch to a standard configuration as rapidly as possible.

Luckily, recent utilities and methods have made it easier to roll out Windows NT and Windows 98—and with them you can use the same noninteractive installation of Office 2000 for users who receive in-place upgrades.

Operating System and Applications Setup

The following sections focus on MCS experience at one company that wanted to deploy Windows NT 4.0 and a locally installed version of Office 2000. As part of this plan, they stopped all Windows 98 deployment so that they could standardize on Windows NT 4.0. Procedures vary slightly between these operating systems but the concepts are much the same—including use of a system preparation utility and optional use of disk duplication utilities. For more information on these deployment methods, check out the white papers and other resources at http://www.microsoft.com/ntworkstation/deploy/resources.asp.

 Note   Problems with duplicated Security Identifiers (SIDs) made it impossible to clone (that is, bit-copy) Windows NT. It now can be done, using Sysprep, a Microsoft approved system-preparation tool released in November 1998.

System Preparation Tool (Sysprep)

Sysprep allows you to use disk duplication software to capture a completely configured workstation, with applications already installed and customized to the site's specifications. You can set up one command to apply the image, and upon rebooting, the new system recognizes that it has been cloned. Sysprep generates a new, unique SID, reboots one last time, and the installation is complete.

This has huge implications for deployment of large applications such as Office 2000 to brand new systems. MCS has found that it normally takes 10–15 minutes to apply a bit-copy image of a Sysprepped Windows NT and a typical suite of applications (off a CD). Unattended installations from CD run 30–40 minutes. And you save more time and effort because the method eliminates the need to prepare a hard disk by partitioning (traditionally with fdisk) and formatting.

You can request Sysprep for Windows NT 4 by going to http://www.microsoft.com /ntworkstation/deployment/sysprep.asp, navigating to the registration page, and entering the address to which you want the utility sent. It comes with documentation that fully explains how to use it.

Unlike the classic unattended Windows NT installation, Sysprep provides no auto-detection of existing video card or NIC. If your environment has many types of video card types and NICs, it is hard to apply images that will not elicit errors due to the mismatched hardware configuration embedded in Windows NT. The company faced this problem, and the next section describes how MCS worked around hardware variation while using disk duplication to deploy.

How to Use Sysprep Effectively

Sysprep typically is used with one or both of these disk duplication methods:

- **Disk Duplication Software (also called bit copy software)**. Disk duplication software that can handle the Windows NT NTFS file system includes Symantec's Ghost, and PowerQuest's DriveImage, which allows you to write an *image* of a hard disk to a file that can later be restored to another hard disk from all sorts of media: CD-ROM, removable disk, external hard drive, or network shares. Several products allow a central server to multi-cast the bits to workstations in one pass.

- **Disk Duplicators (hardware)**. MCS customers have reported that it took only five minutes to duplicate 6-GB disks, four at a time, on some of this equipment. You have to remove hard disks from the machines, connect them to the duplicator, then re-bolt them inside the system. If you have hard disks delivered separately, this is a reasonable option. This is fast: hardware duplication (unlike software duplication) is not influenced by how much data is on the original disk.

The company bought disk duplication software, so MCS had to work out an approach that dealt with the variety of hardware in the field. After determining there were few if any SCSI controllers to consider (all systems were IDE-based), MCS decided to create a *generic* image of Windows NT and Office 2000.

Creating a Suitable Image

Basic steps:

1. Install Windows NT as site specifications require, on a basic machine.
2. Use the customized silent installation to apply Office 2000 (using the site's transform file). This is works better than manual installation because its choices are automated, so you know you are getting consistent images.
3. Add any other software required by all users.

Some things *must not be done* as part of the configuration planned for imaging— they must be done *after* a cloned system logs in for the first time. The list below describes these tasks and discusses command-line utilities you can use after installation to achieve the same result.

1. **Do not join a domain**. Instead, join a *workgroup*. After installation you can use the NETDOM.EXE utility Supplement 3 of the *Windows NT Resource Kit* (NTRK) to join a domain.
2. **Do not add user accounts to the local SAM in User Manager.** After installation you can use the NTRK ADDUSERS.EXE utility (or similar tools, available on the Internet).
3. **Do not apply file permissions.** After installation you can use the NTRK utility XCACLS.EXE.

After installation you can perform all these tasks with a batch file that you insert into the computer's Startup folder *before* imaging. The batch file runs the first time the computer is booted and logged on. The utilities mentioned above are just a few options for automating post-installation tasks; there are lots of others.

To enable any system, regardless of hardware, and to apply the image without generating errors, substitute these drivers:

1. **Video.** VGA Compatible video from the original list offered by Windows NT. Video cards that cannot load this low-end VGA driver are very rare.
2. **Network Interface Card.** MS Loopback Adapter. This serves as a placeholder to which protocols can bind.

Use this command to run Sysprep:

```
Sysprep company.inf
```

The company's .INF file contained something similar to the list below—answers to questions Sysprep normally asks a user when it senses it is running on a cloned machine for the first time. Note that, like the UNATTEND.TXT file used for a Windows NT non-interactive installation, this file is essentially just a series of answers to Setup questions.

```
[NT4Preinstall]
OemSkipEula = YES
ProductID = 123-4567890
FullName = "company"
OrgName = "org"
AdminPassword = "password"
OemBannerText= "Company Workstation Build 1.0"
```

When you have entered license information, make sure there is an MS-DOS boot disk in the floppy drive, then click **OK** to reboot. The system now is ready to be disk duplicated.

Run the disk duplication software or remove the hard disk to install it in the hardware duplicator unit. Follow the manufacturer's instructions.

For convenience, provide a place to run the disk duplication software and store the image by configuring a second hard disk or a second partition on the master system hard disk. Or you can configure the MS-DOS boot disk with network drivers to enable connection to a network share that contains the disk duplication software and enough room to store the image.

Applying the Image

You can apply the resulting image to any number of machines. At this company, MCS chose generic video and adapter drivers, which would come up on any of the configured computers, so in the cloned system installation instructions they included steps to replace the video and NIC drivers with models appropriate to the user's hardware.

To apply the image and work with the newly cloned machine:

1. The installer needs a boot disk with CD-ROM drivers suitable for the target machine and the custom CD with the images upon it.
2. Insert the disks into the machine and reboot.
3. Depending on the type of machine, the installer either responds to choices presented by the MS-DOS boot disk or types in various commands.
4. After you enter the final command, the disk duplication software will begin copying the image to the new machine.

Distribution Methods for Windows NT 4.0 and Office 2000

There are two common methods for getting a customized Windows NT and Office 2000 desktop image to users' machines: working with a central deployment location (called the Central Warehouse in the scenario on the following page) and dealing with situations where regions or departments far from the main office get their own equipment and must deal with the installations as the systems arrive.

Distribution Media

Regardless of whether you use bit-copy software or scripting, choose distribution media carefully. Consider these advantages and disadvantages:

CD-ROM

Lots of advantages. Downloading a bit-copy image from CD is only slightly slower than using a hard disk (*if* SMARTDRV.EXE is loaded properly from the MS-DOS boot disk). Depending on CIW choices, it usually takes less than ten minutes to download Windows NT with the Office suite. Compact discs are cheap, drives are everywhere, and the discs are easy to carry from site to site.

If you want to use CDs, consider investing in a good CD-ROM recorder. MCS has found recorders to be fickle, although some systems perform solidly and consistently. Keep these criteria to keep in mind:

- Get a recorder with a healthy amount of built-in buffer memory to avoid *overruns* (buffers exceeded by the flow of data), which abort the burning of an image.

- Use *mainstream* software approved by the manufacturer. When evaluating products, research them in an Internet Usenet group to see if they generate a lot of complaints.

- Dedicate a system to the task. Recorders don't tolerate interruptions in data streams, so don't use a machine subject to other network or application requests.

External Hard Disks

If every system has a standardized SCSI controller with an external interface, and external hard disks are available for use by a team of installers, you might consider this method. Hard disk-to-hard disk is still the fastest way to apply images. You might also be able to use a parallel port solution. Whichever you use, make sure MS-DOS boot disks are available with the proper ASPI or other drivers to access the device.

Removable Media

Products such as Iomega's Jazz or Zip drives may be good options for certain sites. Make sure MS-DOS boot disks are available.

Network Installation

There are two methods, and before choosing either you need to consider carefully whether the deployment traffic will justify possible drops in productivity.

- **Standard network share for source.** Images are stored on a central share, which end user systems access after booting from an MS-DOS disk with the proper network drivers.

- **Multi-casting technologies.** Several disk duplication manufacturers have products that allow you to launch installation of several computers simultaneously through the network—without generating traffic to each computer.

Distribution Scenarios

Central Warehouse

In this scenario, the vendor delivers all new hardware to a central site with the custom configuration of OS/Office 2000 and additional applications already installed. Following the custom installation, systems are packed up again and delivered to local and remote-site desktops.

Based on experience with this model, MCS has developed recommendations:

- **Equip the setup room properly.** Set up in a central location large enough to store boxes as they arrive, with plenty of protected electrical power, and with sturdy tables that have access to power. At each station, set up a permanent monitor, keyboard, and mouse.

- **(Optional) Set up network.** Provide a network drop at each station, attached to a hub that is isolated from the production network. In addition, build a server dedicated to the deployment that will provide images and other deployment files. The server can have a single processor but it needs plenty of memory. High speed 100 Megabits/sec network interface cards (NICs) are highly desirable, especially if all distribution of images will go through the network.

- **Standardize hardware.** Order large blocks of the same hardware and stick to one model, if at all possible. If you can't stick with one model, install a standard NIC and video card in all models.

- **(Optional) Set up a multi-casting server.** If you use bit-copy software, consider setting up the multi-casting server described earlier. Study the software manufacturer's documentation. This requires a robust and reliable network setup to avoid complications and halts. Remember, a typical Windows NT and Office installation usually sends more than 250 MB of data over the wire, not counting additional software required by all users. Field studies show that you can load five clients simultaneously in roughly 20-30 minutes, but this varies considerably with network configuration and the server/client hardware speed.

Distributed Regions

In this scenario, the vendor delivers hardware directly to the field with all customized software pre-installed from the image you supply.

Based on experience with this model, MCS has developed recommendations:

- **Use CD-ROMs.** If drives are available on all user systems, record custom CDs with the disk duplication software images. If not, create dedicated network shares at each site. You can also consider using other removable or portable media, such as external hard disks. If your network can't tolerate deployment traffic, use CDs: they are the most portable and familiar means.

- **Create and provide the boot disks.** Send each site a boot disk with the appropriate CD drivers. A popular one such as OAKCDROM.SYS can cover most drives. If you install it from network shares, create a boot disk with network drivers for each NIC in the system.

- **Use a generic image if necessary.** If you have in-place hardware standards, build to them when you create the original images. Otherwise, make one master image that is generic in terms of drivers: VGA Compatible for video, MS Loopback Adapter drivers for the network adapter.

- **Limit choices for installers.** Use command line switches so that a single command installs an image. If several images are available, present users with clear choices on a menu. Put the menu commands on the boot disk provided with the CD. Users might have to perform their own installations, so simplify and limit steps wherever possible—every choice is an opportunity to make a mistake.

C H A P T E R   8

Deploying Outlook 2000

Managing and scheduling messages and contacts—critical for most enterprises—can be handled by users and organizations through the Outlook 2000 messaging infrastructure. This chapter explains how to plan, execute, and optimize Outlook 2000 deployment; it assumes that you have read Chapter 4, "Customizing an Office 2000 Installation," and Chapter 5, "User Settings."

What You'll Find in This Chapter

- How to best deploy Outlook 2000 before, during, or after deploying Office 2000.

- How to best plan the stages of your deployment.

- How to avoid common migration and deployment issues.

- How to best use the Custom Installation Wizard to deploy Outlook 2000.

Outlook 2000 Deployment and Migration Strategies

Outlook 2000 can function as a standalone messaging application or as an integrated component of the Office 2000 suite. You can deploy it before, after, or with Office 2000. Each method requires a slightly different deployment path.

The Office Resource Kit (ORK), available at http://www.microsoft.com/office/ork, or on CD, contains the Office Profile Wizard, the Custom Installation Wizard, and other utilities and tools that help deploy Outlook 2000 successfully. Specific tools are covered in detail later in this chapter.

Note   ORK tools are added and updated regularly. Check the ORK Toolbox to make sure you are using the latest versions.

Anticipating Schedule+ and Calendar Migration Issues

The first step in formulating a deployment strategy is to investigate potential migration issues. For example, are you upgrading from an Exchange client? If so, you have to understand *how* Outlook handles scheduling differently.

Outlook 2000 supports legacy Schedule+ files or newer Outlook calendar files, since enterprises occasionally prefer to retain legacy technology. If you want to ease into Outlook 2000, you can take advantage of the fact that it does not delete the original Schedule+ files to migrate Schedule+ files and not delete them until later.

If you plan to migrate users in phases, you need to identify groups that share calendar information and move them together—especially if group members administer each other's calendar information (that is, are in *delegate relationships*) and use automatic resource scheduling. Under Outlook 2000, Schedule+ users can read Outlook information but cannot modify an Outlook user's calendar. To compensate for these restrictions, you can migrate in this order:

- Upgrade users in delegate relationships at the same time, regardless of their workgroups. Members of delegate relationships must be able to open each other's calendar information, which requires that they use the same client and backend.

- If possible, upgrade all members of a workgroup at the same time.

- Upgrade users first, then upgrade resource accounts, such as conference rooms.

- During the Outlook upgrade, you must decide to whether to continue using the Schedule+ calendar or upgrade to the Outlook Calendar, which offers more features (such as Outlook Today) and is of course integrated in Outlook. Continuing to use Schedule+ can confuse users because Outlook still displays its own calendar module. You should avoid using Schedule+ *unless* people need to share their calendars with non-Outlook users who cannot be upgraded to Outlook 2000.

 You can use the Custom Installation Wizard (CIW) to configure Outlook 2000 so that it imports Schedule+ data automatically, by adding this key:

```
HKEY_CURRENT_USER\Software\Microsoft\Office\9.0\Outlook\Import
Value Name: ImportDetection
Value Type: DWORD
Value Data:
1 = Prompt user to import Schedule+ information
2 = Import Schedule+ information without prompting user
```

The first time a user launches Outlook, this occurs:

1. Outlook looks for Schedule+ data for the Exchange user's mailbox. If it finds none, it takes no further action.

2. If it finds Schedule+ data, it prompts the user to convert the data or it automatically converts it (depending on the ImportDetection value). At this point, Outlook copies the user's schedule data to Schedimp0.scd in the user's local Temp directory.

3. Outlook then imports the Schedimp0.scd file to the user's Outlook mailbox, moving the user's Schedule+ contacts, appointments, and tasks into the appropriate Outlook Contacts, Calendar, and Tasks folders. It displays a status indicator during this process.

 Note Outlook does not migrate Schedule+ permissions; the user has to do this manually on the Calendar folder, which, by default, has no permissions.

4. After importing the Schedule+ data, Outlook deletes the registry ImportDetection key and leaves the .SCD file in the Temp directory, so it can be used for recovery if a problem arises.

5. The user first verifies that the data was imported correctly and then can run Microsoft Outlook with the /CleanSchedPlus parameter to permanently delete the Schedule+ data.

You should not permanently delete Schedule+ files until you are sure the data is no longer needed by any users. Normally, you schedule deletion for a specified date after deployment; waiting helps avoids issues such as deleting files of users on vacation or who do not convert immediately.

Deployment Guidelines

For a large-scale deployment, the Custom Installation Wizard (CIW) is the main tool but not the only one. Before customizing Outlook 2000, you should map out a rollout path. The steps below develop a typical rollout path.

Step 1 – Select the Deployment Share

First, select a deployment share—a CD drive or one or more servers—to serve as the center of the Outlook 2000 deployment. If you plan to deploy Outlook separately from Office, your choice will be influenced by whether you want to run all of your installations from the same shares or different ones.

For server-based installation, you have two options. The first is to put Office in one folder on the server and the standalone version of Outlook into another. This uses server space for Outlook twice (once for Office and once for Outlook) but makes it easier to keep track of the setup and customization files. A disadvantage is that it puts two copies of MSO9.DLL on the client, and this file can be loaded into memory more than once if a user runs both Outlook and another Office application.

The other option is to put administrative installations of both Office and Outlook into the same share. The advantage is that this option does not duplicate files on the server so users can't end up with more than one copy of MS09.DLL. This method requires you to take some extra steps, and you have to work a bit more to document things properly.

You can also create custom Outlook images on CD. For details on this method, see chapter 7, "Distributing Office 2000."

Step 2 – Initial Setup Installation

To begin testing the Office automated install process, you first have to install the main Setup files by running **Setup.exe /a** from the Outlook 2000 distribution medium and directing Office or Outlook to use the share location created earlier. This step is critical for a large organization as it *stamps* each install with the company name and the product license number.

Step 3 – Install the Deployment Tools

When Step 2 is complete, install the Office Resource Kit (ORK) from the distribution medium. It provides the CIW, the Office Profile Wizard (OPW), the Office Removal Wizard, and the Internet Explorer Administration Kit (IEAK), which you need to customize Internet Explorer 5. Be sure to visit the ORK Web site regularly to check for the latest versions of tools.

Step 4 – Create the Deployment Image

Use the CIW, the OPW, and any other tools you need to customize Outlook. For details on using tools, see Chapter 4, "Customizing an Office 2000 Installation," and Chapter 5, "User Settings." Select the settings for your Outlook 2000 configuration, including feature installation states, custom user settings, additional installation points, additional files, and removal policies.

Tip   You should set certain features, such as Collaboration Data Objects and Electronic Forms Designer Support, as *Run From My Computer*. They cannot be *Installed on First Use* and are needed for most messaging solutions.

If you create multiple transform (.MST) files for multiple custom installation types, give each one a *functional* name. For example, if you deploy based on functional unit and there are separate transforms for Accounting and Human Resources, call the transform files OFC2ACCT.MST and OFC2HR.MST. You are not restricted to 8.3 names, but they make it easier to access .MST files from a batch file.

You should also record the Product Code for the transform (right-click the transform file and click on **Properties**), which can help you with maintenance and troubleshooting. In large organizations, users often change departments and configurations; this can require multiple images and re-images, and you must properly label and track them throughout deployment.

You can also consider simplifying the deployment by using a transform and a non-interactive command line to automate the process so that users do not have to make choices. Once you have finished the customization and have built the transform file or files, you are ready to start testing.

Step 5 – Test the Deployment Image

Connect to the deployment share from a test machine and run the customized installation. After Setup is complete, reboot the system and check Outlook 2000 functionality and configuration. Best practice: create a deployment database log of the choices made in each transform and the file's effect on the environment. This information can be helpful as time goes on and version tracking becomes difficult.

Deploying Outlook with Office 2000

When you deploy Outlook with Office, you have to make sure that Outlook settings (including the profile and feature installation states) are properly configured for your environment. For example, the first time Outlook runs the user is asked to specify if Outlook is being used on the Internet or with Microsoft Exchange Server. When you customize your configuration, be sure to make this choice for your user.

Customizing the Outlook 2000 Installation

Chapter 4, "Customizing an Office 2000 Installation," explains how to use the CIW to create a transform file that customizes installation. The CIW displays a series of panes in which you make choices and create settings that determine how Office is deployed. Once you are past the third CIW pane, you can skip to any screen using the list in the upper right part of the pane. This section covers the panes that are of particular interest in customizing Outlook.

Pane 7 Set Feature Installation States lists installation options for each Office application. For Outlook 2000, you can set each feature to be **Run from My Computer**, **Run from Network**, **Installed on First Use**, or **Not Available**. Since e-mail is usually a primary communication tool, it's most common to install and run it from the local computer.

Pane 9 allows you to add custom installation files. This is where you can add content, including sample e-mail files or custom solutions.

Pane 14 Customize Outlook Installation Options (Figure 8.1) allows you to choose **Do not customize Outlook profile and account information** or **Customize Outlook profile and account information**. The first option uses a .PRF file if one is available or prompts the user for information. Because this requires that the registry be modified by a user or an automated process, this option is unavailable if the workstation is locked down (to prevent registry changes). The second option forces you to set default profile information for the user. During initial installation, Setup installs the information but does not remove or change an existing profile.

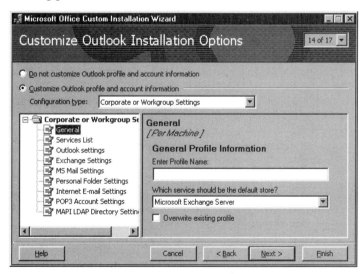

Figure 8.1   Customize Outlook Installation Options pane in the CIW.

The installation options in pane 14 also include choosing **Corporate or Workgroup** or **Internet Mail Only**. For **Corporate or Workgroup**, the first setting is the profile name and default information store location (on the server or in a .PST file). Next, you configure services. If users need Exchange Web Services for Outlook forms, then you need to set Outlook Settings. The Exchange Settings include mailbox name, server, .OST path, and .OAB path. You can also enter MS Mail Settings and Personal Folder Settings for users. **Corporate or Workgroup** also allows you to changes settings for Internet e-mail, POP3 Account, and MAPI LDAP Directory.

The main configurations for **Internet Only Settings** are similar to a corporate configuration. The configuration choices from **General Settings** involve **POP3 Account Settings** or **LDAP Account Settings**. Either one requires you to specify the relevant settings. Internet settings are much more limited.

Note   Whether you choose **Corporate or Workgroup** or **Internet Mail Only**, you can create settings with environmental variables. If you use these variables with Windows 9*x*, you need to define them with the **set** command in **autoexec.bat** and then reboot. Windows NT Workstation and Windows 2000 can process them without any modifications. Unfortunately, these options will not work with NEWPROF.EXE under Windows 9*x* because .PRF files ignore the **set** parameters.

Setting Outlook as the Default Messaging Application

The CIW allows you two ways to specify Outlook 2000 as the default application for e-mail, calendar needs, contacts, and news.

First, you can use pane 16, the CIW **Modify Setup Properties** pane (Figure 8.2).

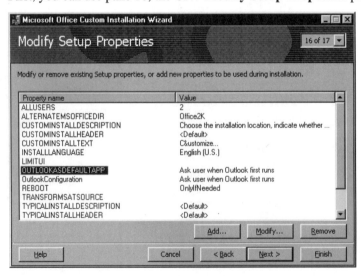

Figure 8.2   Modify Setup Properties pane in the CIW.

Click on **OUTLOOKASDEFAULTAPP** and then click **Modify.** In the Value list, choose between **All**; **Mail Only**; **Mail, Calendar, Contacts**; and **Ask user when Outlook first runs**. If no settings are modified, the first time a user runs Outlook they receive a prompt asking if Outlook should be used as the default messaging system. While you are in the **Modify Setup Properties** dialog, you can click on **LIMITUI** and change the value to **True**. This installs in silent mode, avoiding user interaction if at all possible. If the transform file does not specify settings requiring user input (such as profiles), the user is prompted to specify a setting.

You can also set Outlook as the default messaging manager through Internet Explorer 5 by clicking **Tools | Internet Options**, and then clicking the **Programs** tab and selecting Outlook.

Deploying Outlook Before Office 2000

To deploy Outlook before Office 2000, deploy it as a standalone application and then deploy the rest of Office. The general method is to perform an administrative installation and create separate custom configurations for Outlook and Office. This is described in the following sections.

Perform the Administrative Installation

To perform the administrative installation you can install the standalone Outlook product into its own directory or into the same directory as Office. Installing Outlook into its own directory is simpler but it wastes server space by storing Outlook twice, and it runs some files, such as shared code, twice on user systems.

To Install Outlook and Office in the Same Server Directory

Install the main Setup files by running **Setup.exe /a** from the Outlook 2000 distribution media. Specify a server share—the same administrative installation point you will use for the other Office applications.

Rename SETUP.EXE, SETUP.INI, DATA1.MSI, and AUTORUN.INF in the administrative installation directory and record the names in a deployment log. Names should be consistent because the renamed SETUP.EXE will look for an .INI file with the same prefix. For example, if you run OUTSETUP.EXE, it looks for OUTSETUP.INI.

Edit the renamed Outlook SETUP.INI file to point to the renamed transform, renamed core setup file, and renamed AUTORUN.INF file, or use command-line switches when you run Setup to point to the correct files.

Create Separate Custom Configurations for Outlook and Office

1. Modify the file PROFLWIZ.INI by commenting out all information that does not pertain to Outlook 2000. Save the file with a unique name. Modify it again, this time commenting out only the Outlook 2000 information, and save it with a unique name. Having two separate files allows you to capture settings for only those applications you are distributing.

Note   If you change the name of PROFLWIZ.INI, you have to use a command line to call the file. For details on command-line syntax, see Chapter 5, "User Settings," or see the ORK.

2. Use the CIW to create two transforms: one for Outlook and one for Office. Each has to include a different custom .OPS file created with the OPW and the customized PROFLWIZ.INI files. Make sure that the Office configuration *does not install Outlook* in any way.

For more information on deploying Outlook 2000 before Office 2000, see the topic "Deploying Outlook 2000 Before Office 2000" in the ORK.

Deploying Outlook After Office 2000

The basic method here is similar to the method for deploying after Office 2000: use one of the Office editions (Standard, Professional, Premium) to deploy the rest of Office, and then add the standalone version of Outlook later.

When you create your custom Office configuration, use Pane 7, Set Feature Installation States, to place Outlook in the **Not Available** state and choose **Hide**. This prevents Outlook from installing *and* prevents users from adding it later. Keep in mind that Hide is a permanent state—there is no way to change it.

Another important step in the CIW is to uncheck the box that removes **Microsoft Outlook 97 & 98** in the **Remove Previous Versions** dialog box. If you do not make this setting, Office installation may remove users' existing messaging accounts—recovering from this would mean significant messaging downtime.

Later, after Office has been deployed, you can deploy Outlook from the standalone version using the transform you created specifically for it.

Using the Custom Maintenance Wizard

The Custom Maintenance Wizard (CMW) is designed for making changes to the client computer after deployment. For example, suppose that six months after you deploy Outlook, the messaging group wants to deploy a custom contact management solution that depends on certain files being run from the local computer, which had an initial state of *Installed on First Use*. Use the CMW: it is designed to change the installation state of one or more features on a user's computer. It cannot affect user settings, and it cannot change Hide or Unhide in the Control Panel Add/Remove Programs user interface.

Run the CMW with the transform you used for the client installation. Make the changes, then run it non-interactively on each client with this new transform.

Since you can't use the CMW to make any changes to user settings, you shouldn't use it to add an entire application after an initial distribution of Office; you should instead add the standalone version. If you do decide to use the CMW to deploy an application, you should run the OPW with a specific .OPS file on the user computer to create user settings and change installation states. Keep in mind that any applications that were hidden in Control Panel Add/Remove Programs will remain hidden, making maintenance for them more difficult.

Pulling It All Together

To deploy Outlook 2000 successfully, you have to handle a number of variables. You can customize many features in Outlook, ranging from the Outlook Bar to Outlook Today, and from setting the encryption level to generating an automated profile. While deciding individual settings can be complex, you can follow some general guidelines (based on the issues and choices you have encountered so far) to maximize efficiency, minimize downtime and disruption, and allow you to profit from lessons learned in previous deployments.

Settle backend issues first. Upgrade Exchange Server or relevant e-mail servers before you deploy Outlook 2000. The back end is the foundation for later client support and may obviate any need to modify the client.

Create all necessary transform files and test their interoperability before you deploy. This ensures that configurations work the way you expect them to.

All things being equal, deploy Outlook 2000 with the other Office applications. It is simpler and cheaper to touch client computers only once.

Create profiles, defaults, shortcuts, migration applications, and silent or attended install options in a transform file—in other words, prevent users from having to make choices and IT from having to visit computers later to modify the configuration. A silent install is more desirable than one requiring user input.

Migrate and deploy clients in entire functional, geographic, and/or political units. Migration and deployment issues tend to focus on a closed system when all clients in a common unit are a part of the process.

Special Deployment and Migration Considerations

Along with general deployment and migration issues, some unique issues may arise based on your installed configurations. Some inevitably require research, but issues encountered in the field are documented in the sections below.

Best practice: TechNet is always an excellent source for deployment troubleshooting information. The issues below aren't common, but their resolutions are known, and they may help you in special situations.

Roaming Profiles

Windows 9*x*, Windows NT, and Windows 2000 support roaming profiles, and Office 2000 supports them more than previous versions did. If every roaming workstation receives the same installation package, you shouldn't run into any special issues deploying Outlook 2000 in such an environment. But if different roaming workstations use different packages or are installed in a different order, the following message may appear during installation:

```
Another version of Outlook was installed on your machine prior to
installing Outlook 2000. Did you use that version of Outlook to read
electronic mail?

Answer Yes to allow Outlook 2000 to use the same configuration as the
previously installed version of Outlook. [Yes] [No]
```

Note   Profiles do not roam from one operating system to another.

The installation program detects the presence of Outlook through **HKEY_CURRENT_USER**. This message is triggered by information placed in the key by roaming profiles. The correct answer is **Yes**. It preserves the core type of installation, Corporate or Workgroup versus Internet Mail Only. Failing to do so can corrupt the system and require reinstallation.

Migrating Old Outlook Files

Outlook 97 & 98 offer .PST, .PAB, .OST, and .OAB files. These are stored in the Windows folder unless a different location has been specified. This data is stored in the Application Data subdirectory of Windows in Outlook 2000 to better support roaming profiles and separate data from applications. This is true for both Windows 9*x* and Windows NT/Windows 2000.

Installation does not move these legacy files. If you want all information to be stored in one location—for security or efficiency—make sure to include a migration strategy for these legacy files in the project plan. This is especially true when you use lockdown during installation, preventing users from modifying these files in the Windows directory.

Customization Tips

This section explains how to create customizations for users and groups (functional, geographic, and political) within a corporate environment.

Controlling the Outlook Bar

Outlook allows you to customize the Outlook Bar, but does not provide a simple way to prevent users from customizing it themselves. If you need to provide consistency across the corporate desktop, you can use Visual Basic for Applications to lock down the Outlook Bar. This can prevent support calls from users who lose shortcuts on the Outlook Bar, but it also denies users the productivity gains they sometimes get from custom shortcuts. If you evaluate things and decide to lock down the Outlook Bar, here is how to do it.

On the **Tools** menu, point to **Macro**, and then click **Visual Basic Editor**.

In the Project Explorer pane, expand **Project1** to show entries below it, and then expand **Microsoft Outlook Objects** to show entries below that. Double-click the **ThisOutlookSession** module to open the code window.

Add the following Visual Basic for Applications code to the ThisOutlookSession module:

```
Dim WithEvents oPane As OutlookBarPane
Dim WithEvents oGroups As OutlookBarGroups
Dim WithEvents oShortcuts As OutlookBarShortcuts

Private Sub Application_Startup()
  Set oPane = ActiveExplorer.Panes(1)
  Set oGroups = oPane.Contents.Groups
  Set oShortcuts = oPane.CurrentGroup.Shortcuts
End Sub
```

(continued)

```
Private Sub oGroups_BeforeGroupAdd(Cancel As Boolean)
 MsgBox "Sorry, you cannot add a group to the Outlook Bar."
 Cancel = True
End Sub

Private Sub oGroups_BeforeGroupRemove _
  (ByVal Group As OutlookBarGroup, Cancel As Boolean)
 MsgBox "Sorry, you cannot remove a group from the Outlook Bar."
 Cancel = True
End Sub

Private Sub oPanes_BeforeGroupSwitch _
  (ByVal ToGroup As OutlookBarGroup, Cancel As Boolean)
 Set oShortcuts = ToGroup.Shortcuts
End Sub

Private Sub oShortcuts_BeforeShortcutAdd(Cancel As Boolean)
 MsgBox "Sorry, you cannot add a shortcut to the Outlook Bar."
 Cancel = True
End Sub

Private Sub oShortcuts_BeforeShortcutRemove _
  (ByVal Shortcut As OutlookBarShortcut, Cancel As Boolean)
 MsgBox "Sorry, you cannot delete a shortcut from the Outlook Bar."
 Cancel = True
End Sub
```

Restart Outlook.

This code prevents users from adding to or subtracting from the Outlook Bar: they can still rename its icons and groups. As shown earlier, you can use the **Add Files** pane of the CIW to incorporate VBA code into a transform. With some planning, you can make policies an integral part of customization.

Avoiding Profile Conflict in the CIW

Although the CIW is designed to avoid conflicting settings, there are a few possible trouble spots. One of them is the overlap between Customize Outlook Installation Options (pane 14) and Modify Setup Properties (pane 16). You can choose between **Corporate or Workgroup** and **Internet Mail Only** in pane 14 or in the **OutlookConfiguration** property in pane 16. If you set these values differently, the **OutlookConfiguration** property adopts the setting specified in pane 14. For example, if you set the **OutlookConfiguration** property to **Internet Mail Only** and then set pane 14 to **Do not customize Outlook profile and account information**, pane 16 shows the **Ask user when Outlook first runs** for setting the **OutlookConfiguration** property.

On the other hand, if after pane 14 you create a conflicting setting in pane 16, the pane 16 settings are enforced. For example, you set pane 14 to **Corporate or Workgroup** and then set **OutlookConfiguration** to **Ask user when Outlook first runs**. Users still receive a prompt for what type of Setup they would like when they first run Outlook.

Take pains to avoid this conflict, because once it is in place you cannot modify **OutlookConfiguration** outside of the CIW. For more detail, see http://support.microsoft.com and search for Article ID# Q230835, "Outlook Configuration Property Automatically Reset in the Custom Installation Wizard."

Removing the Outlook Express Icon

Internet Explorer 5 needs a command line switch to make itself the default browser. If you use the CIW to make it the default browser, the Outlook Express icon appears on users' desktops no matter what setup files or modifications you use. To remove the icon you have to create a script or manually run **regsvr32 /n /i:ForceAssoc shdocvw.dll** from the command line.

Granting Access to Web Folders

When this book was written, Outlook 2000 did not allow users to save information to Web Folders if the client was running Windows NT with Service Pack 5 or later or Windows 2000. For earlier versions, you could enable saving to Web Folders by creating an Office Server Extended Web site or virtual directory. This allows you to browse to Web Folders and to choose Web Folders and save successfully to them from the Outlook **File/Save As** menu. A patch is planned for later Windows NT versions.

Successfully Redeploying Outlook 2000

You sometimes need to redeploy Outlook using the transform file from your original installation. The file often contains customized files, registry keys, or installations, and if users have removed, damaged, or modified any of these the reinstallation process will not properly restore or remove the original transform file.

This is because the registry sees files, registry keys, shortcuts, and custom installations as user data. A normal removal does not delete user data, and as long as it remains, the transform file will not completely reinstall added components and modifications. To delete the relevant Registry key, you must first determine the Product Code. Right-click on the transform you used for Setup, click **Properties,** and then click on the **Statistics** tab. The first 36 characters, including the dashes, are the Product Code.

Once you have recorded the Product Code, enter the registry and locate:

```
HKEY_CURRENT_USER\Software\Microsoft\OfficeCustomizedWizard\1.0
\RegKeyPaths
```

Find the subkey of RegKeyPaths that matches the Product Code for the transform, delete the value OCWAddedContentWritten, then either reinstall Outlook or run Outlook Setup again. For more information, see http://support.microsoft.com and search for Article ID# Q229715, "Content Added with a Transform Is Not Added in a Reinstall or Second Install."

Generating a Messaging Profile

It is useful to understand how to create a messaging profile. Most organizations prefer to create these automatically for users, but if you want users to do it themselves, they will have to do it *before* they can run Outlook 2000. When Outlook starts, it looks for a profile, and if it finds one on the computer (from a previous version of Outlook or one that you have supplied with Setup), it uses it. If it doesn't find one, it prompts the user to create one.

Most organizations use the CIW to create new user profiles, but you can use other tools to force the creation of a new profile (even if one already exists) or to create a new one later. Figure 8.3 is an overview of the profile creation process:

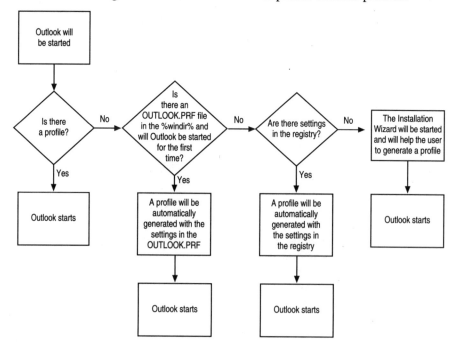

Figure 8.3   Generating a messaging profile.

If you want to integrate your decision-making into the CIW, Figure 8.4 shows how to set up the configuration:

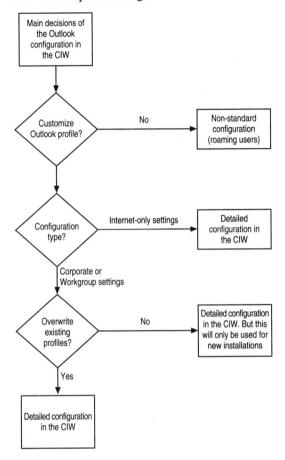

Figure 8.4   Generating profiles in the CIW.

Using NEWPROF.EXE

NEWPROF.EXE is a tool for creating Outlook profiles. Since this can now be done in the CIW, people tend to use NEWPROF.EXE only to force the creation of a new profile on computers that already have one, or to change Setup settings in configurations that do not use a transform file.

To force profile creation, place NEWPROF.EXE in a transform file. If you put it in the CIW, you must also reference a .PRF file with profile settings, so installing a .PRF file becomes the first deployment step. You can download a sample file (to use as a guide) from http://www.microsoft.com/office/ork/2000/appndx /toolbox.htm.

After you finish with the .PRF file, start the CIW, open the **Add Installations and Run Programs** dialog box, and click on **Add**. Enter this command line:

```
%path%\Newprof.exe -p %path%\Outlook.prf
```

where *%path%* represents the path to the file.

Earlier versions of Outlook used NEWPROF.EXE to create profiles. You can use it to generate a messaging profile for a user. The syntax is:

```
NEWPROF [-P <Path to .prf file>] [-S] [-X] [-Z]
```

Where:

- *-P <Path to .prf file>* is the .PRF file with the complete path.
- *-S* causes NEWPROF.EXE to bring up a window, allows the user to choose a .PRF file, and displays status and error messages in this window.
- *-X* causes NEWPROF.EXE to start execution automatically when the *-S* option is used, without waiting for a .PRF file to be selected. Requires that you use the *-P* option or that the DEFAULT.PRF file be present in the Windows directory.
- *-Z* causes NEWPROF.EXE to display MAPI error codes if it encounters errors. This requires the *-S* option.

By design, NEWPROF.EXE versions 5.5.2505.0 or later cannot use variable names with Windows 9*x*. It does not generate any log files when it runs. If you do not specify a file, it looks for DEFAULT.PRF in the Windows directory.

From the Trenches: Deploying Outlook 2000 at Hanson Brothers

Hanson Brothers is a small but growing distributor of corn products. The company currently uses Windows 95 with Office 95 and MS Mail 3.2 as their backbone. Their goal is to upgrade an MS Mail environment and productivity suite to Office 2000 and Exchange Server 5.5 with the client-side employing the advanced features of Outlook 2000. This process will involve assessing the existing infrastructure, designing an Outlook 2000 deployment that matches best practices with business needs, and deploying an automated solution with follow-up training and technical support.

Hanson Brothers owns eight plants in the United States and has its central headquarters in the heart of the Midwest. Over the past five years, the company has used MS Mail with the MS Exchange 4.0 client to handle messaging.

For its productivity suite, Hanson Brothers was using Office 95. As part of an infrastructure upgrade, the company decided it was time to create an Internet presence. Their goal was to upgrade the entire client/server environment and adopt a more powerful messaging client. They opted for Outlook 2000 running with an Exchange Server 5.5 backend.

The company has a small IT presence, so it decided to stage its client upgrades in two parts, upgrading the messaging environment before going to Office 2000. Training sessions were to focus on important changes, such as user interface enhancements, calendaring, and Internet messaging.

Hanson Brothers was making a substantial investment in Outlook 2000 as the centerpiece of their updated Internet and messaging strategy. They saw the introduction of Outlook 2000 with Internet Explorer 5 (for tight Web integration) as a factor that would let them leverage their messaging system to remain competitive.

Once predeployment information was gathered from business units on what they were using and what they most wanted to see, the IT department had to determine what type of deployment it could support. When deploying Outlook 2000, there are two primary choices to make. Should deployment occur centrally or from a central point at each site? What is the best deployment choice based on this decision?

They opted for a decentralized deployment, and then had to choose whether to deploy using the Custom Installation Wizard, burn the installation image onto a CD and then install on individual workstations, or use an alternative setup method.

After careful consideration, the IT department opted for creating an administrative share at each site, producing a primary setup (.MSI) file using the Custom Installation Wizard, and then creating transform (.MST) files for each site that required further customization.

Organizing and Rules   Rules are an important component in Outlook 2000 architecture. Although individuals can set rules for managing their Inbox, enterprise-wide policies can set rules proactively. With the proliferation of junk mail, corporations are configuring messaging clients in an attempt to reduce unnecessary traffic and storage. Hanson Brothers used Outlook 2000's improved Organize tool to create company-wide rules and customize for efficiency.

Outlook Today   The default startup configuration for Outlook is another important design component. For example, the Outlook Today screen allows all aspects of a day, from scheduling to Inbox to Tasks, to be present and ready at startup.

The company had to make a decision by committee, so they enlisted the help of selected power users from each business unit. After viewing different startup options, they agreed on most of the major choices, differing only in subtle cosmetic choices that most users could handle on their own. One of the decisions made was to add a link to the intranet home page from Outlook Today, along with the company logo.

CHAPTER 9

Multinational Deployment

Office 2000 has more options for deploying in multiple languages than did previous versions. By examining how to decide whether to use the MultiLanguage Packs or the localized version, then explaining how to deploy software and settings efficiently, this chapter helps you create a multinational-deployment plan that meets your needs but requires minimal IT effort.

What You'll Find in This Chapter

- In-depth descriptions of the three Office 2000 options for editing in a language other than English.

- How to perform an administrative installation for localized versions or MultiLanguage Packs.

- How to customize a localized version of Office 2000.

- How to decide if you should customize the MultiLanguage Packs and how to customize them once you decide.

- How to balance priorities and objectives to choose the best deployment strategy.

- A table that lists the benefits of using a localized version of Office 2000 versus a MultiLanguage Pack.

Office 2000 Multilingual Capabilities

Users who need to edit in a language other than English can use a localized version of Office 2000, the U.S. English version with the MultiLanguage Pack, or proofing tools for another language. The functionality and characteristics of each option are explained below.

Localized Versions

The localized versions of Office 2000, available in approximately 40 countries around the world, contain native-language content and specialized default settings. These versions must be installed in an operating system in the same language or used to upgrade a previous Office version in the same language. For example, German Office 2000 installs only on German Windows and can upgrade only an earlier version of German Office.

Localized versions are useful for companies that:

- Use only one or a few languages
- Lack client computer hard drive space
- Need to avoid processes that run after the Office 2000 reboot (MultiLanguage Packs are installed after the reboot)
- Can test each language on the matching operating system

Localized versions have the same deployment and installation capabilities as the U.S. English version and you customize them with the same tools. Although the *Microsoft Office 2000 Resource Kit* Toolbox is available only in English, the tools work on all language editions. To customize an edition, you need space on the server for an administrative installation and access to test computers that are running an operating system in the same language.

Microsoft Office 2000 MultiLanguage Pack

To create the MultiLanguage Pack, Office 2000 developers separated all language-dependent items (user interface, Help, error messages, and so on) from the application executable and then designed the U.S. English version to combine with language packs to localize user interface, Help system, proofing tools, font, messages, and default settings such as paper size. (A few items remain in English: the Excel Data Map feature, some wizards and templates, a few Help items, and the **Start** menu shortcuts.)

Consider combining U.S. English Office 2000 with the MultiLanguage Pack if you:

- Use many languages worldwide
- Have machines on which different users use different languages
- Have users who use more than one language

The MultiLanguage Pack is available for Office Standard, Professional, and Premium versions, and consists of eight CDs. It includes the user interface and Help files for more than 25 languages, the Microsoft Office 2000 Proofing Tools for over 35 languages, wizards, templates, add-ons, Input Method Editors (IMEs), and more.

You have to install Office 2000 before the MultiLanguage Pack. Most languages require 150 MB of hard-disk space (over the Office 2000 requirement); Asian languages (with more complex display characteristics) require up to 300 MB more if optional fonts are used.

You can install the U.S. English version installs on any language operating system so long as it runs Office 2000, and can upgrade previous versions of Office in any language. Word can convert language-specific files from previous versions of Word; the other applications can convert earlier language-specific files as long as the default languages and operating systems are the same.

Proofing Tools

If all you need to do is check spelling and grammar in documents that contain text in another language, use the Office 2000 Proofing Tools. The CD contains tools for more than 35 languages. Word 2000 and PowerPoint 2000 allow you to spell check one document using dictionaries in several languages. Word detects language changes and automatically uses the appropriate dictionary within three to five words.

Administrative Installations

To create an administrative installation for localized versions or MultiLanguage Packs you use the command **setup /a** (as you do for other Office 2000 products). You can create an administrative installation on a server then run client installations from that location, or you can distribute CDs to users and let them install.

Customizing a Localized Version of Office

A localized version of Office 2000 is customized with the same process used for the U.S. English version. The *Microsoft Office 2000 Resource Kit* Toolbox tools work on all localized versions. Follow these steps to create a completely customized version for a specific locale:

1. Create an administrative installation from the localized version CD.

2. Run a client installation on a test computer with a matching operating system.

3. Create the customizations.

4. Use the Office Profile Wizard (OPW) to capture the new defaults.

5. Use the Custom Installation Wizard (CIW) to create a transform (.MST) with the appropriate installation states, customizations, and commands.

6. When the software is distributed, the install process performs one reboot.

For more information on customization, see Chapter 4, "Customizing an Office 2000 Installation," and Chapter 5, "User Settings."

Customizing the MultiLanguage Pack

Customizing the MultiLanguage Pack installation can minimize the files installed on the client computer and ensure that the proper language and default settings are installed. This reduces post-installation support because you can create settings that are compatible with existing files and macros, and because users don't have to select installation details or settings.

Customization should be decided by need, however, and not all organizations find the option practical. Some provide one standard image worldwide, or at least per region, figuring that this tactic minimizes deployment costs and the number of images that need to be configured and tested, even though incompatibilities caused by incorrect default settings can raise support issues and costs. If you use the defaults or if different-language users share a computer, you may have to rely on users to install and choose their own languages, which can result in configuration problems and more helpdesk calls.

Customizing the Client Installation

If you don't customize the MultiLanguage Pack client installation on an English language operating system, all languages install on first use and U.S. English remains the default language. On non-English operating systems, both the Office and the MultiLanguage Pack Setup programs detect the operating system's active code page and change the installation states of language-specific features to *Run From My Computer*. For example, if you install Office 2000 on a Korean operating system, the installation state for optional fonts and other Korean-specific tools changes to *Run From My Computer*. When you install the Korean MultiLanguage Pack, the installation state for the most commonly used Korean-language features, such as the user interface and proofing tools, changes from *Installed on First Use* to *Run From My Computer*.

Customizing the client installation of the MultiLanguage Pack allows you to install specific languages and features to the local computer regardless of whether the active code page matches. As with the U.S. English version, you use the CIW and OPW. You can use the Language Version Tool to set the default language, but this resets any existing customized Word settings.

This section explains how to customize a multilingual Office 2000 installation. The method below requires more custom configurations and more steps to create, but it requires fewer steps to install on client computers. For ways of reducing the number of custom configurations, see the "MultiLanguage Pack Deployment Tactics" section that appears later in this chapter on page 260.

Steps for complete customization by locale:

1. Create the customized version of U.S. English that meets your needs. Ensure that any necessary international components in the Office Tools section install to the local computer or on first use.
2. Create the administrative installation(s) of any necessary MultiLanguage Pack CDs.
3. Use the CIW to create a transform (.MST) file to customize the client installation of the MultiLanguage Pack, including setting installation states, adding additional files to the installation, or adding other programs or installations.

4. Run the customized installation on a test computer that already has your base U.S. English Office 2000 and the appropriate language version of the operating system.

5. Use the Language Version Tool from the *Microsoft Office 2000 Resource Kit* CD to set the default language. This sets the user interface, Help, proofing tools, and default settings. The tool resets all Word settings to the Office 2000 defaults—so run it before you apply any custom settings.

6. Create any other custom settings, such as those used for the base U.S. English version and those that may differ by locale, including locations for documents and templates.

7. Use the Office Profile Wizard to capture all custom settings, including those created by the Language Version Tool.

8. Use the Custom Installation Wizard to open the transform (.MST) file for the base U.S. English Office 2000. Save the file with a new name and make this change (your setup may require others):

In pane #13, **Add Installations and Run Programs**, add three commands: one to chain the Language Version Tool, one to run the Office Profile Wizard with the .OPS file you created, and a third to chain the MultiLanguage Pack installation to the U.S. English version so that everything installs with one command.

For example:

```
langver.exe /LCID auto
proflwiz.exe /r German.ops
setup.exe /chained TRANSFORMS=German.MST /qb-
```

German.ops is the name of the file you created with the Office Profile Wizard, and *German.mst* is the transform file you created to only use the German language from the MultiLanguage Pack.

Tip   The MultiLanguage Pack does not install until Office 2000 has rebooted and installed successfully. If your distribution process does not include a way to log back in as the user (such as using Microsoft Systems Management Server's administrative context), users will have go through some installation tasks the next time they log in. Inform users that they have to complete about 15–20 minutes of installation tasks once they log on and tell them that these tasks *must* complete successfully.

Setting the Language

You can set the language two ways: with the Office Language Settings Tool that installs with the MultiLanguage Pack on the client computer, or with the Language Version Tool from the *Microsoft Office 2000 Resource Kit* CD-ROM.

Office Language Settings Tool

The Office Language Settings Tool (shown in Figure 9.1) allows users to change the user interface and enable editing for another language. For example, you have both U.S. English and German installed, and one user uses English as a primary language but allows a visiting German counterpart to use the computer occasionally. The German user can run this tool and choose German without changing the English user's default settings. The next time an Office 2000 application starts up, the user interface, Help, and proofing tools appear in German. This tool does not change the default language to German—that and the default settings remain U.S. English. For example, the paper size is 8 ½ x 11, not A4, and measurements would be in inches rather than millimeters. In this case, this is the desired behavior on the U.S. machine; the German user should use the Language Version Tool to change the default settings on the computer in Germany.

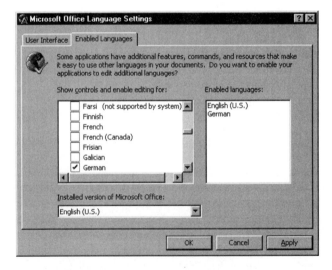

Figure 9.1   The Microsoft Office Language Settings Tool.

Language Version Tool

The default is the language that has the correct default settings for that locale and is used most often to run macros and create documents. The Language Version Tool changes the default language from U.S. English to any of the installed languages (as shown in Figure 9.2).

Figure 9.2   The Language Version Tool allows you to choose a default.

Changing the default language deletes custom settings, but only those stored in Normal.dot for Word, so it's best to set the default language while you are creating the custom installation—before you add custom user settings or users start creating their own. The Language Version Tool defaults to interactive mode but has switches to run it non-interactively.

Switch	Action
Langver.exe /LCID Auto	The Language Version Tool starts up and automatically detects the operating system language, sets the Office 2000 default to match the language, then exits as if the user had clicked **OK.**
Langver /LCID 1041	The Language Version Tool starts up, sets itself to that language, and exits. In this example, 1041 is for Japanese.
Langver /LCID foo	If the Language Version Tool cannot recognize a valid string after the /LCID switch, it simply exits without doing anything.

A list of valid language IDs:

LCID	Language
1025	Arabic
1069	Basque
3076	Chinese (Hong Kong)
2052	Chinese (Simplified)
1028	Chinese (Traditional)
1050	Croatian
1029	Czech
1030	Danish

(continued)

LCID	Language
1043	Dutch (Standard)
1033	English
1061	Estonian
1035	Finnish
1036	French (Standard)
1031	German (Standard)
1032	Greek
1037	Hebrew
1081	Hindi
1038	Hungarian
1040	Italian (Standard)
1041	Japanese
1042	Korean
1062	Latvian
1063	Lithuanian
1044	Norwegian (Bokmål)
1045	Polish
1046	Portuguese (Brazilian)
2070	Portuguese (Standard)
1048	Romanian
1049	Russian
2074	Serbian
1051	Slovak
1060	Slovenian
3082	Spanish (Modern Sort)
1053	Swedish
1054	Thai
1055	Turkish
1066	Vietnamese

Enforcing Corporate Standards

You can create one standard image to use in sites around the world, but this does not change the default language and settings and it can cause compatibility issues for users of certain languages, especially Hebrew, Arabic, and Asian languages. See the "Minimizing the Number of Custom Configurations" section later in this chapter on page 261 for suggestions on how to set up a standard U.S. English configuration with a few other languages.

Adding IMEs and Additional Content

Some content on each MultiLanguage Pack CD isn't installed by default. The **Extras** folder includes localized Add-ins for Excel, the language packs for Internet Explorer 5, and IMEs for Asian languages as well as other items.

If the extra software has its own setup routine, such as an IME, then add a setup command to the CIW's **Add Programs and Installations** pane when you customize the MultiLanguage Pack installation. For files without their own setup routines use the CIW's **Add Files** pane.

Running the Client Installation

Here is how to install the client in a configuration that completely customizes U.S. English Office 2000 as well as the MultiLanguage Pack:

1. Run the Office 2000 installation with the transform that includes all customized settings for that locale and a command that chains the MultiLanguage Pack installation.

2. After Office 2000 reboots the computer, log back in as the user.

3. Once you are logged on, Office 2000 Setup installs the MultiLanguage Pack. You can chain the MultiLanguage Pack to another one for locales requiring languages that are not on the same CD or to content in the Extras folder.

Operating System Considerations

System Locale and the Active Code Page

Every Windows system has a *system locale* setting that determines the system language and a *user locale* setting that sets the defaults for currency, date and time formats, and other regional settings. (Windows 2000 offers a third setting to control the Windows UI language.)

System locale controls the Active Code Page (ACP), which governs what types of legacy software can be run on the machine. For instance, a machine with a German or Swedish system locale can run software that uses the Western European code page (set of special characters), but probably will have trouble with Russian software, which has a different code page. Most of Office 2000 is based on Unicode so that it is independent of the ACP, but some parts still depend on the ACP.

Operating System Detection

Office 2000 Setup uses operating system information to match the installation to user needs on Windows 95/9*x*, Windows NT Workstation 4.0, and Windows 2000. It detects the system locale, changes the installation state to *Run From My Computer* for language-specific features such as fonts and some tools, and enables editing for the language by activating the appropriate UI tools (menu and toolbar options).

The MultiLanguage Pack operates similarly. The default installation state for MultiLanguage Pack features is *Installed on First Use*, but when the Pack detects the enabled editing languages in Office, it changes the installation state to *Run From My Computer* for features that are required to edit in that language.

Note If you are using the CIW to create a transform just to change feature installation states, check the MultiLanguage Pack list of features to see if it has everything your users need. If it does, you may not need the transform: make sure the system locale is set correctly, then simply run Setup in quiet (non-interactive) mode.

Operating System Code Page Support

On Windows 9*x* and Windows NT Workstation 4.0, you need to make sure that the operating system version supports the language the user needs. For example, if you have a user in the Netherlands who needs Hebrew as well as Dutch, make sure the operating system supports Hebrew or the user won't be able to install and switch to it.

To help you determine this, the *Microsoft Office 2000 Resource Kit* Toolbox includes an Access database (Wwsuppt.mdb) you can find on the **Start** menu at **Start | Programs | Microsoft Office Tools | Microsoft Office Resource Kit Documents | International Information**. When you open it, it displays a form (Figure 9.3) you can use to query the database and determine which operating system versions support the Office language you need.

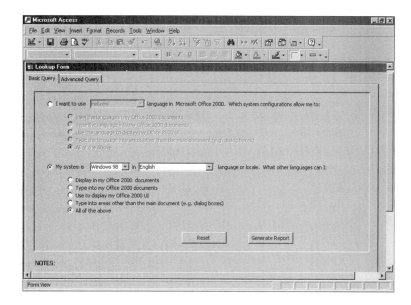

Figure 9.3   Querying Wwsuppt.mdb for operating system language support.

Click on the **Generate Report** button to produce an Access report listing the operating system languages that support your needs. If you were to use the example above, you would find that no Dutch-language operating systems support Hebrew. This result, based on the yes/no condition that every Office application supports Hebrew, is somewhat misleading because every application except FrontPage supports Hebrew. To get more precise results, use the **Advanced Query** tab to report on each application. If you issue an advanced query that leaves out FrontPage 2000, you see that Dutch Windows 2000 supports Hebrew Office 2000, so you can alleviate the user's problem simply by running Hebrew Office without FrontPage. (You could also use U.S. English Windows 2000 and Office 2000, add language packs for Dutch and Hebrew, then switch the user interfaces as needed. See Chapter 14, "Office 2000 and Windows 2000," for more information.)

Internet Explorer and Multilingual Use

If you install Internet Explorer 5 with Office 2000 and include the language packs for it, it follows the user interface language of Office 2000 on Windows 9*x* and Windows NT Workstation 4.0. The same is true for Windows 2000, except that you don't have to install Internet Explorer 5 with Office because it is already present. These language packs are not in the MultiLanguage Pack Setup: get them from the **Extras** folder on the CD.

Office 2000 and Windows 2000

Windows 2000 is similar to Office 2000 in that you can combine the U.S. English version with language packs and change the user interface to any supported language without requiring a dual boot system or the localized version of the operating system. Therefore, combining Office 2000 with the MultiLanguage Pack running on Windows 2000 provides the most flexibility for users, particularly when switching between Hebrew, Arabic, or Asian languages and any other language.

This also simplifies testing in that you don't have to locate and install each localized version of the operating system to test language configurations. For example, a user in Japan works in Japanese but occasionally lets a visiting German counterpart use the computer. The German user can switch the language in Windows 2000, reboot Windows 2000, then switch Office 2000 to German. (The German user can edit documents without any of these modifications. This process is required only to operate completely in German.)

 Note   Outlook 2000 and FrontPage 2000 also require the system locale to match the language the user is switching to.

MultiLanguage Pack Deployment Tactics

This section discusses ways to establish an Office 2000 setup routine that requires no user or technician interaction to install all software and create all custom settings on the client computer. The goal is to:

- Maximize the control over the configuration, including all settings.
- Minimize the amount of work required to create, store, and manage all of the different configurations.
- Minimize user interaction with the installation.

The discussion also explains how to minimize hard drive space requirements, chain installations, and use a software tool to distribute everything together.

Maximizing Configuration Control

To ensure that each installation happens exactly the way you want it to, you should have a custom configuration for each language or locale that your business operates in. Each would install U.S. English Office 2000, the specific language(s) needed, and custom settings that set the default language as well as those that support internal policies—such as default Save formats or locations. The least complex method is to chain the installations, use the *Microsoft Office 2000 Resource Kit* tools, and create complete sets of transforms and profile settings files to accomplish the installation for each locale.

Minimizing the Number of Custom Configurations

You don't have to give up control as you minimize custom configurations, but if you want to use custom user settings you have to build the language installation and default settings logic into a batch file or script. The example below makes no changes to the U.S. English configuration.

1. Use two batch files. The first file puts the second one in the StartUp folder (to run the processes required after Office 2000 U.S. English Setup reboots), and then installs U.S. English Office 2000.

2. After the system reboots and Office 2000 Setup has completed, the second batch file:

   a. Checks a locally stored variable that determines the system locale (for example, Switzerland, rather than Germany or Italy).

   b. Runs the Language Version Tool in Auto mode to set the default language.

   c. Runs the Office Profile Wizard in restore mode with the .OPS file for the appropriate locale.

   d. Matches the locale to a table that correlates transforms to languages, then installs the appropriate MultiLanguage Pack CD.

   e. Removes itself from the StartUp directory.

To minimize custom configurations, take advantage of the fact that both Office 2000 and the MultiLanguage Pack can auto-detect the active code page and change the installation state for features that match that language. In this case, don't use transforms on the MultiLanguage Pack installation because those installation states will override the auto-detected changes. Here is the client installation process:

1. Use two batch files. The first file puts the second one in the StartUp folder (to run the processes required after Office 2000 U.S. English Setup reboots), and then installs U.S. English Office 2000.

2. After the system reboots and Office 2000 Setup has completed, the second batch file:

   a. Runs the Language Version Tool in Auto mode to set the default language.

   b. Matches the locale to a table listing which MultiLanguage Pack CD to install. Auto-detection installs the correct language to run from the local computer.

   c. Removes itself from the StartUp directory.

This eliminates the need for custom Word settings, but there are very few custom configurations. While only one language installs to run from the local computer, other languages on the same CD can still install on first use. You still need to provide a custom configuration for countries that use multiple languages that span different CDs and for users who need to set a default language that does not match the active code page.

From the Trenches:
Deploying Office 2000 in a Large Multilanguage Environment

A large multinational manufacturing company was making plans to upgrade to Office 2000 in conjunction with a general PC upgrade. They have several sites in countries that use more than one language, so they decided to use U.S. English Office 2000 with the MultiLanguage Pack. They tested configurations at one European and one U.S. site, and decided, halfway through the PC upgrade period, to move all users to Office 2000 within 12 months. To accomplish this, they came up with two distribution methods.

The first was for the new computers, which were purchased preconfigured from a single manufacturer. Using the same customized U.S. English version that would be distributed to existing PCs, they installed all appropriate languages, set the default language, then captured from this computer the master image which they handed off to the PC manufacturer.

The second method was for PCs already in use and upgraded to the new hardware standards. This company has over 100,000 PCs, but rather than use a single software distribution tool, they used two batch files. The first file copied the second one into the StartUp directory and then installed the standard U.S. English Office 2000. Office rebooted the computer, so the process stopped until the user came back to work and logged on, at which point Office completed Setup. The second batch file checked the computer's custom ID to determine its location, then ran the appropriate Language Version Tool, set the default language, and started installing the language(s) needed from the MultiLanguage Pack. If a country needed languages from more than one CD, the first installation chained to the next one. The last thing the batch file did was remove itself from the StartUp directory.

The company informed users that these processes have to complete successfully, provided an estimate of how long the process takes, and used command-lines switches to conceal the **Cancel** button, so users would not stop the installation.

Minimizing User Interaction

Chaining Installations

If you are using the MultiLanguage Packs, you can chain their installation to the Office 2000 installation in a single command line. When you use the CIW to create the transform for Office 2000, add a command in the **Add Programs and Installations** pane, and then replace the Setup.exe in the root of the MultiLanguage Pack administrative installation with the new Setup.exe (in the resource kit). While creating a transform for the MultiLanguage Pack that runs the Office Profile Wizard in restore mode with the appropriate .OPS file, you should add another command in the **Add Programs and Installations** pane if you are using custom user settings, especially for Word. An example command for chaining the installations together is:

```
<fully qualified path>\setup.exe /chained TRANSFORMS=lpksettings.mst
/qb-
```

The /chained command tells Office Setup that another Windows Installer process is being chained to this one, and the new Setup.exe is designed to make that work.

For more details on chaining Office products, see README.DOC on the *Microsoft Office 2000 Resource Kit* CD.

Minimizing Hard Drive Space Requirements

If user don't not need English, you can save hard disk space by changing the installation state for all Office applications to *Installed on First Use* and then installing the appropriate MultiLanguage Pack and setting the default language. The first time the Office application starts up, it uses the default language's resources—the English resources are not installed (unless the language is changed to English)—saving 150 MB. Remember: the Windows Desktop Update is required for application-level installation on first use.

A Word About Software Distribution

When you install U.S. English Office 2000 and the MultiLanguage Pack, two factors require a reboot:

- The MultiLanguage Pack does not start installing until Office 2000 is completely installed.
- Office 2000 requires a reboot on all operating systems but Windows 2000.

If you want to have one U.S. English transform file, but to install everything without user intervention—including logging on—you need a software distribution tool that can reboot the computer and log on as the same user. If you use a tool that cannot do this, then events required after the Office 2000 reboot cannot occur until the user logs on, which means you need to tell users what to expect and make sure that everything completes successfully.

Suppose you are doing a very controlled distribution: specific departments on specific nights, during non-working hours, using Microsoft Systems Management Server (SMS) 2.0 to create a multilingual installation of Office 2000 that completes automatically. The key is to use groups that change as machine attributes change (called *dynamic* groups) and assign the jobs to them. Create at least two:

- **Group 1:** Has no Office 2000 software.
- **Group 2:** Has Office 2000, but no MultiLanguage Pack software.

Then create two different jobs: one assigned to Group 1 that installs Office 2000, and a second assigned to Group 2 that installs the MultiLanguage Pack. Use the administrative context for both so that SMS can log back on if the computer reboots. Base the dynamic groups on user groups so that you can schedule and time the distribution by department. Schedule a mandatory time for the first job to make the distribution very specific and schedule the updates for the dynamic groups as frequently as hourly to upgrade all users within the allotted period.

 Note   You can't use dependency relationships in SMS 2.0 to solve this problem. Version 1.0 of the Windows Installer permits only one instance to run at a time, and the dependency relationship method starts installing the MultiLanguage Pack *after* the Office 2000 reboot but *before* all of the Windows Installer tasks are finished. This prevents the MultiLanguage Pack from completing successfully.

Summary

The table below summarizes localized versions and MultiLanguage Pack benefits.

Localized Version	MultiLanguage Pack
Client machine is limited to one UI language. (Asian and bidirectional versions such as Arabic and Hebrew include English as an optional UI language.)	Client machine can switch between UI languages (depending on system capabilities).
All content, UI, and Help are localized.	Same, but there are minor exceptions.
When roaming users switch machines, their UI language does not follow them.	Roaming users can switch machines and their user interface will be as expected, even if no bits were installed on the new machine for that language.

Localized Version	MultiLanguage Pack
Requires test computers with localized operating system to test and build custom configurations.	Can test and build custom configurations on U.S. English operating system.
189–250 MB of client computer hard disk required, depending on Office edition. Asian versions require an additional 150–300 MB if optional fonts are included.	189 MB to 250 MB of client computer hard disk required (if English applications are installed as *Run from my computer*), depending on the Office edition, *plus* 150 MB for each additional language. If the installation state for the applications is *Installed on First Use*, English resources are not installed, and system requirements are still 189–250 MB once the language resources from the MultiLanguage Pack are included. Asian languages require an additional 150–300 MB if optional fonts are included.
Approximately 550 MB of server hard disk required per localized edition. If you used the same 28 languages available in the MultiLanguage Packs, your total server space required would be more than 10 GB if you had all languages on one server.	About 550 MB server hard disk required for U.S. English Office 2000, plus 100–150 MB per language (around 600 MB for each MultiLanguage Pack CD). CDs 1, 3, 5, 6, 7, and 8 each contain 4+ languages at 100–150 MB each, while CDs 2 and 4 contain two Asian languages at 200–300 MB each. Total server space is approx 4.5 GB.
The Thai localized version contains a mini-language pack that allows switching between English and Thai.	Not available for the Thai and Indic language versions, which also support Vietnamese. The Indic languages include Devanagari-based languages (Hindi, Konkani, Marathi, Nepali, and Sanskrit) and Tamil.
Each custom installation requires a full customization of Office for each localized version.	Custom installation requires the standard US customization, plus a customization of the MultiLanguage Pack per language.
One step to install on client with one reboot at end.	Using SMS or a batch file, one step to install on client with one reboot in the middle.
Track transforms easily by storing them with the appropriate localized version.	You must track a single standard US transform and a separate one for each MultiLanguage Pack customization.

CHAPTER 10

Network Bandwidth Considerations

*By Geoff Kenny
and David Chu,
IKON TS,
Vancouver*

This chapter documents network statistics that you can refer to when choosing the most appropriate Office 2000 deployment methods for your organization. These statistics were gathered by performing a variety of Microsoft Office 2000 installations over a network and capturing network statistics—including total_bytes_transferred, bytes_per_second, and elapsed_time. Microsoft Network Monitor was used to capture statistics.

Microsoft Office 2000 is installed using the Windows Installer, which allows for a variety of installation states on a per-feature basis. These installation states include *Run from My Computer, Run from the Server, Installed on First Use,* and *Not Available*. This chapter documents the network load as more and less Microsoft Office features are installed the first time Setup runs and as features are installed on first use. Also reported is the network load generated as Microsoft Office 2000 applications are run over the network from a server.

What You'll Find in This Chapter

- Network bandwidth usage statistics that can serve as a basis for deciding deployment methods for Office 2000.

- A description of the test environment used to capture the network bandwidth usage statistics.

- A detailed description of the tests that were run.

- A comprehensive set of test data that was captured.

- A graphical representation of test data.

- Deployment recommendations and guidelines.

Note   The information and data in this chapter are meant to serve as guidelines only. They are not meant to reflect your actual deployment environment and should not be considered recommendations for how to deploy Office. The test environment used was very basic and the tests were conducted in a way that would allow observation of specific network bandwidth usage levels when deploying and using Office 2000. These conditions do not reflect the typical IT environment but do allow for observation of data that can be analyzed for the purposes of comparison and extrapolation. You will need to draw your own conclusions.

Test Environment

It is important to understand the environment where these tests were done for comparison to real-world complex networks. The simple model employed for these tests allowed an administrator to calculate anticipated network impact before deploying Microsoft Office 2000. The statistics supplied here can also assist when deciding which Office features to install during Setup, which to install on first use, and which to run over the network.

Server Operating Systems

Microsoft Windows NT Server 4.0 with Service Pack 5 - Two servers were installed. One was installed as the PDC, DHCP, and WINS server (called the *Controller*). The other Windows NT Server served as a member server and file server—this was also the server that would run Microsoft Office Setup. Network Monitor was loaded on the *Controller* to minimize the impact on the file server.

Novell Netware 4.11 - Once the tests were completed with Windows NT 4.0 Server, the file server was formatted and reinstalled using Novell Netware 4.11, Support Pack 6 with SMP enabled. During the Netware portion of the tests, Network Monitor was run on the Windows NT *Controller*. Performance Monitor was not used during the Netware tests.

Server Hardware

A Hewlett Packard Netserver LH Pro 512 MB RAM, Dual Pentium Pro 200 served as the file server platform for both the Windows NT and Netware tests.

Client Software

Two client computers were installed with Microsoft Windows 98. During the Windows NT tests, TCP/IP as DHCP clients was configured; the file server and *Controller* only ran TCP/IP.

During the Netware tests, IPX was loaded on the controller. Netware Client 32 software version 3.10 was loaded and TCP/IP was removed.

Norton Ghost 5.1b was used to create images of the Windows 98 machines after the networking components were configured. The Ghost images were used to rapidly *reset* the client computers between tests when required.

Client Hardware

Two clone PII-233 MHz machines were used. Each client had 32 MB RAM.

Network Environment

The following sections describe the network environment in which the tests were conducted.

10BaseT LAN

An isolated Local Area Network was used, employing a 3COM 8-port 10BaseT hub. Network activity was kept to a minimum while tests were performed to keep test results accurate.

Network Bandwidth

Network Bandwidth used as a percentage is not documented in this chapter. You will need to take the statistics documented here and extrapolate them so that they are meaningful to your own network. You will need to consider your network bandwidth (for example, 10BaseT or 100Base), current utilization, whether the network is switched or non-switched, and the number of clients per installation server.

Defining Tests to Be Performed

The following sections describe the tests that were performed to capture the deployment and usage data. The tests performed fall into three categories: installation, running Office 2000, and Office 2000 self repair.

Installation

This category encompasses the majority of tests performed. It includes the execution of Office 2000 Setup, as well as features installed on first use. The following tests were performed:

- **Standard Install** - Word, Excel, Outlook, and Internet Explorer 5.0 are installed to the client hard disk. Most of the remaining Office 2000 features are installed on first use, and some are not available.
- **Complete Install** - All of Office 2000 is installed to the client hard disk.
- **Minimal Install** - All of Office 2000 is installed on first use.
- **Network Install** - Office 2000 will be run from network servers.
- **Language Pack** - Install German from optional Microsoft Office Language Pack CD.
- **First Use Word Features** - Cause *Text with Layout Converter* and *Report Templates* to be installed on first use.
- **First Use Access** - Cause Access to be installed on first use. Then open the Northwind sample database.
- **First Use PowerPoint** - Cause PowerPoint to be installed.
- Repeat the Standard install simultaneously on 11 machines to observe network saturation levels and time increase.

Running Office 2000

When the client is configured to run Office from a server, measure the network impact when the client runs Word, Excel, Outlook, Spell Check, Grammar Check, Insert Table, and Save File.

Self Repair

Remove Winword.exe from the client and attempt to run Word. Office 2000 repairs itself, copying the missing files from the installation point.

Test Methodology

The following sections describe the methodology used in executing the tests.

Setting Up Office 2000 on the File Servers

Administrative installs were done to network share points on the file servers. Use the /A switch when running Microsoft Office 2000 Setup to create an administrative installation.

UNC (Universal Naming Convention) names eliminate the need to map drive letters to network share points. Instead, the UNC name of a share can be supplied. For example, \\SERVER\SHARE points to a share point on SERVER called *Share*. Windows Installer can make use of the UNC name or a mapped drive when installing Office 2000 and remembers the location that Office was installed from. When Office 2000 installs features on first use or performs self repairs, it reconnects to the network share point that Office was originally installed from by using the stored location. The administrator can supply alternate locations in the transform file that Office Setup can use if the original location is unavailable.

Custom Installation Wizard

Microsoft Office 2000 uses Microsoft Windows Installer technology to set up Microsoft Office for use on client machines. This technology allows for the use of transform files (*.MST). Transform files are created using the Custom Installation Wizard, and are read by the Windows Installer during Office installation to change the installation states of the features from the defaults if desired.

The tests performed required four transform (*.MST) files to set feature states during installation to install locally, install on first use, run from network, or not installed. Using the Custom Installation Wizard, the transform files were created and saved on the *Controller* computer. Before each set of tests, the *.MST files were copied to the file server share points where the administrative install of Office 2000 was located.

Installation Rollback

In the unlikely event that Office 2000 fails to complete installation, Office Setup will roll the client back to the state it was in prior to running Setup.

Norton Ghost 5.1b

The tests require that computers running Windows 98 be *reset* periodically in order to run the next set of tests. Norton Ghost 5.1b was used to create images of the Windows 98 client installs and to reload those images when the testing required.

Installing Office 2000 on the Client Machine

Each time Microsoft Office was to be installed, the client was reloaded using the Ghost images. The Microsoft Office Setup program was then invoked, supplying the name of the transform file (*.MST) that was configured to support the desired client setup. The following command line was used:

```
SETUP.EXE TRANSFORMS=XXXX.MST /qn+
```

Note   Because Netware does not support UNC names, a drive letter had to be mapped for the Netware clients to support first-use installs and self-repair tests.

Capturing the Statistics

Network Monitor was run on the Controller computer and was configured to capture all network statistics; no filter was used. After each test, the Network Monitor Capture file was saved for later analysis. The totals statistics were recorded in an Excel Spreadsheet for each test performed.

Office 2000 Setup Command Line

Running Setup Under Windows NT

Use the following command line:

```
\\SERVER\SHARE\SETUP.EXE TRANSFORMS=Standard.mst /qn+
```

where:

Feature	Meaning
\\SERVER\SHARE	UNC location of network share point containing Administrative install of Office 2000.
SETUP.EXE	Office 2000 Setup program.
TRANSFORMS=	Informs Setup that a transform file will be supplied to customize Office 2000 Setup behavior.
Standard.mst	In this example, the name of the transform file configured to perform a Standard setup is supplied.
/qn+	Display options. In this example, no display will show, and there will be no confirmation at the end of Setup.

Running Setup Under Novell Netware

Use the following command line:

```
P:\SETUP.EXE TRANSFORMS=Standard.mst /qn+
```

where:

Feature	Meaning
P:\	Drive letter permanently mapped to the network share point containing the administrative installation of Office 2000.
SETUP.EXE	Office 2000 Setup program.
TRANSFORMS=	Informs Setup that a transform file will be supplied to customize Office 2000 Setup behavior.
Standard.mst	In this example, the name of the transform file configured to perform a Standard setup is supplied.
/qn+	Display options. In this example, no display will show, and there will be no confirmation at the end of Setup.

For a complete listing of Office 2000 SETUP.EXE parameters, refer to your Office 2000 documentation, or run SETUP.EXE with a /? Switch.

Test Results

The following sections show the data that was gathered for the various tests that were run.

Running Microsoft Office 2000 Setup.exe

	Time Elapsed (Minutes)	Frames	Broadcasts	Multicasts	Mbytes	Bytes/Sec	Frames Dropped
Windows NT 4.0							
Standard Install	0:08:52	232,148	6	1	220.41	414,313	0
Complete Install	0:14:00	504,208	7	0	483.63	575,749	0
Minimal Install	0:01:50	59,345	1	0	57.83	525,763	0
Network Install	0:08:47	220,348	5	0	206.53	391,897	0
Install German Language Pack	0:03:22	160,389	2	2	156.01	772,310	0
Standard Install on 11 Machines	0:33:57	2,065,081	106	30	1952.30	958,419	0

	Time Elapsed (Minutes)	Frames	Broadcasts	Multicasts	Mbytes	Bytes/Sec	Frames Dropped
Netware 4.11							
Standard Install	0:10:08	169,776	194	0	219.43	360,897	0
Complete Install	0:15:17	365,875	300	0	482.71	526,396	0
Minimal Install	0:02:03	42,843	37	0	57.94	471,021	0
Network Install	0:10:10	162,920	201	0	205.88	337,510	0

First Use Install Tests

	Time Elapsed (Minutes)	Frames	Broadcasts	Multicasts	MBytes	Bytes/Sec	Frames Dropped
Windows NT 4.0							
First use - Word, Text with Layout Converter	0:00:09	308	0	0	0.26	29,248	0
First use - Word, Report Template	0:00:06	346	1	0	0.32	53,303	0
First use - Access	0:00:29	10,846	0	0	10.64	366,829	0
First use - Northwind Sample Database	0:00:14	2,770	0	0	2.64	188,378	0
First use - PowerPoint	0:00:21	6,963	1	0	6.82	324,654	0
Netware 4.11							
First use - Word, Text with Layout Converter	0:00:14	308	6	0	0.27	19,557	0
First use - Word, Report Template	0:00:11	324	12	0	0.33	29,658	0
First use - Access	0:00:34	7,887	10	0	10.67	313,813	0
First use - Northwind Sample Database	0:00:14	2,063	6	0	2.64	188,887	0
First use - PowerPoint	0:00:25	4,991	8	0	6.78	271,072	0

Running a Network Copy of Microsoft Office 2000

	Time Elapsed (Minutes)	Frames	Broadcasts	Multicasts	MBytes	Bytes/Sec	Frames Dropped
Windows NT 4.0							
Running Network copy of Word, Excel, and Outlook simultaneously. Use Spell Check, Grammar Check, Insert Table, and Save File.	0:00:16	3,759	0	0	3.04	189,908	0
Netware 4.11							
Running Network copy of Word, Excel, and Outlook simultaneously. Use Spell Check, Grammar Check, Insert Table, and Save File.	0:00:28	4,809	9	0	4.84	172,971	0

Self Repair

	Time Elapsed (Minutes)	Frames	Broadcasts	Multicasts	MBytes	Bytes/Sec	Frames Dropped
Windows NT 4.0							
Delete Winword.exe. Then run Word.	0:00:27	9,533	0	0	9.42	348,831	0
Netware 4.11							
Delete Winword.exe. Then run Word.	0:00:36	6,963	10	0	9.46	262,770	0

Installation Graphs Showing Elapsed Time and Bytes Transferred

Figures 10.1 and 10.2 provide a graphical representation of elapsed time and bytes transferred for Standard, Complete, Minimal, and Network installations of Office 2000.

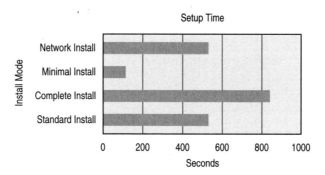

Figure 10.1   Elapsed time for various Office 2000 installation modes.

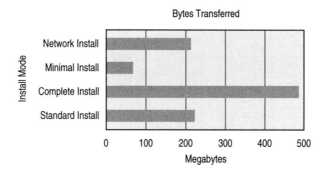

Figure 10.2   Bytes transferred for various Office 2000 installation modes.

Recommendations and Guidelines

The following guidelines will assist deployment managers as they design a network-based implementation strategy for Office 2000.

- Determine current network utilization statistics before deploying Office 2000. Look for periods of low to no network activity and plan to deploy Office 2000 during these times.

- Deploy Office 2000 using a staged approach. In other words, stagger the installation across the organization to avoid congesting your network.

- If you plan to install most of the features to the local computer, schedule the distribution for off-peak hours.

- Place Office 2000 installation points carefully in your network to provide for fault-tolerance and to spread the network load.

- Plan for failed installations. Have procedures in place to determine if Office 2000 Setup completes successfully, and to rerun Setup on machines where Setup originally failed to complete. This could include saving the log files created for analysis.

- Employ the First Use Office 2000 installation feature to reduce the initial network impact if that is a concern. Conversely, the more features that are set to install on first use, the more difficult it will be for the deployment manager to estimate future network load or confine that load to off-peak hours. Theoretically, this option will reduce the amount of data passed over the wire, as some users may never make use of some Office 2000 features. Be aware that users can potentially become annoyed if too many elements are installed on first use. Also, keep in mind that laptop users will not be able to install features on demand when they are not connected to the network. You may want to consider giving laptop users an installation CD to support *Install on Demand*.

- Consider using Microsoft Systems Management Server (SMS) to assist in hardware inventory, software inventory, software distribution, and determining the successes and failures of Office 2000 Setup.

- Conduct a pilot rollout. This will test your deployment procedures and confirm that the options installed are appropriate for the clients.

- If Novell Netware servers are used as installation points, clients will need to have a persistent drive mapping to that installation point. Microsoft Windows NT clients can use UNC names, eliminating the need for persistent drive mappings, although those server names will need to be persistent. Use additional locations (which can be specified in the transform file) to provide for more flexibility.

- A totally silent install is best limited to times when a user is not present. Users will not necessarily realize an installation is being performed and may restart their computer prematurely. Notify users of installation times and durations or use a quiet installation with progress and error dialog boxes. Notify helpdesk staff that network performance complaints may be received during installation times.

CHAPTER 11

Customizing Alerts and Help

By Mark Jennings,
Flywheel Systems,
and Joel Ware,
Boeing Company

In addition to more than 5,000 alerts and 50 MB of compressed Help files, Office 2000 contains methods you can use to customize these systems. This chapter shows why, where, and how to customize, illustrating the process with occasional examples based on the fictional *Northwind* company. The discussion includes:

- An overview of the Office 2000 alert and Help customization features.

- A discussion of the benefits and drawbacks to customization.

- A customization overview.

- Step-by-step processes for various customizations, presented in ascending order of sophistication.

What You'll Find in This Chapter

■ How to best customize your company's Help files and alerts (also known as error messages) by studying the example of the *Northwind* enterprise

■ An overview of the Help and alert options available in Office 2000

■ How to weigh the costs and the benefits of customization, and how to determine which customization efforts will pay off for your company

■ How to perform the actual customizations on your Help files and alerts once you have decided which ones will be of most use to your company

Warning This chapter discusses changing the Windows system registry using the Registry Editor. Using the Registry Editor incorrectly can cause serious, system-wide problems that require you to reinstall Windows. Microsoft cannot guarantee that any problems resulting from use of the Registry Editor can be solved. Use this tool at your own risk.

Enterprise

Northwind is a large, multinational, Fortune 100 manufacturing and systems-integration company. Most of its offices are located in the United States, although there are a few abroad. Most of its 200,000 desktops are Pentium-based.

Network/Applications

Northwind's network runs on Microsoft Windows NT 4.0 servers. Most employees use Windows 95, some run Windows NT 4.0 workstation. Almost all employees use Office 2000 and many desktops support server-based software.

Challenge

Northwind's major challenge is to customize Office 2000 so that employees use internal support resources first.

Solution

Northwind plans to accomplish this by customizing Office 2000 Help files and redirecting Help Web links to direct users to internal support resources.

Customization Overview

This section describes the alerts, Help systems, and customizations available in Office 2000, to help you understand what is available and how it can be changed to suit a specific environment.

Custom Alerts

Alerts are also known as error messages. The *Microsoft Office 2000 Resource Kit* (ORK) refers interchangeably to error numbers and error IDs.

Alerts for each Office 2000 application are documented in an Excel worksheet called ERRORMSG.XLS (on the resource kit CD). Figure 11.1 shows part of the worksheet for Word. (The information in this file is discussed later in this chapter in the "How to Customize Alerts" section on page 290.)

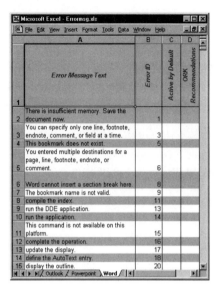

Figure 11.1   A section of ERRORMSG.XLS for Word.

An alert usually displays an error message with an **OK** button that dismisses the alert and takes the user back to the application. For any Office 2000 alert, you can add a button that takes the user to a Web site for more information. Several hundred Office 2000 alerts take users to the Microsoft Office Update Web site for more information, and you can redirect these to your own intranet site. Figure 11.2 shows a customized alert.

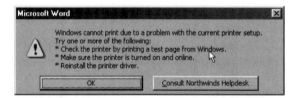

Figure 11.2   Customized alert for a Word printer error.

All customized Office 2000 alerts go to a single Web site, but you can work around this by writing server scripts that direct Office 2000 to pass the error number to the script, which in turn redirects to a page written specifically for the alert.

Custom Help Content

You can add your own custom content to the standard help files. The Answer Wizard searches all content—including custom content—when users submit queries.

From the Trenches: Adding Custom Help Topics to Office 2000 Help

Northwind wanted to make company-specific information available to users. The company recently changed the look of their corporate branding, and it was important that users creating presentations and letters used the appropriate logos and document styles. Northwind created custom Help topics containing information about the changes and how to locate and use updated templates, graphics, and style guidelines. Figure 11.3 shows an Office Assistant screen at the Northwind company. When users submit the highlighted question, the Answer Wizard searches the standard Office 2000 Help topics and Northwind's custom topics. (Users can also search custom content from the Answer Wizard pane of the Help window.)

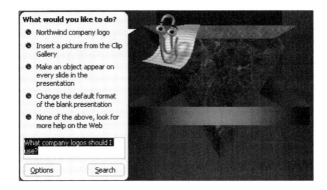

Figure 11.3   Custom Help content from an Office Assistant query.

The Office 2000 Answer Wizard can incorporate pages stored on Web servers as Help window topics, allowing you to integrate existing Web-page Help content into Office.

Architectural issues prevent displaying custom content in the Help window's Contents or Index panes (see Figure 11.4). Instead, you have to point users to the Answer Wizard from either the main Help window or from an Office Assistant.

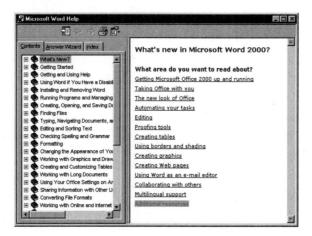

Figure 11.4   Help window Contents pane—no custom content can appear.

You can replace the Office Help files containing Microsoft Technical Support information with internal support information and the files containing links to the Microsoft Web site with links to internal Web sites.

Custom Web Links

Office 2000 can link to additional Help information stored on Web sites and displayed in an Internet browser such as Internet Explorer.

Users can display Web-based Help by clicking hyperlinks within Help topics, by clicking more **Help on the Web** buttons that are provided Office Assistant query results, and by clicking the **Office on the Web** menu item included in each application's **Help** menu. These links connect to various pages in the Office Update section of the Microsoft Web site, pointing users to Microsoft information sources such as the Microsoft Developer Network (MSDN), TechNet, resource kits, developer tools, and so on. You can redirect these links to your company's internal Web site or turn them off altogether.

Links between the Answer Wizard and the Web are generally better to customize by adding material. Then, when a user queries an Office Assistant, Office 2000 uses the Answer Wizard to suggest relevant Help topics and a link to the new material can be can be included in a *Look for more Help at...* bullet in the assistant's text balloon (see Figure 11.5). Clicking on this bullet displays an intermediate dialog box (see Figure 11.6) and the Answer Wizard branches to a Web site where the user's query can be parsed and searched against further Help content. Support staff can log queries to track user issues and improve Help content. Office Assistant Web Help is also connected to the Microsoft Office Update Web site, and you can redirect the link to a custom intranet Web site.

Note   This type of Web customization is available only from Office Assistants and cannot be done from the Answer Wizard pane of the main Help window.

Figure 11.5   Custom Web Help available through the Office Assistant.

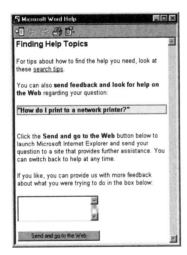

Figure 11.6   Custom dialog for Answer Wizard Help.

The final Web link in the Office Help system is from the **Office on the Web** menu item in the **Help** menu (Figure 11.7). Usually, this connects to the Microsoft Office Update Web page, but you can customize the link to connect to a page on your company's Web site.

Figure 11.7   Office on the Web menu item.

Custom Office Assistants

Office 2000 includes nine different Office Assistants. If you have the appropriate Software Developer Kit (SDK), you can write your own agent.

Should You Customize?

You have to weigh the benefits of customized Help content against the costs of creating it. While Office 2000 provides some fairly easy methods to make the customizations described above, most require some effort and all require resources to implement—especially those that require you to write Web server code. In addition to content development and programming, you typically have to deploy files on the network and maintain them.

Reduced Total Cost of Ownership

Customization usually seeks to lower the total cost of ownership (TCO) for each Office 2000 desktop installation. Using the *better, faster, cheaper* mantra, many large corporations set aggressive goals such as reducing company-wide desktop computing costs by 50 percent.

Gains are achievable because helpdesk support costs typically make up a large percentage of computing costs—as users help themselves more, computing costs decline. The first step in cost-effective customization is to find out which issues cause the most difficulty for users. The next is to assess which of these can be alleviated through improved alerts and better Help systems. This process will help you see if a customization effort is justified.

Rapid Software Deployment

Alert and Help customization can also speed the deployment of complex products such as Office 2000. Without customization, a large organization can take months for rollout, during which time the software's productivity gains are not fully realized. Customization may make it possible to accelerate the rollout so that user productivity is enhanced more quickly.

Internet Restrictions

Office 2000 is much more Web-aware than previous versions. Out of the box, Office 2000 contains numerous links between alerts and supplemental information on Microsoft's Web site.

If you do not provide Internet access to some desktops (for security, cost, or productivity reasons) those users will not be able to use these links and you may want to disable them. But since the links already exist, it makes sense to redirect them to an intranet site that provides support information geared to your environment.

Reduction in Configuration Variations

Downloaded software can cause unplanned and uncontrolled variations in software configurations, especially localized ones, and you may have (or need) a *no Internet downloads* software policy. You can avoid some of these issues by redirecting some Office 2000 Web links to internal Web sites where downloads can be controlled.

Use Helpdesk First Policies

Large companies with centralized helpdesks have found that resolution and diagnosis costs can increase when users ignore these resources and instead call Microsoft or ask friends. Studies show that a direct and accurate answer to a user question costs about 10 percent as much as leaving the question unresolved, working around it, or cobbling together a solution. Customized alerts and Help content can reduce cost by making reliable answers available from the user's desktop.

License Restrictions

Many site licenses do not allow users to call Microsoft directly with questions, so some of the references and resources mentioned in Office 2000 Help files are not accessible. You can change these references to internal helpdesk resources or delete them.

Site-Specific Information

Every company has information specific to network, location, and method of Office 2000 deployment. You can reduce user support costs by seamlessly integrating this with Office 2000 information. If you already have helpdesk information deployed on your network, you should be able to integrate this information into Office 2000 with little or no modification.

Improving Help Resources

Many customizations redirect users to Web sites where Office 2000 provides information about the user, the computer, and the type of problem. You can use server code to log this information, track user issues, and focus Help content in, for instance, Frequently Asked Question (FAQ) screens.

How to Customize: Overview

Now that you know why and where to customize Office 2000 alerts and Help, this section will offer a broad technical overview of *how*. Each process contains a few general steps. All customizations will follow the general sequence, but some steps may not be required for some customizations.

1. Create the custom content

   Write the Web pages and Help topics you want to add. You may not have to write much: if you already have Web-based Help content you can simply add it or leave it where it is and link to it if it is on Web servers. You can create files with any tool that supports HTML Web authoring, including Word, which now supports reading and writing HTML files. The HTML Help Workshop included in the *Microsoft Office 2000 Resource Kit* is the best tool for Help file creation.

2. Distribute the content

   Place the new content on the network, either as individual files or HTML pages on a Web server. Copying Help files to individual desktops provides the best performance but consumes disk space on every desktop and makes it harder to update content.

3. Register the content on individual desktops

   Register new content so that Office 2000 is aware of it. The content can appear alongside standard Office 2000 content or replace some pieces of it. There are several ways to register it. For a single client, the simplest method is to use Registry Editor (RegEdit) to edit the computer's registry. Because this often is impractical for larger rollouts, Microsoft provides two additional tools: the Custom Installation Wizard (Figure 11.8) for new deployments and the System Policy Editor (see Figure 11.9) for post-deployment registration. You can also use Microsoft Visual Basic for Applications (VBA), for registrations that last only while an application is running. The table on page 290 summarizes the different registration methods available to you.

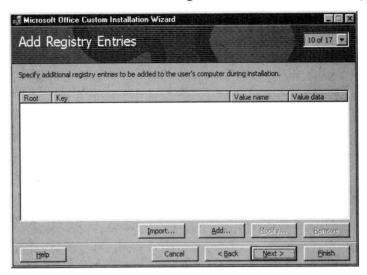

Figure 11.8   Registry edit step in Custom Installation Wizard.

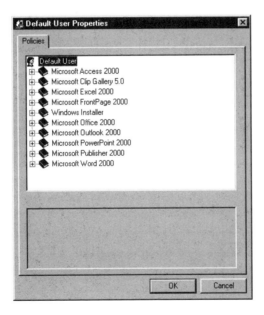

Figure 11.9   System Policy Properties dialog box for Default User.

Summary of client registration methods

Registration Method	Tool	Typical Use	Duration
Manually edit registry on individual desktops	RegEdit	Trial deployments and testing	Persistent
Distribute registry changes during initial Office 2000 installation	Custom Installation Wizard	During initial deployment	Persistent
Register customizations through global system policies	System Policy Editor	After initial deployment	As long as system policy is maintained
Register customization through an Office application	Visual Basic for Applications (VBA)	Customization needed for a specific Office application	As long as application runs

How to Customize Alerts

This section walks you through the alert customization processes. For more information, refer to the *Microsoft Office 2000 Resource Kit.*

Note   The customization processes in this section involve editing the registry, which you can do on a single computer with RegEdit or during deployment with the Custom Installation Wizard. For some client registrations you can use system policy and VBA methods; these are detailed at the end of the chapter.

There is only one way to customize an alert: add a button that links to a Web page. All Office 2000 alert links go to a single Web page, but Office 2000 passes you enough information to write server code to branch to alert-specific pages. You can use the same button test for all customized alerts or different text for each.

First, decide which alerts you want to customize. All Office 2000 alerts are listed in the Excel worksheet ERRORMSG.XLS, which is on the *Microsoft Office 2000 Resource Kit* CD and on the Microsoft Office Web site (Figure 11.1). Each Office application has a separate section in this file, with one alert per row and four corresponding columns of information:

- **Error Message Text.** This is the text the alert displays or a placeholder for passing dynamic information from Office 2000 to the alert.

■ **Error ID.** This is an alert number unique within the application *not* across all Office applications. Complete identification requires the Error ID *and* the application's globally unique identifier (GUID). The list below shows the Office 2000's application GUIDs; they are also available at the Microsoft Office 2000 Update Web site:

Application	GUID
Excel	{CC29E96F-7BC2-11D1-A921-00A0C91E2AA2}
Word	{CC29E963-7BC2-11D1-A921-00A0C91E2AA2}
PowerPoint	{CC29E94B-7BC2-11D1-A921-00A0C91E2AA2}
Access	{CC29E967-7BC2-11D1-A921-00A0C91E2AA2}
Outlook	{CC29EA4B-7BC2-11D1-A921-00A0C91E2AA2}
Graph	{CC29E975-7BC2-11D1-A921-10A0C91E2AA2}
Office 2000 Shared	{CC29E943-7BC2-11D1-A921-00A0C91E2AA2}

■ **Active by Default.** Whether the alert has already been customized by Office in a default setup.

■ **ORK Recommendations.** Whether the *Microsoft Office 2000 Resource Kit* recommends customization. In general, you should consider customizing most alerts dealing with network issues, passwords, disk space, file/record locking, file conversions, printing, and e-mail integration. See the resource kit for more possibilities.

The next sections describe alert customization methods, working from easiest to most difficult. Rule of thumb: the more difficult a customization, the more powerful it tends to be.

Stage 1: Disable Default Web Links

You can disable default Web links to Microsoft's Office Update Web site if you don't want to build an intranet site for handling alerts, if you have users without Web access, or if you want to prevent users from linking to Microsoft's Web site. All you have to do is delete the URL and button text in two registry entries. This removes *all* custom buttons in *all* Office 2000 alerts.

Required Steps

1. Delete the URL. Store a null string in the registry entry named CustomizableAlertBasedURL in the subkey:
   HKCU\Software\Microsoft\Office\9.0\Common\General

2. Delete the Button Text. Store a null string in the registry entry named CustomizableAlertDefaultButtonText in the subkey:
   HKCU\Software\Microsoft\Office\9.0\Common\General

Note Do not delete these registry entries; just set their data to a null string.

Stage 2: Install a Simple Static Custom Web Page for Selected Alerts

You can link customized alerts to a single static intranet Home page, where you can put a Frequently Asked Questions page or general information that helps users with common problems. You can also add hyperlinks that take users to more information—an existing helpdesk page, for instance.

After creating the Web page, enter its URL and the alerts' default button text in the two registry subkeys mentioned in Stage 1. Then go to the application-specific portions of the registry and create entries for each alert you want to link to your Web page. (You can skip this step if you're satisfied with the Office 2000 default choices for customization. If you make new choices, you can make the button text different for each alert.)

Required Steps

1. Create the Web page(s). Using any HTML authoring tool (Word will work for simple pages), create the one or more Web page(s) and deploy them on the network. Be sure to note the Home page's base URL.

2. Register the URL. Store the base URL in a registry entry named CustomizableAlertBaseURL in the registry subkey: HKCU\Software\Microsoft\Office\9.0\Common\General

3. Register the Default Button Text. Store the default button text—the text of any button you don't specifically enter text for in Step 4 below—in a registry entry named CustomizableAlertDefaultButtonText in the registry subkey: HKCU\Software\Microsoft\Office\9.0\Common\General

4. Register Each Alert. For each alert you want to link to the Web site, create an entry in the registry subkey: HKCU\Software\Microsoft\Office\9.0*Application*\CustomizableAlerts where *Application* is the name of the application (such as Word, Excel, and so on).

5. Name each registry entry with the alert error number (see ERRORMSG.XLS) and set the value to the button text. If you don't enter any button text, the default button text is used.

 Note You can skip this step if you just use the default selection of customized alerts that ships with Office 2000.

Stage 3: Install a Scripted Web Site for Customized Alerts

You can use Web server scripts to create a more sophisticated Web site to handle customized alerts. With some server-side code, you can bring up a separate Web page for each customized alert without requiring any action from the user. You can also log the alert to provide real-time feedback on what types of alerts users are encountering most frequently, then use this data to improve your Help resources.

When a user clicks on a customized alert button, Office 2000 links to your Web site and passes three parameters in the QUERY_STRING variable appended to the URL:

Alrt	Error message number (see ERRORMSG.XLS)
HelpLCID	Country code (1033 for English-language countries, for example)
GUID	Application global ID (given earlier)

The server script uses these three parameters to bring up a custom page for a specific alert. If your server handles localized versions of Office 2000, you can use the country code parameter to bring up pages in different languages.

Required Steps

1. Create the Web site. Create the Web pages and server script, deploy the pages on the network, and note the URL for the server script. If your Web server is Microsoft Internet Information Server (IIS) running on Windows NT Server, you'll probably find it easiest to write an Active Server Page (ASP) script. The Office 2000 Resource Kit includes an Excel workbook (ASPSCRPT.XLS) with macros that can generate simple ASP files, or you can modify sample ASP scripts and HTML files in the *Microsoft Office 2000 Resource Kit*. You can use any Web server program, such as a CGI script.

2. Register the URL. Store this URL in a registry entry named CustomizableAlertBaseURL in the registry subkey:
   HKCU\Software\Microsoft\Office\9.0\Common\General

Note   Add a **?** to the end of the URL so that the error message number, GUID, and country code are appended to the base URL. For example:
http://Helpdesk/OfficeAlerts.asp?

3. Register the Default Button Text. Store the default button text for any alert without custom button text in a registry entry named CustomizableAlertDefaultButtonText in the registry subkey:
   HKCU\Software\Microsoft\Office\9.0\Common\General

4. Register Each Alert. For each alert you want to customize, create an entry in the registry subkey: HKCU\Software\Microsoft\Office\9.0*Application*\CustomizableAlerts where *Application* is the name of the application such as Word, Excel, and so on. Name each registry entry with the alert error number (see ERRORMSG.XLS) and set the value data to the custom button text. If you do not enter any button text, the default button text set in step 3 is used.

How to Customize Help

Customizing Help is a bit more complex than customizing alerts because the Office 2000 Help system is more complicated and you can customize its behavior on multiple levels.

First, decide what type of Help customization is applicable to your needs. You can modify the Office 2000 Help system by adding custom Help topics, by writing Office Assistants, and by linking from the Help system to Web pages in three different ways. So, there are five possible Help system customizations:

- **Custom Help content.** This is supplemental Help content that you create with Help authoring tools (HTML Help Workshop, any HTML editor, and Answer Wizard Builder) and add to the Office Help system so that it appears alongside the standard Help content. It is available when the user makes a query with the Answer Wizard—either in the main Help window or from an Office Assistant—and can be stored as standard HTML files on a Web server, as compressed HTML files stored locally, or as compressed HTML files stored on a network share.

- **Help topic links to the Web.** These are supplemental Help pages stored on the Web and accessed by hyperlink from Office Help topics. Office 2000 automatically directs the hyperlinks to supplemental Help pages on the Microsoft Office Update Web site. If you don't need or can't access this resource, you can disable the hyperlinks or redirect them to Web pages on your intranet.

Note   The hyperlinks use Microsoft's associative links (A-links) technology documented in the HTML Help workshop.

- **Answer Wizard Links to the Web.** These are supplemental Help pages stored on the Web and displayed to users who issue Answer Wizard queries from an Office Assistant. After displaying all the topics applicable to a user's query, the Office Assistant can provide a last resort option—linking to the Web to try to find more information there. Office 2000 directs these links to Microsoft's Office Update Web site where the query is logged and a search is made against the latest content. If you don't need or can't access this resource, you can disable the hyperlinks or redirect them to Web pages on your intranet.

Note   This feature is available only for Answer Wizard queries made with an Office Assistant. Queries made from the Answer Wizard pane of the Help window cannot link to the Web.

- **Office on the Web Link to the Web.** These are supplemental Help Web pages stored on the Web and reached by clicking **Office on the Web** on any Office application Help menu. Office 2000 directs these links to an application-specific Web page on Microsoft's Office Update Web site. If you don't need or can't access this resource, you can disable the hyperlinks or redirect them to Web pages on your intranet.

- **Custom Office Assistants.** You can write custom Office Assistants using the Microsoft Agent software development kit available through Microsoft Developer Network. For example, you can create a custom Office Assistant that looks like your company's logo or has a different gesture set that is applicable to your line of business.

It is difficult to generalize which customizations are applicable for different situations, but here are some guidelines:

- Office 2000's Help system now allows you to index, search, and display Web pages as Help topics that look just like the standard Help topics. If you have existing Help content on a Web site, you can index this content with Answer Wizard Builder and make it available alongside the Office Help content.

- If you have a large body of custom Help content already in WinHelp format, you can add it to the existing Office Help content and store it as compressed HTML (.CHM) files—either on individual clients or on a network share. If you have large volumes of information, want the best performance, and want to use all the bells and whistles in the Help authoring environment, use compressed HTML files.

Note   Whether you store your custom Help content as Web pages or as compressed HTML (.CHM) files, it is currently impossible to add your custom Help to the Help window Contents or Index panes. Users who don't use the Answer Wizard will not see your custom content.

- If network performance is an issue, you can provide better performance for users if you store custom Help content in compressed HTML (.CHM) files locally on individual clients. On the downside, this method uses considerable client disk space and makes it burdensome to update client computers. The next best alternative from a performance standpoint is to store the .CHM files on a network share. Web pages stored on a Web server offer the lowest performance, but the generally are the easiest to maintain and they allow you to use the widest assortment of development tools.

- If your Help content is currently on a Web site and you don't want to integrate it with the Office Help content, you can link it to your company's content by using any of the three *link to the Web* methods.

- Hyperlinks from within Office Help topics to the Web are used primarily to tell users where to go within Microsoft to get product updates, development kits, technical support materials, and similar information. The most common customization is to simply disable these links. Office 2000 *bottlenecks* all hyperlinks from Help topics through a few files, so you can easily disable the links by deleting these files. These are the only Help files that can be deleted without breaking other parts of Help.

- Links that send users to the Web from the Answer Wizard (*last resort* links) are most useful when you have a server script that actively searches your intranet for information that might help a user. Server scripts also allow you to log the question—a tremendous resource for improving Help content.

Note   Web links from the Answer Wizard are available only from Office Assistants. If users make their queries from the Answer Wizard pane of the Help window, they will not see a *last resort* Web link.

- The link from the **Office on the Web** menu item on the **Help** menu is the easiest link to set up between a single helpdesk page and Office 2000.

The next sections describe Help customization methods, working from easiest to most difficult. The stages are not mutually exclusive; you can use techniques from one stage within another.

Stage 1: Remove All Web Links

Easiest option: remove all references to the Web from the entire Help system. This is for users who cannot access the Web from their clients and who you don't want to redirect to intranet Web sites. The user won't see any hyperlinks from Help topics, Web links from the Answer Wizard, or the **Office on the Web** menu item in the **Help** menu.

Required Steps

1. Delete or edit the Help files containing Web links. Disable all hyperlinks from Office Help topics by deleting these five Help files: ACWEB9.CHM, OLWEB9.CHM, PPWEB9.CHM, WDWEB9.CHM, and XLWEB9.CHM. Another methods is to decompile these files in the HTML Help Workshop, edit the HTML to remove the hyperlinks, recompile the files, and redistribute them to individual clients. You can use this alternative to create a single Help page in each file that hyperlinks users to your intranet Web site. The topics in these files are generally not useful without the hyperlinks to Microsoft's Web site.

> **Note**   These are the only files in the Office 2000 Help system you can delete without breaking other parts of Help.

2. Register a null string for the Answer Wizard URL. Disable links between the Answer Wizard and the Web by storing a null string in a registry entry named AWFeedbackURL in the subkey: HKCU\Software\Microsoft\Office\9.0\Common\Internet

3. Register a null string for the *Office On The Web* URL. Disable the link between the **Office on the Web** menu item on the **Help** menu and the Web by storing a null string in a registry value named OfficeOnTheWeb in the subkey: HKCU\Software\Microsoft\Office\9.0\Common\Internet

Stage 2: Redirect All Web Links Back to a Static Intranet Web Site

This stage can be simple or complex—depending on the complexity of your intranet Web site.

Required Steps

1. Build the Web site. Create the site and note the Home page base URL.

2. Edit Help files with Web links. Redirect hyperlinks from Help topics to your Web site by editing the hyperlinks in these five files with HTML Help Workshop: ACWEB9.CHM, OLWEB9.CHM, PPWEB9.CHM, WDWEB9.CHM, and XLWEB9.CHM. For each file, decompile, edit the HTML to redirect the hyperlinks, recompile, and store the files for later distribution.

> **Note**   The Help topics in these files aren't very useful without the links. You may prefer to delete the files or replace each one with a single page directing users to your Web site (as discussed in Stage 1, above).

3. Register the URL with Answer Wizard. Redirect the link from the Answer Wizard to your Web site by storing the URL in a registry entry named AWFeedbackURL in the subkey: HKCU\Software\Microsoft\Office\9.0\Common\Internet

4. Register balloon text with Answer Wizard. You can store your own *balloon label text* in a registry entry named AWFeedbackBalloonLabel in the same subkey. (This is text that appears in the balloon next to the Office Assistant— the default Web prompt is *None of the above, look for more Help on the Web.*)

5. Register dialog text with Answer Wizard. You can also store your own *dialog text* in a registry value named AWFeedbackDialogText in the same subkey. (This is a special line of text that appears in the Help dialog above the feedback text edit box—there is no default text.)

6. Register the URL with the **Office on the Web** menu item on the **Help** menu. Redirect the item to your Web site by storing the URL in a registry entry named OfficeOnTheWeb in the same subkey.

Stage 3: Replace the Technical Support Help File with the Custom File

One compiled HTML Help file (PSS9.CHM) contains Microsoft Technical Support Information, including phone numbers. Figure 11.10 shows this file open in the Office 2000 Help window. Users reach these Help topics through the Help window or by clicking the **Tech Support** button on the **About Application** dialog.

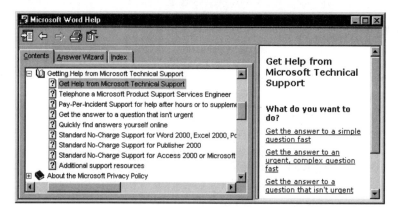

Figure 11.10   Microsoft Technical Support topics in PSS9.CHM.

To supersede this information and redirect calls back to your own technical support services, replace the PSS9.CHM file with your own but make sure it has the same name.

Required Steps

1. Create a custom compressed HTML Help file. Create a file with technical-support topics applicable to your system. If you have an existing technical-support page in WinHelp format (perhaps from an Office 97 deployment) you can import it into the HTML Help Workshop, recompile it, and save it as PSS9.CHM. (This technique is discussed in more detail in Stage 5.) You can also use HTML Help Workshop to decompile the PSS9.CHM file that ships with Office 2000, edit it to reflect your own technical support phone numbers and other information, recompile it, and save it as PSS9.CHM.

Note   You *must* name this file PSS9.CHM. The Help system has *hard links* to this file and there is no way to link to a file with another name. You also *must* create a content (.HHC) file for your custom file to work properly.

2. Build an Answer Wizard file. You can do this with the Answer Wizard Builder (AWB). Open AWB and enter a path to your new PSS9.CHM file. AWB will parse the file into topics and allow you to add specific questions for each topic that will lead users to the correct topic when they ask a question in the Answer Wizard.

3. Register your Answer Wizard file. If you created an Answer Wizard file, register its location by storing the location in a registry entry named with any unique name and with a value that is the full path (including the file name) where the Answer Wizard file is stored. Store this registry entry in the subkey: HKCU\Software\Microsoft\Office\9.0*Application*\Answer Wizard where *Application* is the name of the Office application (Word, Excel, and so on). You may need to create the subkey if this is the first Answer Wizard file to be registered on the client.

4. Distribute files. Distribute the .CHM and (optional) Answer Wizard files to client computers. You can use the Custom Installation Wizard or other methods. You must store these files in the same folder as other .CHM and Answer Wizard files, which must be where the original PSS9.CHM file was stored.

Stage 4: Add An Existing Web Site to the Office Help Content

You can index any Web site so that its content can be accessed from the Answer Wizard in Office 2000. This makes it possible to integrate large amounts of existing, site-specific Help content with the standard Office Help material. The key tool for this customization is Answer Wizard Builder (AWB) included in the *Microsoft Office 2000 Office Resource Kit*. The AWB indexes the Web site and makes the full text available for Answer Wizard searches. It also allows you to associate typical user questions with each Help topic, which can dramatically improve the AWB's accuracy with free-format queries.

Required Steps

1. Create a new Answer Wizard project by entering the path to your existing Web Help content. The AWB parses and indexes the HTML pages in the Web site. When the process is complete, it displays a list of Help topics.

2. Add user questions. You can add *user questions* that address typical issues and improve Answer Wizard searching accuracy. You can enter one or more questions for each Help topic.

3. Build an Answer Wizard (AW) file by clicking the **Build** button in the main AWB window. Store the file in the same directory as the AWB project file.

4. Deploy the custom Answer Wizard file to its final location. This can be on individual clients or on a network server. Deploying the file on individual clients obviously reduces network overhead but it requires copying the file to each client. You don't need to deploy the Web site content—the AW file includes the full URL to find the Help content in the location from which it was parsed.

5. Register the location of the custom AW file on each client. Do this by storing the location in a registry entry named with any unique name and with a value that is the full path (including the AW file name) where it is stored. Store this registry entry in the subkey:
HKCU\Software\Microsoft\Office\9.0*Application*\Answer Wizard
where *Application* is the name of the Office application (Word, Excel, and so on). You may need to create the subkey if this is the first AW file to be registered on the client.

Stage 5: Add WinHelp Content to the Office Help Content

If you already have a significant amount of custom Help content in WinHelp format, you can import these files in the HTML Help Workshop, make modifications, compile this content into compressed Help format (.CHM) files, and then use the Answer Wizard Builder to parse these files for access from the Answer Wizard.

Required Steps

1. Import your WinHelp project into the HTML Help Workshop. Start a new project by clicking **New** on the **File** menu, then clicking the checkbox that indicates you are starting with an existing WinHelp project. Enter that path (or browse) to locate the WinHelp project (.HPJ) file. When you click **Next** the HTML Help Workshop converts all the elements of the Help project.

Note   You can only import WinHelp *projects* to HTML Help Workshop, not individual WinHelp content (.HLP) files. If you have WinHelp content but don't have the original project files used to create them, you'll have to cut and paste content from the WinHelp browser to the HTML Help Workshop.

2. Edit the project. Use HTML Help Workshop to make any necessary modifications to individual Help topics.

3. Build a compressed HTML Help file. Compile your project and save it as a compressed HTML (.CHM) file.

4. Create a new Answer Wizard project (use the AWB) by entering the path (or browsing) to the location of your .CHM file. The AWB parses and indexes the file and displays a list of Help topics when it is done.

5. Add user questions. You can add typical questions you think users may ask in the Answer Wizard. These can improve Answer Wizard searching accuracy. You can enter one or more user questions for each Help topic.

6. Build an Answer Wizard file. Click the **Build** button in the main AWB window. Store the AW file in the same directory as the AWB project file.

7. Deploy the AW and .CHM files to their final locations. This can be on individual clients or a network server. Deploying on individual clients reduces network overhead, but it requires copying the files to each client.

8. Register the AW file by storing the location in a registry entry with any unique name, then setting the value to the full path and file name where the file is stored. Store this registry value in the subkey: HKCU\Software\Microsoft\Office\9.0*Application*\Answer Wizard where *Application* is the name of the Office application (Word, Excel, and so on). You may need to create the subkey if this is the first Answer Wizard file to be registered.

9. Register the .CHM file location. Do this by storing the location in a registry entry with any unique name, then setting the value data to the path (without file name) where the .CHM file is located. Store this registry value in the subkey: HKLM\Software\Microsoft\Windows\HTML Help

Stage 6: Log User Queries to Your Own Web Server

The link between Answer Wizard and the Web allows you to track user queries with a Web server script. In the default configuration, when users go to the Microsoft Office Update Web site with a query, the query is parsed and used to search the site for information. The query is logged so that Microsoft can get feedback to improve the Help system.

You can log user queries and do your own searches by redirecting the links from the Answer Wizard to your own server and writing a server script to process and log the query.

Required Steps

1. Create your Web site and write a server script to log and process user queries. The form that appears after the user clicks the **More Help on the Web** balloon uses the POST method to pass these form elements to your server script:

DCC	Application global ID (table shown earlier)
HelpLCID	Country code (for example, 1033 for English-language countries)
AppName	Application name (for example, Microsoft Word)
UQ	Text of the user query
IAP	Additional feedback text entered by the user

2. Register the URL with the Answer Wizard. Redirect the link from the Answer Wizard to your Web site script by storing the URL in a registry entry named AWFeedbackURL in the subkey:
HKCU\Software\Microsoft\Office\9.0\Common\Internet
An example: http://Helpdesk/myfeedback.asp.

3. Register balloon text with the Answer Wizard. This is text that appears in the balloon next to the Office Assistant—the default Web prompt is *None of the above, look for more Help on the Web*. You can store your own balloon label text in a registry entry named AWFeedbackBalloonLabel in the same subkey.

4. Register dialog text with the Answer Wizard. This is a special line of text that appears in the Help dialog above the feedback text edit box—there is no default text. You can store your own dialog text in a registry value named AWFeedbackDialogText in the same subkey.

Custom Office Assistants

Office 2000 ships with nine different Office Assistants—characters (such as Clippit) that appear on the screen, make suggestions as a user works, and pass user-submitted questions to the Answer Wizard. See Figure 11.10 on page 298 for an example.

Assistants are Microsoft Agents. You can create your own versions by using the Microsoft Agent software development kit, available through MSDN. Creating an assistant takes some effort, but registering it with Office 2000 is easy.

Required Steps

1. Write an Office Assistant. You can implement as many agent UI features as you like, as long as the agent can accept user text input for Answer Wizard queries.

2. Register the Office Assistant. Store the file name of the assistant in a registry entry named AsstFile in the subkey:
HKCU\Software\Microsoft\Office\Common\Assistant

3. Distribute the Office Assistant. Copy the office assistant file to client desktops, either as part of installation or as a later update.

Registering Customizations with System Policies

These system policies are available for handling client registration. You can set them with the System Policy Editor:

- User*Application*\Miscellaneous\Custom Answer Wizard database path
- User\Microsoft Office 2000\Assistant\Help on the Web\Feedback button label
- User\Microsoft Office 2000\Assistant\Help on the Web\Feedback dialog text
- User\Microsoft Office 2000\Assistant\Help on the Web\Feedback URL

- User\Microsoft Office 2000\Help on the Web\Office on the Web URL
- User\Microsoft Office 2000\Customizable error messages\Base URL
- User\Microsoft Office 2000\Customizable error messages\Default button text
- User\Microsoft Office 2000\Customizable error messages\List of error messages to customize
- User\Application\Customizable error messages\List of error messages to customize

Registering Customizations with Visual Basic for Applications (VBA)

These VBA methods are available for handling client registration. They remain in effect only as long as the application is running:

- Application.Assistant.Filename (Office Assistant file)
- AnswerWizard.ClearFileList (Clears AW file list)
- AnswerWizard.ResetFileList (Resets AW file list to default stored in registry)
- AnswerWizardFiles.Add (Adds a file to AW file list)
- AnswerWizardFiles.Delete (Deletes a file in AW file list)
- CommandBarButton.OnAction (Can be used to redirect **Office on the Web** menu item)

C H A P T E R   1 2

Deploying Office 2000 on Windows Terminal Server

Deploying Office 2000 on Windows NT Server 4.0, Terminal Server Edition helps contain support costs by simplifying client configurations and making more efficient use of hardware. Users still have access to all Office 2000 features.

Designed as the model Windows Terminal Server application, Office 2000 offers *intelligence,* central control, and scalability to boost productivity and decrease total cost of ownership (TCO). (See "Running Office 2000 with Windows Terminal Server" at http://www.microsoft.com/Office/enterprise/deployment /termserv.htm for more information.) This chapter describes how to deploy and customize Office 2000 on Terminal Server.

What You'll Find in This Chapter

■ An overview of possible solutions and strategies for your Office 2000 deployment on Windows Terminal Server—including tools required and a step-by-step overview of deployment

■ How to incorporate the specific requirements of an Office 2000 deployment into your deployment plan and troubleshoot common issues that arise

■ How to use pre-deployment testing and pilot rollouts to your best advantage

■ How to successfully implement your solution—minimizing downtime and user issues

■ How to troubleshoot your deployment by learning from the other companies' experiences

■ An overview of custom settings used to deploy Office 2000 on Windows Terminal Server

Solutions and Strategies

Northwind Traders wanted to deploy Office 2000 to 1,500 clients across 700 sites (some with low bandwidth). The IT team picked Windows NT Server, Terminal Server Edition, to simplify the Office 2000 deployment—the most important factor in a project to use about 150 Terminal Servers. (The decision also created some unique requirements, described in the section "Office 2000–Specific Planning" on page 308.)

Northwind Traders considered two deployment strategies. The first strategy was to use *SysPrep* and Ghost to make images of the Terminal Servers and then deploy Office 2000 on the Terminal Server as part of the cloning procedure. The second was to provide the Terminal Server administrator with customized builds of Microsoft Internet Explorer 5 and Office 2000, along with installation procedures. Northwind Traders went with this strategy because it was more flexible than the first: the customized build could be used on an existing Terminal Server or incorporated into the scripted installation of a new Terminal Server.

Tools and Technologies Required

These *Microsoft Office 2000 Resource Kit* tools were used:

- Custom Installation Wizard (CIW).
- Internet Explorer Administration Kit (IEAK).
- Policy Editor (POLEDIT).
- Office Profile Wizard (PROFLWIZ).

TermSrvr.MST (from the resource kit Terminal Server tools) was used as a basis for a customized transform file containing the registry and configuration settings needed to install and operate Office 2000 on Terminal Server. Customization added command line arguments to control non-visible features and other MSI properties, and it added pre-set Office feature install states to avoid poor performance. *TermSrvr.MST* has no features set to *Install on First Use* or *Run from Source*. For details on transform file settings, see the *Microsoft Office 2000 Resource Kit*.

The team also installed the office assistant; it has no animation, thus reducing bandwidth requirements for a Terminal Server session.

Deployment Overview

As this was a new deployment of Terminal Server servers and clients, not an upgrade, the method was fairly straightforward:

1. The Terminal Server servers were built using a scripted installation, located in the data center, and assigned static IP addresses.
2. For each Terminal Server client, files required by the user were moved to a file server.
3. Users' systems were rebuilt with a standard operating environment based on Windows 95 OSR-2 and the Citrix MetaFrame client software.

In execution, of course, the plan was a little more complex. With the Terminal Servers in the data center, it made sense to move users' data stores and Microsoft Exchange mailboxes to data center servers too, and this data transfer used slow links.

Users had to be trained on Terminal Server and Office 2000, which lock down parts of the system and no longer permit you to save files on the workstation.

Office 2000–Specific Planning

Deploying Office 2000 on Terminal Server introduces some new requirements and eliminates many standard ones (such as having the Desktop Update on clients). The sections below describe Terminal Server requirements, deployment recommendations, and issues such as Office 2000 dependencies.

Identifying Office Components and Configurations

At Northwind Traders, MCS installed all of the Internet Explorer 5 components included in a *typical* installation, including Outlook Express, which is required for Outlook 2000 to operate correctly.

Almost all Office 2000 Professional components were installed on the Terminal Servers. Some components of note that were not installed are:

- Symantec Fax Starter Kit
- Office Assistants
- Language Selection Tools

Terminal Server is a shared system. The Windows Installer's *Detect and Repair* and *Install on First Use* features cannot be used because a *repair* run in one terminal session could overwrite files that are open in another terminal session. You have to install every application users might need.

From the Trenches: Saving CPU Time and Bandwidth While Implementing Support Technologies

At Northwind Traders, non-essential features that use up bandwidth and CPU time were made *Not Available*. Office Assistants use more bandwidth because they move when the screen is otherwise idle, so Northwind Traders installed the *Still Logo* Office Assistant (included in the resource kit) because it is not animated and saves bandwidth on the Terminal Server client connections. (Rather than including the *Still Logo* in the CIW, you should install it with the resource kit so that it is registered with Darwin.)

Northwind Traders also plans to implement supporting technologies, such as Web-extended error messages and Web-extended Help files. This will be handled by the team deploying Office 2000 for Windows 95 and is not part of this project.

Support for Roaming Users

Because Northwind Traders users *roam* and can attach to any Terminal Server, the deployment included the use of the Citrix Metaframe Load Balancing services. Office 2000 had to be configured to support Terminal Server profiles and to transfer user settings with Window NT user profiles to provide a consistent user experience on any Terminal Server.

Customization Requirements

Using the Internet Explorer Administration Kit (IEAK), the team customized the Internet Explorer 5 installation to conserve disk space on the Terminal Servers, to reduce bandwidth use, and to prevent users from changing settings. For more details of the IEAK settings, see the "Internet Explorer Administration Kit Settings" section later in this chapter.

In the course of customizing Internet Explorer, MCS found that the version 4.0 Desktop Shell Update (which includes the Active Desktop) caused Terminal Server sessions to run very slowly and must not be installed. The team created a custom Terminal Server transform (.MST) file by copying TermServ.MST (from the resource kit, ORK) to *MyTransform.MST* then using the CIW to add and remove application components.

Most CIW modifications (such as adding System Policy Editor) were made to minimize bandwidth use. For more details on settings, see the "Custom Installation Wizard Settings," and "System Policy Settings" sections later in this chapter.

The CIW was also used to create a custom transform file for the *Microsoft Office 2000 Resource Kit*, which is installed using the same Windows Installer technology as Office 2000, and can be modified with the same tools. Northwind Traders installed only the Terminal Server Tools (which include the non-animated office assistant), omitting the other tools to conserve disk space.

You have to install the non-animated office assistant file (StilLogo.ACS) through the resource kit SETUP.EXE; you cannot copy it onto the Terminal Server system, as you could with Office 97. Office 2000 applications are enabled for Windows Installer, so *all* add-in files must be installed by the Windows Installer. For details on the CIW settings for installing the resource kit, see the "Custom Installation Wizard Settings" section later in this chapter.

MCS created a batch file to automate the installation of Office 2000 (including Internet Explorer 5) and the ORK. The file:

1. Put the Terminal Server into *install* mode (CHANGE USER /INSTALL).

2. Copied the KIX32.EXE script processor to the operating system directory (%SystemRoot%). This is required because the deployment team added a Kix script to the customized Office 2000 installation.

3. Ran the Office 2000 SETUP.EXE and executed the installation using the custom transform file (specified in the SETUP.INI for Office 2000). Internet Explorer 5 was installed as part of the Office 2000 Setup (by including the IE5SETUP in the custom transform file). The ORK was installed using the updated SETUP.EXE, which supports chained installations with the **/chain** switch, so the ORK Setup could be run from within the custom transform file as an additional command line. When these are completed, the batch file reboots the system through the **/qb-** switch, which provides the *basic* progress bars and reboots without question.

A short batch file like this allows you to use the installation script on an existing Terminal Server (perhaps as an upgrade to Office 97) or integrate it into the unattended installation script for Terminal Server.

Defining Acceptance Criteria

When you work with Terminal Server and products such as Internet Explorer 5 and Office 2000, no one—not the project team, operational administration teams, or users—knows enough at first to clearly formulate acceptance criteria.

For example, Northwind Traders stipulated that Outlook 2000 performance should be *fast enough*. This is easy to say, but it is impossible to quantify. Realizing this, the project team chose a **Microsoft Solutions Framework** (MSF) approach: they configured Internet Explorer 5 and Office 2000 to meet as many user requirements as was practical, ran tests and pilot installations to assess performance and define needs, refined the configuration by incorporating feedback, then implemented it company-wide. Microsoft uses this approach to develop products; beta cycles for large products such as Office 2000 and Windows 2000 can become extensive.

Iterations of *criticism and refinement* educated users on the products and the systems, allowing them to set more reasonable acceptance criteria, and resulted in a configuration that suited their needs.

On Terminal Server, it is easier to run pilots, so you can run a larger number of shorter ones. When you deploy Office 2000 to Windows 95 or Windows NT Workstation you are probably going to stick with a single minor pilot (approximately 10 users) and a single major pilot (approximately 50 users). Redeploying each pilot release is so labor-intensive as to be prohibitive. But if you start the Terminal Server pilot with two Terminal Servers and ten clients, then increase these numbers over the course of the pilot phases, you can have five to ten phases. This is possible because at the start of each pilot phase you have to rebuild only the servers, not the client workstations.

Developing a Training and Support Plan

Since most users are experienced with Office 97 and the Windows 95 interface, Northwind Traders decided to use computer-based training (CBT). They checked the options and chose *Microsoft Office 2000 Step by Step Interactive*, which is an electronic version of the *step by step* book that allows you to tailor the course work and check on students' progress. When assessing training, Northwind Traders considered:

- **A Web-based course.** Northwind Traders considered creating Web pages—with snapshots (bitmaps) and diagrams—that users could browse for instructions on new and standard Office 2000 features. Development time was estimated at two to three weeks. Biggest advantage: material could be tailored to the employee work practices and environment.

- **A paper-based quick guide.** About 10 pages of text and graphics that users could browse through to learn about features. Biggest disadvantage: to be practical, the book had to be short, but if it made users want more information, there was no way to provide it.

- **Microsoft Press titles.** *Quick Course in Microsoft Office 2000, Microsoft Office 2000 8-in-1 Step by Step, Running Microsoft Office 2000 Premium,* and *Microsoft Office 2000 Professional at a Glance.* Biggest disadvantage: the opposite of the short book—the full texts probably offer too much information and no way to tailor it. Users take books, lose them, ignore them, and so on, but seldom read through them carefully.

- **Personalized CBT title created by contractor.** Biggest disadvantage: timing—at that time Office 2000 was new, so it was hard to find a third-party CBT vendor familiar enough with Office 2000 to be able to create good training materials.

- **Citrix MetaFrame.** This allows a tutor to *shadow* a user's session and work with the student from a remote locale. Biggest disadvantage: too labor intensive for a large user base. Biggest advantage: makes a good troubleshooting and training tool for helpdesk.

- **Classroom training.** Terminal Server presents users with the same environment regardless of where they log in from, which means that classroom training mirrors employees' typical workday experiences. Biggest disadvantage: bringing students to a classroom is costly and logistically hard.

There are lots of options for training Terminal Server users on Office 2000. Choose the one the best suits your environment and users. For large deployments consider Microsoft Press's self-training/CBT materials.

Implementation

This section describes and explains pre-deployment testing and pilots at a division of Northwind Traders that deployed Office 2000 and Internet Explorer 5 on Windows 95 (upgrading from Internet Explorer 3.02 and Office 97).

Test Plan/Methodology

Testing Office 2000 and Internet Explorer 5 on Terminal Server presented some interoperability and compatibility issues that needed to be addressed in the test plan.

Lab Environment

The development lab contained this hardware:

- One server of the same make and model used in the production environment. This was used for developing the scripted installation of Terminal Server, Citrix MetaFrame, Office 2000, Internet Explorer 5, and the other core applications.

- One workstation of each type used in the production environment. These allowed developers to create a standard operating environment (operating system and applications) for Terminal Server clients, and to test the Terminal Server environment performance on each of type of workstation.

- A 64-Kbps ISDN link for simulating a slow speed connection from client to Terminal Server.

- A number of other development workstations running the Internet Explorer Administration Kit (IEAK) and Office 2000 Resource Kit so that they could be used to modify the installation images.

- A file server with enough disk space (20+ GB) to hold the installation images.

- A CD-recordable writer for shipping installation images to the test and pilot engineers.

Test lab workstations all had enough disk space to configure an extra D: drive, on which testers used Norton Ghost to image the C: drive. This allowed them to reset workstations to the baseline, which proved very useful as the project progressed.

File Conversion Issues

One company was moving some users from Windows 95 and Office 97 to Terminal Server and Office 2000. There were no file conversion issues for Word, Excel, and PowerPoint, but Access 2000 uses a different file format than Access 97, so automatic conversion failed 6 to 7 percent of the time. The error messages returned all were described in the ORK, but some databases still required time-consuming syntax changes, which in turn often required retesting to make sure the database still worked as intended.

These were essentially the same conversion issues the company encountered when migrating Office 97 users to Office 2000 on Windows 95—see Chapter 2, "Migrating Files, Templates, and Custom Solutions," for details.

LAN/WAN Considerations

This was a large installation of Terminal Server (1,500 clients and 100 servers). To address server availability concerns, MCS implemented the load-balancing add-on to the Citrix MetaFrame product, added user profiles, and stored users' files and Exchange mailboxes on separate servers.

If a server goes offline, its users can still function by simply logging on to another available server, which downloads their profiles and lets them go back to work. MCS tested this in the lab and in the pilot by switching off one server and measuring the reaction.

Pilot Rollout

The pilot rollout lasted for only three weeks and was used primarily to gauge performance issues and users' acceptance of the system.

Performance Tuning

This company decided early to purchase high-specification servers and to *over engineer* the solution, by, for instance, loading only 15 users/server, well below Terminal Server limits. They had several reasons:

- **Business-justification process.** At this company, only one hardware cost can be justified during the project's three years. Hardware had to last three years without an upgrade.

- **Growth allowance.** They figured that over time the Terminal Server client software would require more RAM and CPU power and that more IT applications would be loaded onto the Terminal Servers.

- **Out of service allowance.** If a server went offline, its users would be switched to another, which would have to handle the extra load without loss of performance.

All of the servers are Pentium II 266MHz or better, with 256 MB RAM and RAID 5 disk arrays. The pilot demonstrated that these servers had acceptable performance with an average load of fifteen users, approximately what is recommended for this hardware configuration. The performance did not noticeably decrease when the load was increased to twenty-five users. Based on these results and its own policies, the company was willing spend more to over-engineer the solution so that it would last at least three years without updates.

Terminal Server's symmetric multi-processing uses multiple-processor machines efficiently. In a dual-processor system, one processor system handles CPU spikes (a user opening a large document, for example) and the other maintains service to other users.

Refining the Configuration

Based on user feedback from the pilot, the company refined the configuration, primarily by removing the adaptive menus for Office 2000 applications. Early feedback indicated that these took too long to appear on a Terminal Server system. To remove the menus, the team simply changed the policy settings. Other minor configuration changes (Internet Explorer 5 and Office 2000) were made as part of the MSF refinement process.

Scalability

The pilot showed that the Terminal Server solution was easy to implement and to scale.

The pilot started with a single server and a handful of users, then added a server, then users, and so on until the final target number was reached. The team did not have to make any changes to servers in order to add users, and did not have to make any changes to clients in order to add servers. Scaling from the pilot rollout to the full deployment required only that the team add the servers and roll them out to clients.

Implementing the Solution

Rollout Strategies

The rollout plan had two steps:

- A team began building servers on day one of the rollout. Four weeks were allotted for server building, but scripted installation helped the team finish in less time.

- After about half of the servers were built, the client installation team began converting users over to Terminal Server. Sites are geographically separated, so the team went to each site, converted its users to Terminal Server, then moved on to the next site. Six weeks were allotted for this process.

Deployment Tools

As noted, the team built servers from scratch. They used a scripted installation of all components, including Windows NT 4.0, Terminal Server Edition, Citrix MetaFrame, Internet Explorer 5, and Office 2000 and its applications.

The client software was delivered on the workstations by rebuilding each system using a standard operating environment (SOE) based on Windows 95 OSR-2 and the Terminal Server client. The team built the SOE on a reference machine, imaged it using Norton Ghost, transferred the image to a CD, then used the CD to reload each system (which took about 10 minutes). This saved time and ensured consistent Terminal Server client installations.

The team investigated an alternative solution: build a scripted installation procedure to install Windows 95, the Terminal Server client, and a virus protection package. This method was dismissed, because the team calculated that each installation would take 35 minutes, and (more important) because developing and perfecting the script would take several days. Using imaging, the team could build a reference machine in half a day, then image and transfer the system to CD in an hour. Imaging also makes it easier to make changes in mid-stream, which can be difficult when you are working with a script. With imaging, it takes about an hour to make changes to the reference machine, retake the image, and transfer it to CD.

User Training

When the client installation team visited sites to install the client systems, they often ended up with some extra time there. They put this to good use by developing a 10-minute *getting started* presentation that showed users how to:

1. Start the system.
2. Connect to Terminal Server.
3. Log on and off.
4. Start applications, especially Outlook 2000.
5. Start the online CBT course.

This introductory lesson gave users the background they needed to start learning their way around the system.

Lessons Learned

This company was fortunate in that all of the servers were new, and all of the workstations could be rebuilt with a standard operating environment. This made it particularly effective to automate server installation and image the workstation. Internet Explorer 5 and Office 2000 fit in very well with this strategy. The ORK tools made it easy to create a customized Internet Explorer 5 setup image and a customized Office 2000 transform file.

The work on the Windows 95 deployment was very helpful in developing configurations for the Office 2000 applications. The project showed that the best approach is to develop a standard configuration for Windows 9*x,* or Windows NT workstation, then use what you learn to build the Terminal Server environment.

The Terminal Server environment presented its own challenges, particularly its requirement to *lock down* the environment so that users cannot modify the server. Office 2000 system policies and restrictions are much more extensive than the options in Office 97. System policies (particularly when configuring Internet Explorer 5 and Office 2000) improved the environment's stability and security.

The project generated a large number of script files, transforms, and IEAK setup files, and put them through many revisions—hundreds in some cases. To solve the logistical problem of tracking and identifying files, the team used Microsoft Visual SourceSafe (VSS) to store and organize all files and design documents.

Custom Settings Described

The sections below describe the Custom Installation Wizard (CIW), Internet Explorer Administration Kit (IEAK), and system policy settings used in the deployment of Office 2000.

Custom Installation Wizard Settings

These CIW defaults were changed for Terminal Server:

P7 Install all to hard disk, except:

- PowerPoint

  Presentation Broadcasting (Do Not Install)

- Outlook for Windows

  Symantec Fax Starter Edition (Do Not Install)

  FrontPage for Windows (Do Not Install)

- Office Tools

  International Support (Do Not Install)

  Lotus VIM Mail (Do Not Install)

Note   These options are *hidden.* These applications are bandwidth-intensive or unnecessary for Northwind Traders, which wanted to keep Terminal Server deployment consistent with the Office 2000 deployment to Windows 95 (international support was removed, and so on).

P8 Use the COMPANY.OPS profile.

Note To create this profile, the team used the Office Profile Wizard (from the *Microsoft Office 2000 Resource Kit*) and included the company standard application configurations.

P9 Copy two files (DelIEIcon.KIX, DelOLIcon.KIX) to <Program Files\Microsoft Office>\Company.

Note The team used these Kixtart scripts to delete the icons for Internet Explorer, Outlook Express, and Outlook from the desktop and the **Start** menu.

P11 Set Office Applications to have icons on <StartMenu>\Standard Apps.

■ Remove all other **Start** menu icons, leaving only toolbar icons.

Note Northwind Traders chose this **Start** menu location for *all* users.

P12 Additional Drives. Add \\%O2KSRVR%\PUBLIC\O2K. The variable %O2KSRVR% will be set in the logon script.

P13 Include two command lines:

```
C:\WINDOWS\KIX32.EXE "C:\Program Files\Microsoft
Office\Company\DelOLIcon.KIX"
C:\WINDOWS\KIX32.EXE "C:\Program Files\Microsoft
Office\Company\DelIEIcon.KIX"
```

The team saved the transform file with these settings to the administrative share point as **CompanyTS.MST.**

Internet Explorer Administration Kit Settings

These IEAK configuration options require special attention:

P5 Set the Destination Folder to *D:\IE5_CUST* or a drive with suitable amount of disk space.

■ Click **Advanced Options.**

Note When you run the IEAK for the first time you must synchronize (use AVS) and you must have access to www.microsoft.com. If you have run the IEAK before, **do not** do AVS (it should already have been run), and make sure you set the .INS file to *D:\IE5_CUST\CD\win32\EN\bin\Install.ins* (which is the Internet Explorer Settings file from the last time the IEAK was run).

- Set the Component Download Folder to *C:\Program Files\IEAK\download.*

P7 Select **Flat.** Deselect all other options.

P10 AVS.

Note   If you are running the IEAK for the first time, you need to synchronize. This doesn't take long if you already have the most recent files. If you aren't running AVS, the components are displayed with yellow symbols. This is OK.

P16 Silent Install.

- Select **Hands-free Install.**

P17 Installation Options.

- Select **Minimum.** Click **Delete.**
- Select **Full.** Click **Delete.**

Note   This forces installation of the *Typical* configuration.

P19 Install Directory.

- Install in the specified folder within the Program Files folder.
- Folder name: Internet Explorer.

P20 Corporate Install Options.

- Disable saving uninstall information [checked].
- Internet Explorer is set as the default browser.

P21 Components on Media.

- Click **Deselect All.**

P32 Channels.

- Select **Delete existing channels**, if present.
- Deselect **Turn on desktop Channel Bar** by default.

Note   Northwind Traders did not want to install the channel bar.

P34 User Agent String.

- Set the custom string to *Company SOE 2.0 (WTS).*

> **Note** Applications on the intranet server use this agent string to tell Terminal Server users from Windows 95 users.

P35 Automatic Configuration.

- Deselect **Enable Automatic Configuration.**

P36 Connection Settings.

- Select **Import the current Connection Settings.**
- Select **Delete existing Connection Settings**, if present.

> **Note** This picks up the current Internet Explorer 5 installations connection settings, which must be set correctly before this process is started.

P37 Proxy Settings.

- Select **Use the same proxy server for all addresses.**
- Set the HTTP proxy server address to *internetproxy.company.com.au.* Set the port to *8080.*
- Insert exceptions for the following:

  http://interweb*

  http://10.*.*.*

  ftp://interweb*

  ftp://10.*.*.*

  https://interweb*

  https://10.*.*.*

- Select **Do not use proxy for local addresses.**

P39 Security Settings.

- Select **Custom Security Zone Settings.**
- Click **Modify Settings.**
- Click **Custom.**
- Select **Automatic Logon with current username and password.**
- Click **OK.**
- Click **OK.**
- Select **Do Not Customize Content Ratings.**

P41 System Policies and Restrictions.

- Microsoft NetMeeting

NetMeeting Settings

- Check all boxes.

NetMeeting Protocols

- Check both boxes.

Note   Northwind Traders considered NetMeeting too bandwidth-intensive and did not want it used on the network.

Internet Settings

- Component Updates

Periodic Check for Internet Updates and Bug Fixes.

Set the Update Frequency to 365 days.

Note   The component updates were set as low as possible to reduce the possibility of one user overwriting program files due to a periodic update.

- Install on Demand Setup of Internet Explorer Features and Add-on Components.
- Disable Install on Demand Setup of Internet Explorer Features and Add-on Components.

Note   This stops users from installing additional program files.

- Offline Pages
  - Disable adding channels
  - Disable removing channels
  - Disable channel user interface completely
  - Disable password caching for offline pages
  - Disable downloading of site subscription content
  - Maximum size of subscriptions in kilobytes: 1
  - Maximum number of offline pages: 1
  - Minimum number of minutes between scheduled updates: 1,440
  - Time to begin preventing scheduled updates: 0
  - Time to end preventing scheduled updates: 0
  - Maximum Offline Page Crawl Depth: 0

Note   This restriction prevents users from storing pages on the Terminal Server: they wind up in the user's profile and can, if they grow too large, increase logon times and gobble up Terminal Server disk space.

Internet Restrictions

- Internet Property Pages

  Disable viewing the Security Page

  Disable viewing the Programs Page

  Disable viewing the Advanced Page

- General

  Disable changing Home page settings

- Security

  Use *only* machine settings for security zones

  Do not allow users to change policies for any security zone

  Do not allow users to add/delete sites from a security zone

- Content

  Disable changing ratings settings

  Disable changing Profile Assistant Settings

  Do not allow users to save passwords in AutoSuggest for forms

- Connection

  Select all restrictions, except **Disable Internet Connection Wizard**

- Programs

  Select all restrictions

- Advanced

  Disable changing settings on **Advanced** tab

- Code Download

  Disable software update shell notifications on program launch

- Periodic Update Check

  Disable Periodic Check for Internet Explorer software updates and bug fixes

- Offline Pages Settings

  Disable adding schedules for offline pages

  Disable editing schedules for offline pages

- Browser Menu Restrictions

  Disable **Save As Web Page Complete** format

Note   Most of these restrictions prevent users from changing Internet Explorer connection and security settings. With many users (Northwind Traders has 1500) you should use standard connection settings and keep users from changing them.

System Policy Settings

To create the new system policies you need the System Policy Editor (from the ORK) and the modified ADMIN.ADM file (based on the original Windows 95 file).

Office 2000 and Internet Explorer 5 Settings

Default Computer

NetMeeting Protocols:

- NetMeeting Protocols [checked]
- Disable TCP/IP [checked]
- Disable Null Modem [checked]

Note   Northwind Traders prevented the use of NetMeeting, feeling that it used too much bandwidth for this environment. (Terminal Server does not support NetMeeting.)

Periodic Check for Internet Explorer Updates and Bug Fixes:

- Periodic Check for Internet Explorer Updates and Bug Fixes [unchecked]
- Options left at default

Install on Demand Setup of Internet Explorer features and Add-on Components:

- Install on Demand Setup of Internet Explorer features and Add-on Components [checked]

Note   The team set these restrictions on *periodic check for updates* and *install on demand* to prevent updates to the Internet Explorer files on the Terminal Server.

Windows Installer:

- Always install with elevated privileges [grey]
- Disable Windows Installer [checked]

Note   The team disabled Windows Installer to prevent updates to the executable files while the system was in use.

Domain Users (Default User has been removed)

NetMeeting Settings:

- Restrict the use of File Transfer [checked]
- Prevent the User from Sending Files [checked]
- Prevent the User from Receiving Files [checked]
- Restrict the Use of Application Sharing [checked]
- All Options are Checked
- Restrict the use of the Options Dialog [checked]
- All Options are Checked
- Prevent the User from Answering Calls [checked]
- Prevent the User from Using Audio Features [checked]
- Restrict the Use of Video [checked]
- Prevent the User from Sending Video [checked]
- Prevent the User from Receiving Video [checked]
- Prevent the User from Using Directory Services [checked]
- All Other Options are Grey

Note   To economize bandwidth, NetMeeting was restricted.

Advanced Settings:

- Browsing [checked]
- Automatically Check for Internet Explorer Updates [unchecked]

Note   This was disabled so that Internet Explorer updates could not be applied to the system while it was in use by multiple terminal sessions.

- Security [checked]
- Delete Saved Pages When Browser Closed [unchecked]
- Do not save Encrypted Pages to Disk [unchecked]

Note   These settings conserve Terminal Server disk space by preventing the saving of additional pages there.

Offline Pages:

- Offline Pages [checked]
- Disables Adding Channels [checked]
- Disables Removing Channels [checked]
- Disables Channel Interface Completely [checked]
- Disable downloading of Site Subscription Content [checked]
- Maximum Size of Subscriptions: 1
- Maximum Number of Offline Pages: 1
- Minimum Number of Minutes: 480
- Time to begin preventing scheduled updates: 1
- Time to end preventing scheduled updates: 1
- Maximum Offline Page Crawl Depth: 1
- All other options are unchecked

Note   These settings conserve Terminal Server disk space by preventing the saving of additional pages there.

Microsoft Access 2000:

All options as per default (grey) except for:

Disable Items in User Interface

- Predefined
  - Disable Command Bar Buttons and Menu Items [checked]

    Tools | Online Collaboration [checked]

    Help | Office on the Web [checked]

    Help | Detect and Repair [checked]

    All other options unchecked

Note   These settings disable online collaboration (bandwidth intensive) and self-repairing features (which might repair files being used in another session).

Microsoft Clip Gallery 5.0:

- Disable Clips Online access from Clip Gallery [checked]
- Check to Enforce Setting On [checked]

Microsoft Excel 2000:

All options left as default (grey) except for:

- Tools | Options
  - General

    Default File Location [checked]

    Default File Location : h:\documents

Note   These options were set for all Office applications to *encourage* users to save files on the server.

- Disable Items in User Interface
  - Predefined

    Disable Command Bar Buttons and Menu Items [checked]

    Tools | Online Collaboration [checked]

    Help | Office on the Web [checked]

Note   Online Collaboration was disabled to reduce bandwidth use. Office on the Web was disabled to prevent users from accessing the Microsoft Web site.

- Miscellaneous
  - Enable Four-Digit Year Display [checked]

    Check to Enforce Setting On [checked]

Note   This very important setting enforces the year 2000 settings.

Windows Installer:

- Always Install with Elevated Privileges [grey]
- Search Order [checked]
- Search Order: n
- Disable Browse Dialog for New Source [grey]
- Transform Location [checked]
- Cached Transform Location: Copy transform to User Profile
- Disable Rollback [grey]

Note   These settings direct the Windows Installer to the most appropriate source file location.

Microsoft Office 2000:

All components are unmodified (grey), except for:

Tools | Options | General | Web Options

- Files
    - Download Office Web Components [unchecked]

Note   In a controlled environment, you do not want modifications or downloads.

- Shared Paths
    - Shared Templates Paths [checked]
    - Shared Templates Path: P:\templates

Note   This setting sends all users to the same place for shared templates.

Assistant

- Feedback Button Label [checked]

    Feedback Button Label : Go To Company Internal Web

- Feedback URL [checked]

    Feedback URL:
    http://interweb.boral.com.au/test/office_pilot_feedback.htm?DPC=%ProductC
    ode%&AppName=%ApplicationName%&HelpLCID=%HelpLang%&UILang
    =%UILang%&

Note   These settings are required for extended Help.

Language Settings

- User Interface
    - Display Menus and Dialog Boxes In [checked]
    - Display Menus and Dialog Boxes In: English (U.S.)
    - Display Help In [checked]
    - Display Help In: English (U.S.)
- Enabled Languages
    - Show Controls and Enable Editing For

        English (Australian) [checked]

        Check to Enforce Settings On [checked]

        English (Canadian) [checked]

Check to Enforce Settings On [checked]

English (U.K.) [checked]

Check to Enforce Settings On [checked]

English (U.S.) [checked]

Check to Enforce Settings On [checked]

- Installed Version of Microsoft Office [checked]

Installed Version: English (Australian)

Note These settings ensure that only versions of English are used.

Customizable Error Messages

- Base URL [checked]

Base URL:
http://interweb.boral.com.au/test/alert.asp?DPC=%ProductCode%&AppName
=%ApplicationName%&HelpLCID=%HelpLang%&UILang=%UILang%&

- Default Button Text

Default Button Text: Go To Company Internal Web

Note These settings are required for extended Help.

Microsoft Outlook 2000:

All options are Unselected (grey) except for:

- Disable Items in User Interface
  - Predefined

  Disable Command Bar Buttons and Menu Items [checked]

  All Folders | Go Internet Call [checked]
  - Miscellaneous

  Net Folders [checked]

  Net Folders is Available [unchecked]

Note These settings reduce bandwidth use.

Microsoft PowerPoint 2000

All options are unselected (grey) except:

- Slide Show | Online Broadcast | Set Up and Schedule
  - Broadcast Settings
    Send Audio [checked]
    Check to Enforce Setting On [unchecked]
    Send Video [checked]
    Check to Enforce Setting On [unchecked]
    Camera/Microphone is Connected to Another Computer [checked]
    Camera/Microphone is Connected to:
    Recording [checked]
    Check to Enforce Setting On [unchecked]

Note   These settings reduce bandwidth use.

- Disable Items in User Interface
  - Predefined
    Disable Command Bar Buttons and Menu Items [checked]
    Tools | Online Collaboration [checked]
    Help | Office on the Web [checked]

Note   These settings reduce bandwidth use.

Microsoft Word 2000

All items are unmodified except for:

- Tools | Options
  - File Locations
    Documents [checked]
    Documents: h:\documents

Note   These settings *encourage* users to save files to the server.

- Customizable Error Messages
  - List of Error Messages to Customize [checked]

    The following error messages were added:

44	&Web Suggestions
46	&Web Help
121	&Web Help
474	&Web Printing Info
832	" " "

Note   These settings provide error messages with Web-based extensions.

- Disable Items in User Interface
  - Predefined

    Disable Command Bar Buttons and Menu Items [checked]

    File | Save as Web Page [checked]

    Tools | Online Collaboration [checked]

Note   These settings reduce bandwidth use.

- Miscellaneous
  - Custom Answer Wizard database path

    Custom Answer Wizard database path:
    p:\AnswerWiz\CompanyWebHelp.aw

Note   These settings implement the customized Answer Wizard Help.

CHAPTER   1 3

Deploying and Managing Office Server Extensions

By Chris Kunicki, Micro Modeling Associates, Inc.

The deeper you can extend Web technologies into departments or workgroups, the greater the benefits you will derive from them. Office Server Extensions (OSE) facilitate collaboration by helping users get Office documents onto the intranet quickly and easily. Office publishing simplifies the process of putting documents on the intranet, inline discussions allow users to share ideas, and key Web features help users view, search, and retrieve documents stored on Web servers.

The OSE are a set of Web applications built on the FrontPage 2000 Server Extensions, Active Server Pages, and ActiveX Data Objects. They run on the Windows NT 4.0 Workstation operating system with Personal Web Server 4.0, or on Windows NT Server 4.0 with Microsoft Internet Information Server 4.0 (IIS—the built-in Windows NT Web server that provides additional publishing, collaboration, and searching capabilities). The extensions work with client-side software in Office 2000, Windows Explorer, and the Web browser to provide:

- **Web publishing.** You can save, edit, open, and delete files on Web servers from within Office 2000 applications, and you can navigate a Web site just as you currently navigate a hard drive or network file share.

- **Web discussions.** You can discuss intranet documents by adding comments to HTML or Office binary format documents from your browser or an Office 2000 application. Multiple users can comment simultaneously.

- **Subscription and notification.** You can subscribe to Web discussions, documents, or folders and be notified automatically (by e-mail) of changes. This speeds up discussion and feedback, and helps users stay current.

- **Search.** You can search on text or on title, author, category, keywords, or a custom property.

- **Start page.** You can use this to manage Web subscriptions. It also provides access to OSE features, even for users who are not running Internet Explorer 4.0/5.0 or Office 2000.

What You'll Find in This Chapter

- How to best install and configure Office 2000 to meet your company's needs—including useful reference tables such as the System Requirements Table

- An in-depth description of the Windows NT security platform that Office 2000 utilizes, and security strategies your company can explore

- How to best accomplish capacity planning in a Web environment

- How to protect your company's work by implementing a solid backup plan with consideration for three key areas: documents, collaboration database, and Windows NT settings

Office 2000 provides native support for HTML and improves control over the level of HTML produced. You don't need OSE to use HTML, but along with the new Office Web Components, the extensions help you add interactivity to Web pages. To create documents, you can use the native binary Office file format, rich text (RTF), and HTM, all of which are supported by OSE features. To distribute documents, you should take into account how users will access and use them. If lots of users just have to *read* the document, publish it in HTML. If users have to *work* with it using application-specific functionality, leave it in the native binary Office file format.

Installation and Configuration

System Requirements

The Office Server Extensions architecture uses client-side components and server-side services. Client requirements vary with functionality; servers require Windows NT and a Microsoft-compatible Web server. Figure 13.1 below illustrates how various client components and server services interact.

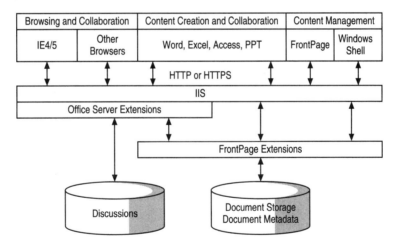

Figure 13.1   Office server extensions client and server architecture.

Client Hardware Requirements

Client computers must be capable of running Office 2000 or a browser equal to or newer than Netscape Navigator 3.0 or Internet Explorer 3.0.

Client Software Requirements

The Office and browser software versions determine the quality of the user experience. For basic functionality, the client computer requires only a Web browser. Users with Netscape Navigator or Internet Explorer 3.0 can access OSE discussion and subscription features through the Start Page via a frames-based version of the **Discussions** toolbar. Users with Office 2000 and Internet Explorer 4.01 or higher can access OSE features directly from an Office application or the browser.

Server Hardware Requirements

Minimum OSE hardware requirements are a 166-MHz Intel Pentium processor, 120 MB of hard disk drive space, and 64 MB of RAM.

Note Because Windows NT 4.0 treats the Cyrix CPU as compatible with the 486 CPU instruction set, it installs and works without problems. But SQL Server and MSDE require a Pentium-class processor because they make full use of the 586 instruction set. Older versions of Cyrix chips do not support the complete Pentium instruction set: SQL Server and MSDE Setup detect these chips and do not install.

Server Software Requirements

OSE has been integrated with a number of key Windows NT platform services for file serving, security, search support, and e-mail.

For these services...	You need one of these software components:
Operating System	Windows NT Server 4.0 with Service Pack 4 or later
	Windows NT Workstation 4.0 with Service Pack 4 or later
	Windows 2000 Premium or Server edition
Web Server	Internet Information Server (IIS) 4.0 or later
	Microsoft Personal Web Server
	World Wide Web service (Windows 2000)
Discussion Database	Microsoft SQL Server 7.0
	Microsoft SQL Server 6.5
	Microsoft Data Engine (MSDE)
	(The SQL Server database can also exist on a remote server)
Notifications	Microsoft Exchange Server or other SMTP mail server
Others	Internet Explorer 4.01 or later

Note   Do not use Windows NT Service Pack 3 with OSE: incompatibilities can disrupt client/server communications. In extreme cases, the IIS service may become unresponsive, temporarily shutting out all HTTP traffic before eventually recovering. Service Pack 4 corrects the problem and should be considered a basic system requirement for all OSE deployments.

Client Installation

Users can access OSE functionality from a Web browser and from Office 2000. If the browser conforms to the browser requirements above, users can participate in online discussions and notification services. To use the OSE content-publishing features, users must have Office 2000.

You can customize user settings during installation. The table below shows what can be customized and what tools are needed.

Tool	Customizable Features	Description
Custom Installation Wizard	Web Discussions	Screen 7: Office Tools I Office Server Extension Support I Web Discussions
	Web Publishing	Screen 7: Office Tools I Office Server Extension Support I Web Publishing
	Built-in Themes	Screen 7: Office Tools I Themes
	Custom Themes	In the Add Files step of the Custom Installation Wizard, custom themes can be distributed and marked for installation into the themes directory.
	Web Components	Screen 7: Office Tools I Office Web Components
	HTML Source Editing	Screen 7: Office Tools I HTML Source Editing
Office Profile Wizard	Web Folders	Edit the PROFLWIZ.INI and remove the # before <NetHood> to capture Web Folders.
	Collaboration Databases	Capture the key **HKCU\Software\Microsoft \Office\8.0\Web Server** It contains the settings for the default collaboration database and others. By default, this key is defined so that it is retrieved from PROFLWIZ.INI.
System Policy Editor	Various Publishing Settings	Use the policy editor to control various Office publishing capabilities. For example, to specify a target browser version for Word HTML output.
IEAK Profile Manager	Proxy Server Settings	Deploy custom proxy settings. (See the "Proxy Server" section later in this chapter.)

To learn how to use the Custom Installation Wizard and the Office Profile Wizard to control feature deployment, refer to Chapter 5, "User Settings."

Note   When you use the Office Profile Wizard to capture the key **HKCU\Software\Microsoft\Office\8.0\Web Server**, make sure there is no default e-mail address defined for receiving notifications: the wizard captures it and deploys it to users. If one has been defined, delete it (Default Email Address).

Server Installation

OSE Setup has two steps: install the OSE files to the hard disk drive, then use the Configuration Wizard to extend a Web server for OSE. The OSE Setup application that installs the OSE files to the hard disk drive is not part of Office 2000 Setup: it is named SETUPSE.EXE and can be found on these Office 2000 CDs:

- Office 2000 Standard (Disc 1)
- Office 2000 Professional (Disc 1)
- Office 2000 Premium (Disc 3)

OSE Setup runs the OSE Configuration Wizard, which configures OSE and enables the Web server for publishing, discussions, and subscriptions.

Installation Details

The OSE Setup Wizard walks you through OSE setup, but you must have Windows NT *administrator* privileges. When you are prompted for the username and licensing information, point Setup to the installation location. You can install some or all of these items:

- FrontPage 2000 Server Extensions
- Microsoft Data Engine (MSDE)
- Windows Installer service pack

After setup, the Configuration Wizard begins walking you through the process of extending the Web server for OSE. It presents defaults that should work for most installations. When this process is finished, an OSE-extended server is configured and available to Office 2000 users. You can use the wizard to customize these settings:

- **Discussion database.** If Microsoft Data Engine (MSDE) is installed, you must supply the database name and password. If SQL Server is installed on the Web server already, you must use that installation of SQL Server, and supply the existing SQL Server database name, SQL Server username, and SQL Server password (see Figure 13.2). For example, you cannot install MSDE on a server that is running SQL Server 6.5 already.

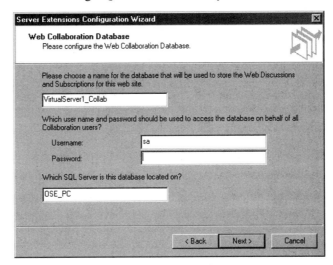

Figure 13.2   OSE Configuration Wizard prompting for Web Collaboration database.

MSDE or SQL Server 7.0 create the collaboration database automatically when OSE is configured. With SQL Server 6.5 you must create the collaboration database *before* you can install and configure OSE. This involves creating a database device, a database, and an ODBC connection. For detailed steps on installing SQL Server 6.5, see the *Microsoft Office 2000 Resource Kit* or http://www.microsoft.com/office/ork/2000/journ/OSEonSQL.htm.

- **Windows NT account use.** The wizard asks if it should create user groups and an administrator account for Windows NT File System (NTFS) security. This creates four groups (OSE administrator, author, browse, and collaborate) on the OSE server. These are needed to manage OSE publishing and collaboration features. Refer to the "NTFS" section later in this chapter for details on why you should use NTFS with OSE.

- **Access rights to discussion database.** Use this to grant access to the Web Discussions feature. The options are: **all users** or **all users with a known Windows NT account** (the default).

- **Browser support.** Use this to enable non-Internet Explorer browsers. The default is **yes**. This uses Basic authentication (usernames and passwords are transmitted over the Internet in clear text) which is the only option for users without Internet Explorer for accessing the OSE-extended Web server through a proxy server or firewall. Since version 3, Internet Explorer has supported Windows NT Challenge/Response, which is a more secure authentication method than Basic, but it will not work over a proxy or firewall.

  If the Web server has been configured with Secure Sockets Layer (SSL) and is used in combination with Basic authentication, information between the browser and Web server is encrypted for a more secure environment. For more information on SSL, see the *Microsoft Windows NT 4.0 Resource Kit*, Internet Guide, Chapter 3, "Server Security on the Internet."

- **AutoNavigation.** Use this to enable AutoNavigation pages (a browser-based file navigation interface) for the Web root, so that users can browse the Web server file system. The default is **yes**.

  Some organizations consider this a security risk because it exposes the Web server's root file structure. If you prefer to avoid this risk, you can disable AutoNavigation during Setup and still allow browsing through a custom AutoNavigation page. After OSE has been installed, you can configure subwebs for directory browsing by editing their properties in the IIS Administrator, then customize the AutoNavigation page link to refer to the correct subwebs. The link would look like:

  http://<webserver>/msoffice/folder.asp?URL=/<subweb name>

  Users will then be able to browse that folder and any subfolders.

- **Subscriptions and Notifications.** The Notifications feature requires an SMTP Mail server. Setup requires the SMTP Mail server name, a FROM address that is used when notifications are sent to users, and a REPLY-TO Administrator address that is used as an administrator point of contact for OSE. If this information is not available at installation or if you are not going to use Subscriptions and Notifications, you can skip this step. You can configure this feature later from the OSE Administration Home Page.

Quiet Mode Installation

To install the OSE in quiet mode, use this command syntax:

<drive>:\Setupse.exe /i ows.msi /q

where *<drive>* refers to the CD drive letter or the network path to the extensions. If you want to specify the custom settings, edit the CFGQUIET.INI file in the OSE Setup directory. The following table shows the CFGQUIET.INI settings in the order they appear:

Setting	Description
ServerType	A string identifying the type of server being extended.
FriendlyName	FrontPage requires this field for non-Microsoft Web servers.
VRootMDPath	For Microsoft IIS\PWS 4.0 and higher Web servers. Metabase path for Web site to extend.
Discussions	Controls whether OSE Web Discussions are available.
Notifications	Controls whether OSE Subscriptions and Notifications are available. You must define these three parameters: *EmailServer, AuthorEmail,* and *ContactEmail.*
EmailServer	Mail server for OSE Notifications and FrontPage Forms Bot.
AuthorEmail	SMTP address of person or alias to contact for assistance stopping or modifying notifications.
ContactEmail	*Reply To* address for e-mails sent by OSE.
AllowDirBrowsing	Controls whether directory browsing is allowed for the root Web.
AllowAnonymous	Controls whether *Anonymous* access is permitted.
AllowBasic	Controls whether Basic authentication is available.
AllowEveryone	Adds **Everyone** group to NTFS ACL in /MSOffice Start Page virtual directory.
CreateLocalGroups	Controls whether Authors, Administrators, Browsers, and Collaborators are created as Local groups.
GroupNamePrefix	Prefix to be used for Local group names. Blank or absent defaults to IIS Web site name (%WebSiteName%).
AdminAccount	FrontPage Administrators account. Leave to use Windows NT Administrators Group.
Server	SQL Server machine name. Leave blank to use current machine.
DatabaseName	Collaboration database name. Leave blank to default to %WebSiteName%_Collab.
UserName	SQL Server user account. Leave blank to use as a SQL Server account.
Password	SQL Server user account password. Leave blank for no password.

NTFS

It is highly recommended that you install IIS and OSE on an NTFS-formatted drive. Although Windows NT supports FAT and NTFS file systems, FAT provides only minimal access control to the file system. OSE and the FrontPage extensions use NTFS for its simplified administration of role-based security. NTFS allows administrators to assign Access Control List (ACL) settings at folder and file levels—which is much more granular than the control possible in FAT.

FrontPage Server Extensions

OSE uses the FrontPage server extensions to publish content to a Web server and manage it. The FrontPage 2000 Server Extensions provide backwards compatibility, permitting FrontPage 97/98 clients to connect to a FrontPage 2000 Extended Web server, although only FrontPage 2000 clients can use the new features. When you install OSE, the FrontPage 2000 Server extensions are installed on the Web Server, upgrading any earlier versions that are already present. OSE cannot work with earlier versions of the FrontPage extensions.

For further details on FrontPage Server extension architecture, administration, security, and command line options, see the *Microsoft FrontPage Server Extensions Resource Kit*, which you can install with Office 2000.

Note   Without OSE, Office 2000 can use the FrontPage Server extensions only to publish and manage content. To participate in discussions or use the subscriptions and notifications service you must install OSE.

Index Server

From the OSE Start Page, users can search an OSE-extended Web server for documents by text, by server location, by date values, and by document properties set when editing documents in Microsoft Office.

Searching requires that Index Server be installed and enabled. Install it from the Windows NT 4 Option Pack, then use the Index Server Manager to configure and manage it. The default installation meets most users' needs, although it can place a significant load on a server when dealing with numerous documents or large ones. For more information, see the "Capacity Planning" section later in this chapter.

SMTP

You need a Simple Mail Transfer Protocol (SMTP) mail server to use the Subscriptions and Notifications feature. If you don't already have an SMTP server configured, you can install the IIS SMTP service along with IIS from the Windows NT 4.0 Option Pack, or use Exchange Server's Internet Mail Service feature as an SMTP mail server. If you already have an SMTP server or you don't want to use Web Subscriptions, you don't need an SMTP service.

Windows NT Domain

OSE will work on a standalone server, but putting it on a server that is a member of a Windows NT domain allows you to use the Windows NT infrastructure for authentication and access control, and to use existing administrator and user accounts. This can be especially helpful for IT support staff that has to troubleshoot remote Web servers.

If you want to configure authentication and access control to a stand-alone server, simply create the user accounts and groups on that server. This allows you to isolate Web server settings and configurations, which can be useful in IT or Internet Service Provider (ISP) environments where a server is configured for use by only one company or department and all configuration options should be local to that server.

Proxy Server

OSE uses HTTP for all communications, so users need proxy server settings to pass through a proxy server to reach OSE servers. Office 2000 and Internet Explorer both enable proxy server access. To use OSE through a firewall, a client must have Internet Explorer 4.01 or later installed. You can use the Internet Explorer Administration Kit to automate Internet Explorer installation and integrate it with the Office 2000 installation—deploying Office, Internet Explorer, and the custom settings at the same time.

Office Server Extension Installation Scenarios

Organizations deploy and maintain networks to meet specific needs, most of which can be accommodated by OSE. The three OSE models below are the most common.

Centrally Managed

In this OSE model, a central organization (such as IT) provides OSE hardware, software, installation, and maintenance. This arrangement uses the existing infrastructure for backup/restore and dedicated staff to handle issues. It benefits users by insulating them from OSE server configuration and operations, which in turn benefits support staff by reducing the chances that a user will cause OSE server problems by making improper or inadvertent changes. Its disadvantage is that it may require more dedicated support and maintenance personnel, and it compels users to rely on support staff for OSE matters they could otherwise take care of themselves.

This model is ideal for organizations that host multiple servers or multiple virtual sites on one computer. IIS and Windows NT can run up to 200 virtual sites on one server, although this requires advanced planning and configuration well beyond the scope of the average user. This model also works well for IT groups and ISPs who need to run numerous virtual teams on one server in a Web farm environment.

Workgroup Server

OSE was designed for teams and workgroups. If central administration is unnecessary, departments or power users can handle OSE installation and support. In this model, workgroups acquire hardware and software, and handle installation, configuration, and maintenance. Each Workgroup typically has one physical Web server that hosts its Web.

Jointly Managed

This model is a blend of the other two: a central organization works with workgroups to provide the hardware, software, installation, and original configuration to get the OSE-extended Web server up and running, after which the workgroups assume responsibility for day-to-day operations. This gives a workgroup more control and direct access to the Web server, but allows it to rely on internal support for backup/restore, troubleshooting, and other standard services.

Security

For security, OSE uses the underlying Microsoft Windows NT platform and its components. Figure 13.3 shows how clients access OSE services through the various layers of Windows NT. At each layer, the granularity of control increases until, at the final NTFS level, you have access control per object by user or group. As an administrator, the various layers can be configured to control the level of access and permissions you want your users to have. The following section discusses how those layers affect security.

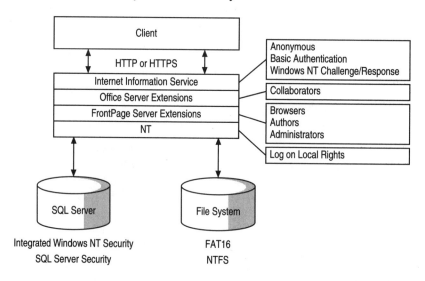

Figure 13.3   A depiction of the various layers of OSE.

Client Security

OSE uses the Hypertext Transfer Protocol (HTTP). Users connect to an OSE-extended Web server from either Office 2000 clients or Web browsers running HTTP. The server must be running IIS, which handles all client requests down into the Windows NT subsystems.

OSE must use Port 80 on the Web server—the default port used by IIS. This presents no issues for normal Web access. When access is through a firewall or proxy, some additional setup is required: you must configure and enable the correct proxy settings for clients and users. You can use the Internet Explorer Profile Manager (shown in Figure 13.4) to deploy proxy settings to users during Office 2000 installation, or you can do it later.

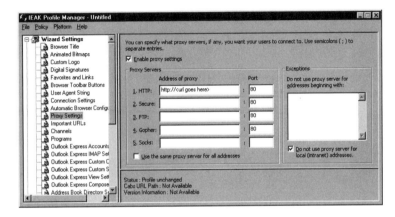

Figure 13.4   The Internet Explorer Administration Kit Profile Manager is used for deploying and updating Internet Explorer settings to users.

Note   OSE cannot use a proxy server that requires authentication.

Internet Information Server

Internet Information Server (IIS) brokers all clients requests and insulates the client from OSE's internal operations. It also validates clients for access to the Web server using one of the following three authentication mechanisms. Each has advantages and disadvantages you should consider when you deploy OSE.

- **Anonymous.** IIS creates a standard Windows NT user account named IUSR_*computername,* which allows unauthenticated users to browse the Web and even use OSE collaboration features, but not to participate in publishing or site administration. Anonymous intranet and Internet sites are handled the same way.

- **Basic.** This is a good solution when users' browsers do not support Windows NT Challenge/Response or when HTTP access is through a firewall or proxy server. Users respond to a prompt for a Windows NT username and password, which are sent over the network unencrypted in clear text. This potential security risk can be avoided by combining Basic authentication with Secure Socket Layers (SSL). This creates a secure communication line between the client and the Web server, and encrypts the transmission.

- You can configure a Web server to require SSL. In the IIS Administrator, right-click on the Web server and select **Properties**. Select the **Server Extensions** tab and check **Require SSL for authoring**. You will have to get an SSL Certificate from a certificate authority and install it in the IIS Key Manager.

Note If a Windows NT group has collaboration access, Basic authentication also grants it *Log-on-locally* privileges to the local computer.

Note When possible, use Internet Explorer 5 or later. It offers the most current version of these features and includes improved support for certificates.

OSE and FrontPage Server Extensions

To provide users with secure publishing and collaboration access, the OSE and FrontPage Server extensions work together by using a role-based security mechanism at the Web-boundary level. (In OSE, a Web is defined as a set of documents and folders that are managed together. It is the scoping mechanism used to manage security.) At this level, OSE and FrontPage Server extensions provide Web management, link fixup, reporting views, themes, bots, and category lists.

Typically, there is one Web per team—an arrangement that mirrors organizational boundaries—although it can have subwebs (others nested below the root). You can set security levels for each Web or subweb, controlling browsing, authoring, and administration rights.

From the Trenches:
Using Role-Based Security on the Corporate Intranet

The Northwind company wanted to restrict user access in certain areas of the company intranet. Northwind has a top-level URL (http://nwinternal/) to which all users can browse. This root level itself is a Web, and under it other Webs are organized by division, department, team, and so on. Human Resources (http://nwinternal/hr) has a recruiting team with its own root Web (http://nwinternal/hr/recruiting) to which all team members have access. The Human Resources recruiting management team wanted to create a subweb that would permit access only to specific users. This Web would need to be secure from the rest of the team. After reviewing their needs, the Webmaster used the FrontPage client **Permissions** dialog (under **Security** in the **Tools** menu) to allow only managers to access http://nwinternal/hr/recruiting/managers. (See Figure 13.5.)

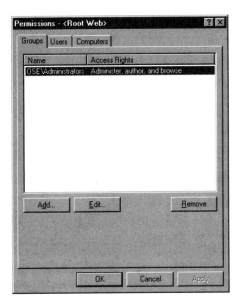

Figure 13.5   FrontPage Client Permissions Dialog. This dialog allows users and groups to be assigned various access rights to a specific Web.

User Roles

OSE and FrontPage define four user roles, each with certain rights. Roles simplify the assignment of access rights. You can control the first three below on a per-Web basis (collaborators have server-level rights).

- **Browsers.** These users can browse Webs, but have no publishing or collaboration rights.
- **Authors.** These users can browse and collaborate on Webs, and can publish to the Web—create, rename, move, and edit documents.
- **OSE Administrators.** These users have the same rights as authors, but can also create Webs, change Web settings, and assign Author and Collaborator access (see below) to users.

Note	Windows NT Administrators by default are also OSE Administrators, but an OSE Administrator does not have to be a Windows NT Administrator.

- **Collaborators.** These users can participate in online discussions and take advantage of Notifications. These rights are at the Web *server* level (the other three are Web-level only) so users with these rights can use the collaboration tools site-wide. They can also give groups of users rights to participate in a Web discussion without giving them unrestricted access to the entire Web.

Each client engaged in a document discussion can select a discussion server and can configure multiple discussion servers for use with the same document. Clients should use the same discussion server; when they choose different ones, users cannot see discussions or be seen by other users. To correct this, users should open the **Discussions Options** dialog (from the **Discussions** toolbar) and select the correct collaboration database.

Windows NT

When you install OSE, you can create four Windows NT local groups designated *Webname Role*. For example, for the Web server *MARS* you create: MARS Admins, MARS Authors, MARS Browsers, and MARS Collaborators. With User Manager you can add or delete users' Windows NT Domain accounts or local machine accounts within these groups. Groups are given Log on Locally rights to the server. Users not assigned to one of these groups must have Log on Locally rights enabled or they will not be able to use the Web server.

To use roles you must use NTFS because it provides Access Control Lists (ACL) to the file and folder levels. Further, you can create security issues during OSE Setup if your C:\ drive is FAT formatted. OSE Setup first copies the OSE support files to the hard disk drive, then starts the Configuration Wizard to OSE-extend the Web server. This creates two virtual directories:

- **MSOffice.** The Office Server Extensions Start Page for the Web server.

- **MSOffice/MSOAdmin.** The Office Server Extensions Administration Home page that the wizard puts in a new directory called *scripts1* under the OSE support files directory. If the C:\ drive is FAT, anyone who can browse the site can access these pages. To ensure the security of these important directories, you must install the OSE support files to an NTFS drive.

 Note   If the Web server hosts multiple virtual sites, the OSE Configuration Wizard creates a separate *scripts* directory for each Web server—*scripts1*, *scripts2*, *scripts3*, and so on—corresponding to the number of OSE-extended Virtual sites.

Security Strategies

To create an OSE security strategy, consider which functions will be used, who needs them, and how they will be used, then use OSE installation options to configure appropriately.

OSE works by extending one or more virtual servers on a machine. If you create multiple virtual servers, you can run the OSE Configuration Wizard on each, creating unique collaboration databases and multiple Webs (and nested subwebs) with different sets of authors, browsers, and administrators. In this way you can create many sites on one machine, and structure them to meet various organizational boundary, department, or team needs.

Keep these points in mind when planning security:

- *Discussions* and *publishing* permissions are separate. Users with permissions to the collaboration database can participate in a discussion on a document even if they do not have editing or other publishing rights.

- Subscriptions allow users to receive notifications of changes to folders for which they do not have read permission. This merely keeps them informed, it does not grant them any other permissions.

Here is an example. You can give each user something similar to a private, *home* directory on a file server—a set of individual folders with various access permissions: an *inbox* folder to which other users have only write permissions (to send documents to the inbox owner), a *private* folder to which only the owner has access, and a *shared* folder to which designated users have read and write access.

Members use the *shared* folder to post documents and obtain feedback. The Office 2000 Web Subscription feature notifies users by e-mail of modifications in the *shared* folder.

Other Security Issues

Virus Scanning

Macro viruses, unfortunately, seem to be proliferating, so the need for protection is likewise increasing. For information on Office 2000 antivirus features, see the *Microsoft Office 2000 Resource Kit*, Chapter 9, "Managing Security." Because OSE is hosted on a server, you can use third-party macro virus scanners to analyze files, capture viruses, and eliminate them before they spread.

NTFS

OSE is optimized for the Workgroup Web. Permissions are typically assigned at the Web level, but if you need a finer level of control you can create subwebs and use the FrontPage client to assign security settings to them. This allows power users or departments to control their site's structure and security.

If you customize the ACL settings of an NTFS folder or file manually, you can cause contention between custom settings and OSE. Customized ACL settings are overwritten if users change Web permissions in the FrontPage permissions dialog. In an OSE environment, use FrontPage to control security by manipulating Web permissions; use another method to create ACL settings manually.

Changing NTFS ACL settings can cause issues in OSE by preventing OSE from accessing needed resources or by allowing unauthorized users to access resources not intended for their use. Plan carefully before changing them.

Capacity Planning

In a Web environment, capacity planning is more of an art than an exact science. A typical client/server application tends to maintain a stateful, long running, and constant connection to server resources—Web server connections may last only a few seconds: a client connects to a Web server, sends a request, the Web server processes the request, and returns the results. At this point, the client-server connection is dropped, and the server frees up resources for the next connection.

OSE components place different demands on the CPU, hard drive, memory, and machines subsystems. This section discusses OSE characteristics to help you plan for capacity loads.

Structural Factors

- **Number of Webs.** A single Web with many documents can degrade OSE performance. OSE maintains metadata on OSE features such as links, categories, security permissions, documents, and so on, within each Web. If possible, split a large Web into subwebs to reduce the amount of per-Web processing required by OSE. Of course, the logic used to split Webs must adhere to the site's use and objectives.

- **Number of documents.** In each Web, OSE parses documents to maintain their metadata. The more documents a Web contains, the more processing OSE requires. OSE can handle 10,000–15,000 documents in a Web before performance begins to decline, at which point you can try distributing documents to reduce per-Web processing.

  Versions of Windows NT before Windows 2000 do not allow you to limit the amount of content a user can save to a directory, but there are third-party tools that do.

- **Size/richness of documents.** OSE handles 200–200 KB documents efficiently but because it has to parse each document to maintain its metadata, multiple-MB or multiple-link documents can take longer to process and you may be able to improve performance by splitting them.

- **Total number of discussions.** Each time a discussion-enabled client accesses a document, the server must request the discussions from SQL Server. OSE is optimized for this and the process usually creates minimal overhead on the OSE server. But if a collaboration database grows to 25,000–30,000 discussions, users may begin to notice delays. In this unlikely event, use the Administration Home page **Configure Web Discussion Settings** dialog (shown in Figure 13.6) to delete discussions automatically after a certain number of days, weeks, months, or years.

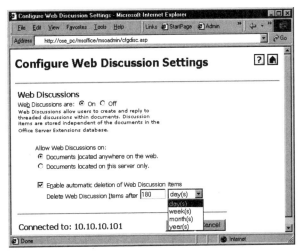

Figure 13.6   The Configure Web Discussion Settings page.

- **Discussion Items.** Client performance can also be affected by rendering discussion items, which can occur in two places. When users access the online discussion feature through the down-level OSE Start Page, the server processes and renders discussion items, and this may affect server performance slightly. When users access online discussions through the **Web discussions** toolbar in Office 2000 or from Internet Explorer, the client CPU processes and displays the discussions. Users with older CPUs may see slower performance, but in this case it is not a server issue.

Operational Factors

- **Number of simultaneous saves.** OSE allows only one file per Web to be saved at a time. If one user is already saving a document, another user trying to save a document to the same Web will have to wait. In a typical team environment, this rarely causes conflicts and when it does the delays are minor. It can have a greater impact when many users are saving to a Web at the same time or when one user is saving a large document. Users can also face delays when saving across a slow LAN connection, and the extended duration of this can block other users longer.

  To alleviate these issues, split the Web into subwebs. The *save* block is at the Web level; nothing prevents other users from saving to other Webs at the same time.

- **Browsing load.** IIS is optimized for Web browsing, and OSE benefits from these optimizations because it installs as an IIS component. For suggestions on improving browsing access, see the *Microsoft Internet Information Server Resource Kit* and related documentation.

- **Index Server.** You can use Index Server to create indexes for full-text searching on Web server documents, but indexing can place significant demands on a CPU. If there are a lot of saves over an extended time, Index Server activity can tie up CPU resources, blocking OSE from fulfilling other requests.

  You can configure and tune Index Server to better support the specific needs of various Web environments. You can put Index Server on another CPU so that the Web server doesn't have to perform CPU-intensive indexing. You can also configure Index Server to run off-peak, when CPU utilization is low. See the Index Server documentation for configuration options.

- **Administrative operations.** Administration tasks such as moving a large number of documents can retard OSE performance by loading the CPU (in this case with link and metadata updates). To reduce impact on users, perform bulk moves or changes during off-peak hours.

Performance Rules of Thumb

Here are some rules to keep in mind when tuning performance.

- Publishing usually consumes the most server resources, followed by collaboration services.
- Create more subwebs with fewer documents to improve OSE performance.
- The FrontPage 2000 Server extensions that OSE utilizes have been improved to increase scalability.
- Often, perceived performance issues can be traced to the client CPU and can be fixed by upgrading.
- Down-level collaboration support through the OSE Start Page can load the server CPU.
- Bulk/stress operations may result in temporary notification backlogs.
- Because OSE runs as a service on Windows NT, it benefits from many of the Windows NT optimizations: multiprocessor support, disk striping, ability to utilize large amounts of physical RAM, and other hardware enhancements available for the Windows NT platform.

Back Up and Restore

To safeguard work and material, you should ensure that an OSE-extended Web server is backed up properly and consistently. Develop a backup plan. Consider three areas:

- **Documents.** For these you can use the Windows NT Backup program.
- **Collaboration database.** OSE uses a SQL Server database to store discussions and subscription information. Back up each collaboration database on a server; you can use SQL Server's built-in backup facilities.

Note   The online version of the *Microsoft Office 2000 Resource Kit* includes an Exporting and Importing utility for a collaboration database (the Server Extensions Migration Utility) which you can use to reset or upgrade a Web server. You can export the database, upgrade your computer and then import the database again, without losing any data.

- **Windows NT settings.** Back up settings such as the registry, users, groups, NTFS ACL, and so on, with the standard Windows NT backup utilities.

CHAPTER 14

Office 2000 and Windows 2000

This chapter discusses how to deploy Office 2000 in a Windows 2000 environment that includes Windows 2000 Server and Windows 2000 Professional. It concentrates on large organizations to help you understand their special challenges, and to demonstrate the advantages of several built-in deployment and installation tools and methods. It was written while Windows 2000 was in beta release.

What You'll Find in This Chapter

- An overview of deploying Office 2000 to Windows 2000 Professional computers.

- A description of enhanced Office 2000 Setup capabilities on Windows 2000.

- How to deploy Office 2000 using Windows 2000 Server software installation and maintenance, and the advantages and disadvantages of this method in very large organizations.

- How to decide which is better for distributing and maintaining Office 2000 in your organization: Windows 2000 IntelliMirror software installation and maintenance or Microsoft Systems Management Server 2.0.

Windows 2000 Change and Configuration Management

Windows 2000 IntelliMirror and Remote OS Installation provide change and configuration management features you can use to manage the Windows 2000 Professional user community through a centrally administered Group Policy. IntelliMirror supplies:

- **User data management.** Defines the properties and location of a Windows 2000 user's files, documents, workbooks, and other information. Makes the user's data available from any networked computer or when the user is offline.

- **User settings management.** Defines both customizations and any restrictions that should be applied to the operating system, desktop environment, and applications for each user.

- **Software installation and maintenance.** Defines how to install, configure, repair, and remove applications, service packs, and software upgrades.

Using a Windows 2000–based server as the remote source, Remote OS Installation is the network equivalent of a CD-based installation of Windows 2000 Professional or an installation of a pre-configured Windows 2000 Professional desktop image. It works in one of these ways:

- **CD-equivalent installation.** Similar to setting up a computer directly using the unattended install options available on the Windows 2000 Professional CD, except that the source files reside on Windows 2000 Remote Installation Server (RIS) computers rather than on CD.

- **Pre-configured desktop image.** Allows you to create a standard corporate desktop configuration image (complete with operating system configurations, desktop customizations, and locally installed applications) then store it on Windows 2000 Remote Installation Server computers, which downloads it on request to computers that support Remote OS Installation. Except for power management, the receiving hardware can differ from the hardware on which the image was created: Windows 2000 Professional plug and play adjusts for differences.

The next sections discuss how Office 2000 works with these features and how to successfully plan their implementation. For details on the requirements for Remote OS Installation, see the paper *Microsoft Windows 2000 Server Remote OS Installation Technical Walkthrough* on the CD in the back of this book.

User Data Management

User data management stores data files on the Windows 2000 server, but caches and updates them locally if the user indicates they are used offline or if the administrator enables auto-caching on the share. Most large organizations already have users store files on the server for backup and restore.

When you use IntelliMirror user data management, you should handle Outlook and Access storage differently than storage for spreadsheets and documents. Microsoft Exchange Server is designed to provide users with access to Outlook items regardless of where they are and whether the user is working online or offline. Users tend to store items in their mailbox on the server, and use an Offline Storage File (OST) if they frequently use Outlook offline. Exchange optimizes synchronization for cases in which many users have very large mailboxes or mail is stored in a .PST file (which can grow very large) instead of in the mailbox. In sum, Exchange Server handles Outlook storage very efficiently: don't use IntelliMirror User Data Management with these files.

Access databases are also excluded from IntelliMirror management by default. Access provides its own synchronization capabilities because its databases can become so large they take a long time to synchronize by other methods.

If you want to exclude other files from IntelliMirror user data management, add them to the list of excluded files managed by Group Policy (see Figure 14.1).

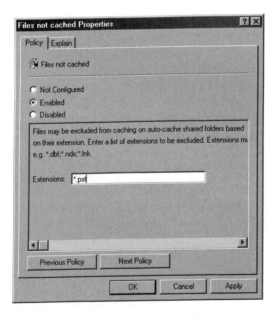

Figure 14.1   Excluding file types through Group Policy.

Finally, be sure to include server size limits when you determine user data management policies. Many organizations use the Windows 2000 Disk Quotas feature to limit users to 50 MB of server space, which limits network traffic and provides a better user experience.

User Settings

Office 2000 supports user setting management on a Windows 2000 server. For more information about creating, managing and controlling user settings in Office 2000, see Chapter 5, "User Settings." In the Windows 2000 environment, administrators can manage user settings by Group Policy and the Windows 2000 Active Directory. The policy templates in the *Microsoft Office 2000 Resource Kit Toolbox* work for Windows 2000 and other operating systems.

For more information on Windows 2000 Group Policy, see the *Group Policy* white paper and the *Group Policy Technical Walkthrough* on the Windows 2000 Web site.

Software Installation and Maintenance

If you have to distribute Office 2000 to Windows 2000 users, you will probably spend most of your planning time working out whether you should use IntelliMirror software installation and maintenance and, if so, how. It allows you to manage applications for computers or users that are managed by a Group Policy Object (GPO) associated with an Active Directory site, domain, or organizational unit (OU). For example, to manage Microsoft Project for engineers that are part of the Engineering OU, you can associate a GPO with that OU, then assign or publish Microsoft Project to that GPO.

There are two ways to manage software packages:

- **Assign.** When you assign software to a user, the shortcuts for applications are advertised on the user's desktop and **Start** menu the next time the user logs on to the network. Assigned applications are not optional—they are provided to all users who are managed by the GPO with the assigned application. It is installed on first use, so original installation to the client computer is quick and does not have a great impact on the user. If a user removes the application, the removal process recreates the shortcuts on the desktop and **Start** menu, so the software reinstalls the next time the user selects the shortcut. Virus checking software is a good example of software you want every user to have.

- **Publish.** Published applications are listed in the Control Panel's Add/Remove Programs application. You can categorize the list to make it easier for users to find and use an application that is not a required installation component. For example, you can *publish* your organization's standard graphics or flow-charting package, because you want users to have access to it but don't necessarily need to provide it to every user. You can also make published applications available by associating filename extensions. For example, if you associate the .DOC file extension with Word 2000, Word installs if a user double-clicks on a Word document, wherever it is—on the network, on the user's computer, or in an e-mail message.

Assigning an Application

When you assign Office 2000 to users within a GPO associated with an OU, all users managed by the GPO get the Office application shortcuts on their Programs menu the next time they log on to the network, but the applications are not installed until the user first accesses the shortcuts. This method does not delay users when they log on, provides them with quick access to applications, and uses very little network bandwidth to advertise the applications.

On the other hand, users have to wait each time they access an application that isn't yet installed locally. Feedback from the field shows that users don't mind having a few less commonly used features install the first time they need them, but don't like *Installed on First Use* for major applications such as Word, commonly used shared features such as the spell checker, or a large quantity of features. You can make users happier by using a transform that installs all of the application to the local computer. For instance, if you do this for Word, it installs all features in the Word sub-tree at one time, reducing the number of times users have to wait for features to install on first use.

There are a couple Software Installation snap-in features that are useful with Office 2000. When you begin the management of the application package, and choose whether to assign or publish it, you must choose **Advanced** if you want to use the custom configuration you have created for Office 2000 and to have maximum control over it (see Figure 14.2).

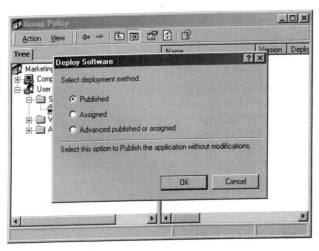

Figure 14.2   Software deployment with Group Policy.

Once you add the package to the Software Installation snap-in, you use several tabs to completely configure it; of these, the **Deployment** and **Modifications** tabs are of special concern here. Use the **Deployment** tab (shown in Figure 14.3) to set whether the application is assigned or published and to decide when it is installed.

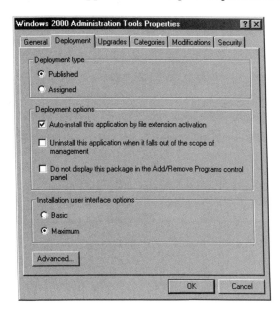

Figure 14.3   Configuring advanced options for application deployment.

This dialog box allows you to set the software for automatic installation based on file extension activation. For instance, you can assign Office 2000 to a user and select auto-install. The user logs in for the day and starts up Outlook, which installs on first use. The user starts reading e-mail, comes across a message with an attached Word 2000 document, double-clicks on it, and Word 2000 automatically installs and opens the document.

When you assign or publish Office 2000 software in a GPO, the *uninstall* option allows you to remove it for users or computers that later are moved out of the GPO and are no longer managed by it. For example, if a user moves to a GPO that does not manage a particular piece of software, that software is removed.

To speed up the installation of Office 2000 and prevent user interaction, use the Basic UI parameter, which is similar to the **/qb** command-line switch for Office 2000 Setup. The user is not prompted for any interaction with the Setup application, and the application installs quickly, using the parameters defined in the Office 2000 Windows Installer package and an associated transform. Basic UI shows only progress messages and error codes.

Use the **Modifications** tab (shown in Figure 14.4) to tell Windows 2000 Server which transform to use with this package. Although you can use more than one transform for a specific package, this is not recommended for Office. Using multiple transforms is only additive if there is no value for an area in the first transform. For example, if you add four files to the Office configuration with the first transform, and add one more file with the second transform, the net result is that the only file added is the one file in the second transform. Because it can be difficult to track the various transforms and test and predict the results, avoid this practice.

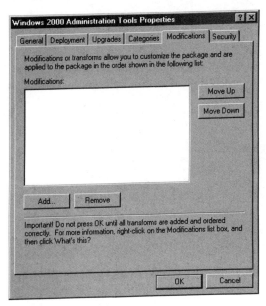

Figure 14.4   Specifying which transform Windows 2000 will use.

You can assign applications to a computer rather than just to users, so that they install the next time the computer reboots. This is particularly useful for computers with multiple users.

Publishing an Application

When you publish an application, you don't actually install any software—you simply make it available from the Active Directory through the Control Panel's Add/Remove Programs and file name extension association. Users can install the software whenever they like in the manner you have determined. This is a good way to provide access to Office applications such as Publisher 2000 that some, but not all, users require.

If you publish a lot of applications, you can create categories and then associate applications with categories so that users can find them more easily in Add/Remove Programs (see Figure 14.5).

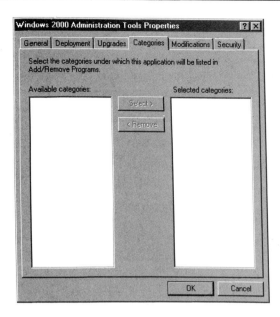

Figure 14.5   Creating categories for published applications.

For more information on software installation and maintenance, see the *Microsoft Windows 2000 Server Software Installation and Maintenance Walkthrough* on the Windows 2000 Server Web site.

Remote OS Installation

The Remote OS Installation feature makes it easier to deploy the Windows 2000 Professional operating system without visiting each computer. Once you have set up this capability and configured everything properly, the user can start the Remote OS Installation process by pressing the F12 key when the computer starts up.

Remote OS Installation allows you to deploy Office 2000 with the operating system as one action. There are several advantages to distributing Office 2000 to new computers this way:

- It requires fewer steps to get all software on the client computer.

- It's significantly faster than remotely installing Windows 2000 Professional and then running the Office 2000 installation separately. Field tests on Windows 2000 Beta 3 (under similar network conditions) showed that it took only slightly longer to remotely install both Windows 2000 and Office 2000 than it took to run through an attended installation of Windows 2000 alone.

- The Office 2000 software is actually installed to the local computer instead of simply being available to install on first use or from Add/Remove Programs.

- It makes it quick and easy to get a user up and running again if there are significant problems with a client computer.

Install and configure Windows 2000 Professional on a base or standardized computer for your organization, then install Office 2000 on the same computer, ensuring that it is configured properly for your purposes. Then run the Remote Installation Preparation wizard (RIPrep.exe) from the Remote Installation Services (RIS) server that will receive the image.

For more information on Remote OS Installation, see the *Microsoft Windows 2000 Server Remote OS Installation Technical Walkthrough* white paper on the Windows 2000 Server Web site.

Reboots

During installation, Office 2000 reboots to update critical DLLs and finish setting up Internet Explorer 5 Setup, but all of these files are already present in Windows 2000 so no reboot is necessary. In most cases, this simplifies software distribution. In all cases, Setup completes without rebooting and logging on again, and you can use this to your advantage, particularly by chaining. For instance, you can chain Publisher 2000 from the second CD to the installation, or chain the MultiLanguage Pack to Office 2000.

See Chapter 4, "Customizing an Office 2000 Installation," and Chapter 9, "Multinational Deployment," for more information about chaining installations.

The MultiLanguage Pack

Windows 2000 is similar to Office 2000 in that you can combine the U.S. English version with language packs and change the user interface to any supported language without requiring a dual-boot system or a localized version of the operating system. Combining Office 2000 with the MultiLanguage Pack running on Windows 2000 provides the most flexibility for users, particularly when switching between Hebrew, Arabic, and Asian languages and any others. It also simplifies testing because you don't have to locate and install each localized version of the operating system to verify language configurations.

Example: A user in Japan works in Japanese but occasionally lets a visiting German counterpart use the computer. The German user can switch the language in Windows 2000, reboot Windows 2000, then switch Office 2000 to German. (The German user can edit documents without any of these modifications. This process is required only to operate completely in German.)

Note   Outlook 2000 and FrontPage 2000 require the system locale to match the language to which the user switches.

Determining Management Methods

Permanently assigning or publishing an application to an organizational unit through Windows 2000 Server IntelliMirror software installation and maintenance has advantages and disadvantages (especially in very large organizations).

Advantages:

- You can enforce a specific configuration.

- You do not have to visit each computer to provide users with the applications they need.

- You can control whether specific users have the right to install software, or can make it possible for users to install specific packages without giving them the right to install all software.

Very large organizations managing Office 2000 for very large groups can encounter the limitations of Windows 2000 software installation and maintenance:

- You can't control exactly when installation occurs. For user-assigned software, the shortcuts appear the next time the user logs on and it's very quick, but actual installation does not occur until the user accesses the shortcut for the first time. If, for example, it happens when a lot of users log on to their systems in the morning and check e-mail it can generate high volumes of Outlook and Word traffic. Further, computer-assigned software installs the entire package the first time the computer reboots, and this can take a long time for the complete Office package.

- Users who rarely or never log on (some lock their workstations for security purposes rather than logging off) may never get the applications.

- There is no reporting mechanism to find out the success or failure of each installation.

- Windows 2000 software distribution works only for Windows 2000 Professional clients, not Windows 9x or Windows NT Workstation.

- Many users dislike having major applications install on first use.

If any of these represent serious concerns in your environment, you may be better off using a change and configuration management tool such as Microsoft Systems Management Server instead, or, for new Windows 2000 computers, the Remote OS Installation.

You can use some Systems Management Server features such as its software distribution model, with Windows 2000 Software Installation and Maintenance's ability to target users by Group Policy. If you deploy Windows 2000 Professional and Office 2000 before you have enough of the Windows 2000 Server and Active Directory infrastructure in place to use the IntelliMirror software installation and maintenance features, you should install Office 2000 per-computer from the same software distribution point (Windows 2000 Server share) that you will use once the rest of the infrastructure is in place. You will have to test these scenarios to determine if the product combination works in your environment.

When you create the Group Policy Object (GPO) to assign Office 2000 to the computer, point the assigned package to the same software distribution point that you used previously. *This must be the same configuration of Office 2000* down to the Windows Installer package transform and the distribution point (unless you are using the Distributed File System). If *everything* is the same, the Windows Installer quickly turns the unmanaged installation into a managed one; users don't notice any change, but if they try to remove the software or change the configuration, Windows 2000 restores the proper configuration. If everything is *not* the same, the Windows Installer removes the existing Office 2000 and reinstalls the assigned version of Office 2000 the next time the computer starts.

You can use a similar process to deploy Office 2000 through Remote OS Installation, but still assign it to computers in a GPO. Make sure the Office 2000 configuration (software distribution point, package, and transform) is the same.

INDEX

Symbols and Numbers

X

Y

Z

System Requirements

To use the *Deploying Microsoft Office 2000* companion CD, you need a computer with the following minimum configuration:

- 486 or higher processor (Pentium CPU recommended for Windows 98 or later operating system).
- Microsoft Windows 95, Windows 98, Windows NT 4.0 or later.
- RAM:
    - 4 MB of RAM for Windows 95 (8 MB recommended).
    - 16 MB of RAM for Windows 98 (24 MB recommended).
    - 16 MB of RAM for Windows NT 4.0 (32 MB recommended).
- CD-ROM drive.
- Mouse or other pointing device (recommended).
- Hard drive space: varies depending on the tools you download from the disk.
- Internet Explorer 4.0 or higher (5.0 recommended).

MICROSOFT LICENSE AGREEMENT
Book Companion CD

IMPORTANT—READ CAREFULLY: This Microsoft End-User License Agreement ("EULA") is a legal agreement between you (either an individual or an entity) and Microsoft Corporation for the Microsoft product identified above, which includes computer software and may include associated media, printed materials, and "on-line" or electronic documentation ("SOFTWARE PRODUCT"). Any component included within the SOFTWARE PRODUCT that is accompanied by a separate End-User License Agreement shall be governed by such agreement and not the terms set forth below. By installing, copying, or otherwise using the SOFTWARE PRODUCT, you agree to be bound by the terms of this EULA. If you do not agree to the terms of this EULA, you are not authorized to install, copy, or otherwise use the SOFTWARE PRODUCT; you may, however, return the SOFTWARE PRODUCT, along with all printed materials and other items that form a part of the Microsoft product that includes the SOFTWARE PRODUCT, to the place you obtained them for a full refund.

SOFTWARE PRODUCT LICENSE

The SOFTWARE PRODUCT is protected by United States copyright laws and international copyright treaties, as well as other intellectual property laws and treaties. The SOFTWARE PRODUCT is licensed, not sold.

1. GRANT OF LICENSE. This EULA grants you the following rights:

   a. Software Product. You may install and use one copy of the SOFTWARE PRODUCT on a single computer. The primary user of the computer on which the SOFTWARE PRODUCT is installed may make a second copy for his or her exclusive use on a portable computer.

   b. Storage/Network Use. You may also store or install a copy of the SOFTWARE PRODUCT on a storage device, such as a network server, used only to install or run the SOFTWARE PRODUCT on your other computers over an internal network; however, you must acquire and dedicate a license for each separate computer on which the SOFTWARE PRODUCT is installed or run from the storage device. A license for the SOFTWARE PRODUCT may not be shared or used concurrently on different computers.

   c. License Pak. If you have acquired this EULA in a Microsoft License Pak, you may make the number of additional copies of the computer software portion of the SOFTWARE PRODUCT authorized on the printed copy of this EULA, and you may use each copy in the manner specified above. You are also entitled to make a corresponding number of secondary copies for portable computer use as specified above.

   d. Sample Code. Solely with respect to portions, if any, of the SOFTWARE PRODUCT that are identified within the SOFTWARE PRODUCT as sample code (the "SAMPLE CODE"):

      i. Use and Modification. Microsoft grants you the right to use and modify the source code version of the SAMPLE CODE, *provided* you comply with subsection (d)(iii) below. You may not distribute the SAMPLE CODE, or any modified version of the SAMPLE CODE, in source code form.

      ii. Redistributable Files. Provided you comply with subsection (d)(iii) below, Microsoft grants you a nonexclusive, royalty-free right to reproduce and distribute the object code version of the SAMPLE CODE and of any modified SAMPLE CODE, other than SAMPLE CODE (or any modified version thereof) designated as not redistributable in the Readme file that forms a part of the SOFTWARE PRODUCT (the "Non-Redistributable Sample Code"). All SAMPLE CODE other than the Non-Redistributable Sample Code is collectively referred to as the "REDISTRIBUTABLES."

      iii. Redistribution Requirements. If you redistribute the REDISTRIBUTABLES, you agree to: (i) distribute the REDISTRIBUTABLES in object code form only in conjunction with and as a part of your software application product; (ii) not use Microsoft's name, logo, or trademarks to market your software application product; (iii) include a valid copyright notice on your software application product; (iv) indemnify, hold harmless, and defend Microsoft from and against any claims or lawsuits, including attorney's fees, that arise or result from the use or distribution of your software application product; and (v) not permit further distribution of the REDISTRIBUTABLES by your end user. Contact Microsoft for the applicable royalties due and other licensing terms for all other uses and/or distribution of the REDISTRIBUTABLES.

2. DESCRIPTION OF OTHER RIGHTS AND LIMITATIONS.

   • **Limitations on Reverse Engineering, Decompilation, and Disassembly.** You may not reverse engineer, decompile, or disassemble the SOFTWARE PRODUCT, except and only to the extent that such activity is expressly permitted by applicable law notwithstanding this limitation.

   • **Separation of Components.** The SOFTWARE PRODUCT is licensed as a single product. Its component parts may not be separated for use on more than one computer.

   • **Rental.** You may not rent, lease, or lend the SOFTWARE PRODUCT.

   • **Support Services.** Microsoft may, but is not obligated to, provide you with support services related to the SOFTWARE PRODUCT ("Support Services"). Use of Support Services is governed by the Microsoft policies and programs described in the user manual, in "on-line" documentation, and/or in other Microsoft-provided materials. Any supplemental software code provided to you as part of the Support Services shall be considered part of the SOFTWARE PRODUCT and subject to the terms and conditions of this EULA. With respect to technical information you provide to Microsoft as part of the Support Services, Microsoft may use such information for its business purposes, including for product support and development. Microsoft will not utilize such technical information in a form that personally identifies you.

   • **Software Transfer.** You may permanently transfer all of your rights under this EULA, provided you retain no copies, you transfer all of the SOFTWARE PRODUCT (including all component parts, the media and printed materials, any upgrades, this EULA, and, if applicable, the Certificate of Authenticity), **and** the recipient agrees to the terms of this EULA.

- **Termination.** Without prejudice to any other rights, Microsoft may terminate this EULA if you fail to comply with the terms and conditions of this EULA. In such event, you must destroy all copies of the SOFTWARE PRODUCT and all of its component parts.

3. **COPYRIGHT.** All title and copyrights in and to the SOFTWARE PRODUCT (including but not limited to any images, photographs, animations, video, audio, music, text, SAMPLE CODE, REDISTRIBUTABLES, and "applets" incorporated into the SOFTWARE PRODUCT) and any copies of the SOFTWARE PRODUCT are owned by Microsoft or its suppliers. The SOFTWARE PRODUCT is protected by copyright laws and international treaty provisions. Therefore, you must treat the SOFTWARE PRODUCT like any other copyrighted material **except** that you may install the SOFTWARE PRODUCT on a single computer provided you keep the original solely for backup or archival purposes. You may not copy the printed materials accompanying the SOFTWARE PRODUCT.

4. **U.S. GOVERNMENT RESTRICTED RIGHTS.** The SOFTWARE PRODUCT and documentation are provided with RE-STRICTED RIGHTS. Use, duplication, or disclosure by the Government is subject to restrictions as set forth in subparagraph (c)(1)(ii) of the Rights in Technical Data and Computer Software clause at DFARS 252.227-7013 or subparagraphs (c)(1) and (2) of the Commercial Computer Software—Restricted Rights at 48 CFR 52.227-19, as applicable. Manufacturer is Microsoft Corporation/One Microsoft Way/Redmond, WA 98052-6399.

5. **EXPORT RESTRICTIONS.** You agree that you will not export or re-export the SOFTWARE PRODUCT, any part thereof, or any process or service that is the direct product of the SOFTWARE PRODUCT (the foregoing collectively referred to as the "Restricted Components"), to any country, person, entity, or end user subject to U.S. export restrictions. You specifically agree not to export or re-export any of the Restricted Components (i) to any country to which the U.S. has embargoed or restricted the export of goods or services, which currently include, but are not necessarily limited to, Cuba, Iran, Iraq, Libya, North Korea, Sudan, and Syria, or to any national of any such country, wherever located, who intends to transmit or transport the Restricted Components back to such country; (ii) to any end user who you know or have reason to know will utilize the Restricted Components in the design, development, or production of nuclear, chemical, or biological weapons; or (iii) to any end user who has been prohibited from participating in U.S. export transactions by any federal agency of the U.S. government. You warrant and represent that neither the BXA nor any other U.S. federal agency has suspended, revoked, or denied your export privileges.

6. **NOTE ON JAVA SUPPORT.** THE SOFTWARE PRODUCT MAY CONTAIN SUPPORT FOR PROGRAMS WRITTEN IN JAVA. JAVA TECHNOLOGY IS NOT FAULT TOLERANT AND IS NOT DESIGNED, MANUFACTURED, OR INTENDED FOR USE OR RESALE AS ON-LINE CONTROL EQUIPMENT IN HAZARDOUS ENVIRONMENTS REQUIRING FAIL-SAFE PERFOR-MANCE, SUCH AS IN THE OPERATION OF NUCLEAR FACILITIES, AIRCRAFT NAVIGATION OR COMMUNICATION SYSTEMS, AIR TRAFFIC CONTROL, DIRECT LIFE SUPPORT MACHINES, OR WEAPONS SYSTEMS, IN WHICH THE FAILURE OF JAVA TECHNOLOGY COULD LEAD DIRECTLY TO DEATH, PERSONAL INJURY, OR SEVERE PHYSICAL OR ENVIRONMENTAL DAMAGE. SUN MICROSYSTEMS, INC. HAS CONTRACTUALLY OBLIGATED MICROSOFT TO MAKE THIS DISCLAIMER.

DISCLAIMER OF WARRANTY

NO WARRANTIES OR CONDITIONS. MICROSOFT EXPRESSLY DISCLAIMS ANY WARRANTY OR CONDITION FOR THE SOFTWARE PRODUCT. THE SOFTWARE PRODUCT AND ANY RELATED DOCUMENTATION ARE PROVIDED "AS IS" WITHOUT WARRANTY OR CONDITION OF ANY KIND, EITHER EXPRESS OR IMPLIED, INCLUDING, WITHOUT LIMITATION, THE IMPLIED WARRANTIES OF MERCHANTABILITY, FITNESS FOR A PARTICULAR PURPOSE, OR NONINFRINGEMENT. THE ENTIRE RISK ARISING OUT OF USE OR PERFORMANCE OF THE SOFTWARE PRODUCT REMAINS WITH YOU.

LIMITATION OF LIABILITY. TO THE MAXIMUM EXTENT PERMITTED BY APPLICABLE LAW, IN NO EVENT SHALL MICROSOFT OR ITS SUPPLIERS BE LIABLE FOR ANY SPECIAL, INCIDENTAL, INDIRECT, OR CONSEQUENTIAL DAMAGES WHATSOEVER (INCLUDING, WITHOUT LIMITATION, DAMAGES FOR LOSS OF BUSINESS PROFITS, BUSINESS INTERRUP-TION, LOSS OF BUSINESS INFORMATION, OR ANY OTHER PECUNIARY LOSS) ARISING OUT OF THE USE OF OR INABILITY TO USE THE SOFTWARE PRODUCT OR THE PROVISION OF OR FAILURE TO PROVIDE SUPPORT SERVICES, EVEN IF MICROSOFT HAS BEEN ADVISED OF THE POSSIBILITY OF SUCH DAMAGES. IN ANY CASE, MICROSOFT'S ENTIRE LIABIL-ITY UNDER ANY PROVISION OF THIS EULA SHALL BE LIMITED TO THE GREATER OF THE AMOUNT ACTUALLY PAID BY YOU FOR THE SOFTWARE PRODUCT OR US$5.00; PROVIDED, HOWEVER, IF YOU HAVE ENTERED INTO A MICROSOFT SUPPORT SERVICES AGREEMENT, MICROSOFT'S ENTIRE LIABILITY REGARDING SUPPORT SERVICES SHALL BE GOV-ERNED BY THE TERMS OF THAT AGREEMENT. BECAUSE SOME STATES AND JURISDICTIONS DO NOT ALLOW THE EXCLUSION OR LIMITATION OF LIABILITY, THE ABOVE LIMITATION MAY NOT APPLY TO YOU.

MISCELLANEOUS

This EULA is governed by the laws of the State of Washington USA, except and only to the extent that applicable law mandates governing law of a different jurisdiction.

Should you have any questions concerning this EULA, or if you desire to contact Microsoft for any reason, please contact the Microsoft subsidiary serving your country, or write: Microsoft Sales Information Center/One Microsoft Way/Redmond, WA 98052-6399.

PN 097-0002297

Proof of Purchase

0-7356-0727-3

Do not send this card with your registration.
Use this card as proof of purchase if participating in a promotion or
rebate offer on *Deploying Microsoft® Office 2000*. Card must be used in conjunction
with other proof(s) of payment such as your dated sales receipt—see offer details.

Deploying Microsoft® Office 2000

_____

WHERE DID YOU PURCHASE THIS PRODUCT?

_____

CUSTOMER NAME

Microsoft® *Press*

mspress.microsoft.com

Microsoft Press, PO Box 97017, Redmond, WA 98073-9830

OWNER REGISTRATION CARD   *Register Today!*   0-7356-0727-3

Return the bottom portion of this card to register today.

Deploying Microsoft® Office 2000

FIRST NAME	**MIDDLE INITIAL**	**LAST NAME**

_____

INSTITUTION OR COMPANY NAME

_____

ADDRESS

_____

CITY	**STATE**	**ZIP**

( )

E-MAIL ADDRESS   **PHONE NUMBER**

U.S. and Canada addresses only. Fill in information above and mail postage-free.
Please mail only the bottom half of this page.

For information about Microsoft Press®
products, visit our Web site at
mspress.microsoft.com

Microsoft ® *Press*